OUDTESTAMENTISCHE STUDIËN

DEEL XXIV

OUDTESTAMENTISCHE STUDIËN

NAMENS HET OUDTESTAMENTISCH
WERKGEZELSCHAP IN NEDERLAND

UITGEGEVEN DOOR

A. S. VAN DER WOUDE

GRONINGEN

DEEL XXIV

LEIDEN
E. J. BRILL
1986

CRISES AND PERSPECTIVES

Studies in Ancient Near Eastern Polytheism, Biblical Theology, Palestinian Archaeology and Intertestamental Literature

PAPERS READ AT THE JOINT BRITISH-DUTCH
OLD TESTAMENT CONFERENCE
HELD AT CAMBRIDGE, U.K.
1985

LEIDEN
E. J. BRILL
1986

*This volume contains the papers read at the Joint British-Dutch Old Testament
Conference held at Fitzwilliam College, Cambridge, England, from
16-18 July 1985*

Contributions by
J. C. DE MOOR, N. POULSSEN, G. I. DAVIES, E. W. NICHOLSON,
K. A. D. SMELIK, L. DEQUEKER, J. D. MARTIN, and T. RAJAK

BS
1192
.J64
1985

ISSN   0169-9555
ISBN   90 04 07873 8
Copyright 1986 by E. J. Brill, Leiden, The Netherlands

PRINTED IN THE NETHERLANDS BY E. J. BRILL

INHOUD

THE CRISIS OF POLYTHEISM IN LATE BRONZE UGARIT[1])

BY

JOHANNES C. DE MOOR
Kampen

1. *Introduction*

The theme of this paper was inspired by the sub-title of an impressive monograph called "Re und Amun" from the hand of the German Egyptologist ASSMANN[2]). In this book ASSMANN describes how Egyptian polytheism went through a crisis during the period of the New Kingdom. We all know about the monotheistic revolution of Amenophis IV/Akhenaten who ascended the pharaonic throne ca. 1365 B.C.[3]). ASSMANN shows that already long before Akhenaten there was a movement towards the henotheistic worship of the national god Amun-Re. In a kind of counter-reformation after the death of Akhenaten this movement gained a lot of momentum. Amun-Re becomes "the one who created everything that exists, the solitary one who created what is". He is the eldest god who has neither father nor mother, "the one who created himself out of the seed of his own body". He is also the creator of heaven and earth, and the father of gods and man. Amun-Re cannot be portrayed because he transcends the conceptive faculties of man.

To be sure, all these rather exclusive qualities were thought to be fully compatible with polytheism. According to this theology all the other gods of Egypt were nothing more than manifestations of Amun-Re, "the one who transforms himself into millions". Nevertheless it is clear that one might just as well call these ideas a reduction of the polytheistic principle. It is for this reason that ASSMANN speaks of a crisis in the polytheism of Egypt.

Although ASSMANN was the first to give a proper assessment of the magnitude and depth of the Amun-Re movement, many of the phenomena he describes have long been known. The first who saw the truly international dimensions of the trend toward henotheism at the end of the Late Bronze Age was W. F. ALBRIGHT[4]). In Babylonia Marduk was elevated to a rank comparable to that of Amun-Re in Egypt. All deities were viewed as mere aspects of Marduk. In Assyria the same was said of Assur, "the king of the gods"[5]).

ALBRIGHT saw this as a development towards monotheism, an evolutionary process on the road "from the Stone Age to Christianity". It is questionable, however, whether it was correct to use a loaded term like "monotheism" in connection with a fundamentally different concept such as henotheism[6]). Moreover, it seems far more likely now that monotheism was not the ripe fruit of a long evolutionary process, but rather the result of a violent reaction to the spirit of the time. Monotheism was a revolutionary concept[7]).

ALBRIGHT failed to take into account that the Late Bronze Age was also a period of deep dissatisfaction with established religion and of fundamental doubts as to the true nature of the relationship between god and man. Especially in the wisdom literature of the time we encounter a very pessimistic view of this relationship[8]). Several Babylonian myths and epics that received their final redaction towards the end of the second millennium B.C. centre upon the problem of the relentlessness of death[9]). We know that these texts were very popular and were read as far away as in Egypt[10]). Texts like the sceptic Egyptian Song of the Harper and the Babylonian Epic of Gilgamesh are full of bitterness about the fate of mortal man and reveal an astonishing lack of reverence for the gods and for generally accepted religious principles[11]).

Manetho tells us that during the New Kingdom a certain Osarseph, an ex-priest from Heliopolis, would even have instigated his followers to abandon all worship of the gods[12]). Thus far the iconoclastic revolution of Osarseph has not been confirmed by any ancient Egyptian source. But even if it did not come to a total rejection of all religion the New Kingdom doubtlessly remains a period of shocking religious developments that seem to have reverberated far beyond the borders of Egypt.

HORNUNG surmises that also outside of Egypt the monotheistic reformation of Akhenaten must have caused quite a stir[13]). This is confirmed in an indirect way by the Amarna-letters, the diplomatic correspondence between Egypt and other nations, especially in the region we are used to call "Canaan". In this period the city-states of Canaan were to a large extent under the political, commercial and cultural influence of Egypt[14]). Their kings were well aware of the fact that Amun-Re was the national god of Egypt. In accordance with the accepted practice of those days they greeted the pharao with benedictions in the name of his god Amun-Re in the older letters of the Amarna-archive.

However, this soon stops under Akhenaten. The message that it had become very undiplomatic to mention the name of Amun-Re must have spread like wildfire throughout Canaan. The uncertainty of the petty kings about the new situation created by the reformation of Akhenaten is reflected in their letters. They do not mention Amun anymore, but they also refrain from praising Aten.

So we may conclude that the Canaanite kings were kept relatively well-informed about the religious developments in Egypt. It is fairly certain that they also succeeded in obtaining Egyptian texts to learn more about the new religion. Psalm 104 for example closely resembles a well-known hymn to Aten. However, since this Psalm at the same time exhibits the typical local colour of Canaan it is more than likely that the Israelites did not borrow this hymn directly from Egypt but used a Canaanite translation which formed an intermediary link[15]).

It may be safely assumed that the polytheists of Canaan awaited in suspense what would happen after the death of Akhenaten. Shortly afterwards the king of Ugarit appears to know exactly that Amun-Re was the highest god of Egypt again, though not its only god[16]). The kings of Byblos even sacrificed to Amun-Re[17]) and in doing so recognized him as a universal god whose power extended as far as their own territory[18]).

Because there are other proofs of a significant Egyptian influence on the religious conceptions of the Canaanites during the Late Bronze Age[19]) it is legitimate to assume that also the further development of the crisis of polytheism did not go unnoticed in Canaan. The main thrust behind the henotheistic movements in Mesopotamia came in the thirteenth and twelfth centuries B.C., *i.e.* shortly after the counter-reformation with Amun-Re as its centre had started in Egypt. It is hardly conceivable then that the geographic area in between would have been unaffected by this fundamental change in religious outlook. Although the Canaanite sources for the period in question are far less abundant than those of Egypt and Mesopotamia we are fortunate enough to have the Ugaritic tablets dating from the fourteenth and thirteenth century B.C. They enable us to study at least some of the effects of the international crisis of polytheism on the religion of the Canaanites.

2. *The pantheon of disillusion*

Certainly there is a high god at the head of the Ugaritic pantheon. His name was Ilu, ''god'' *par excellence*. He is the creator of heaven and earth. He resides at the horizon of the habitable world where he keeps the cosmic waters under control. He is called the ''father'' of gods and man. Ilu does create not only by procreation, he also models his creatures from clay. Sometimes he creates simply by uttering his authoritative word. Being the potent creator-god he bears the epithet of ''bull'', just like Amun-Re in Egypt[21]). Ilu is the only one who can bless people with children. No other god, not even Baᶜlu, is able to do that. Ilu is called the Lord of the gods and probably also the Most High[22]).

Ilu is very old. He is called "the Father of Years". Even Ba'lu wishes him eternal life (KTU 1.10:III.4ff.). No major decision in the world of the gods can be made without the consent of Ilu. He is the overlord who personally picks younger gods to exercise the kingship for him. Only Ilu can decide who among the gods is allowed to build a palace of his own (KTU 1.1:I; 1.2:III; 1.3:V; 1.4:I-V). Just as he has the power to decide on birth he can decree death (KTU 1.14:V; 1.18:I).

Ilu possesses unlimited wisdom[23]). He is a merciful and gracious god whose compassion is praised[24]).

Almost everything that has been said so far about the Ugaritic god Ilu has a close parallel in the Egyptian hymns and prayers praising the qualities of Amun-Re. Often the resemblence is so striking that it makes one wonder whether a direct influence may be assumed. As long as no special investigation into this matter has been carried out this hypothesis is of a speculative interest only of course. However, it might be that it was exactly this close resemblance that made it impossible for the Egyptian theologians to incorporate Ilu into their pantheon whereas many other Canaanite gods, including Ba'lu, were freely admitted[25]). In this connection it is worth noting that when the name of Ilu did occur in a Canaanite text being translated into the Egyptian language his name was replaced by that of Amun-Re[26]). In any case this proves that even according to outsiders Ilu did occupy the most exalted position in the pantheon of the Canaanites at the end of the Late Bronze Age.

Yet it is certain that in Ugarit Ilu was not worshipped in a henotheistic way. Nowhere he is called the one of whom all other gods would have been nothing but aspects. This alone makes a big difference with Amun-Re, Marduk and Assur. On the contrary, the Ugaritic tablets expressly describe Ilu's most important rival, the younger god Ba'lu, as a newcomer in the family of Ilu. He is only a son of Ilu in so far as he is his son-in-law. Ba'lu was the physical son of Daganu of Tuttul. So Ilu is definitely not the one who generated all other deities.

It has often been pointed out that there is a palpable tension between Ilu and his family on the one side, Ba'lu and his supporters on the other. The star of Ba'lu was clearly rising. Yet according to the religious texts of Ugarit he is still in many respects the inferior of Ilu. He does repair the wings of some birds (KTU 1.19:III.12ff.), but he is unable to create anything new[27]), not even when Ilu more or less challenges him to do so (KTU 1.16:V). What then did people see in this young rain-god?

In contrast to Egypt and Mesopotamia Canaan was totally dependent on rain for its agriculture and cattle-breeding. In this semi-arid region sufficient rainfall in the period from October through April was crucial to the sustenance of life. The Canaanites have tried to explain the rhythm of the seasons that was so vitally important to them in composing a masterful mythological narrative around the figure of Baʿlu. His vicissitudes in the distant past of primordial times would be reflected, be it on a smaller scale, in the normal course of every year. In this myth of Baʿlu it is expressly stated that it is he who has to take care of the sustenance of gods and man[28]). This too is a big difference with the henotheistic cult of Amun-Re and Marduk. Whereas in these gods the functions of creator and sustainer had been combined in one divine person, these functions were divided over two different gods in the religion of Late Bronze Ugarit. As a result of this fundamental division the crisis of polytheism which, as we shall see, has also occurred in Ugarit developed in a direction totally different from that of the henotheistic movements in Egypt and Mesopotamia. In Ugarit the crisis took the form of a relentless struggle for power between opposing parties within the pantheon[29]).

The world of the gods of Ugarit is the scene of many low intrigues. Ilu deliberately deceives his son-in-law Baʿlu to deliver him up to his new favourite Yammu, the god of the sea (KTU 1.2:I). When Baʿlu with good reason becomes angry at the lackeys of Yammu who have come to demand his extradition it is his own spouse ʿAnatu/ʿAthtartu who prevents him from acting forcefully (KTU 1.2:I.38ff.). Later on, when Baʿlu succeeds in vanquishing Yammu, it is again his wife who prevents him from dealing the sea-god the final blow (KTU 1.2:IV).

In a later episode of the myth Baʿlu suffers defeat against another son of Ilu, the god of death Motu. On that occasion ʿAnatu reproaches her kin with making merry at the expense of her husband (KTU 1.6:I.39ff.). In KTU 1.12 Ilu creates two monsters to which Baʿlu appears to be unable to stand up.

So young Baʿlu is not yet of the same calibre as his old father-in-law. When he finally gets permission to build a mansion of his own it is only because he has succeeded in bribing Ilu's wife Athiratu behind the back of his father-in-law (KTU 1.4:I-III). When the house has been built, he displays a curious irresolution. At the very last moment he reverses a firm previous decision not to put a window in the house. Immediately it proves to be a fatal error. Enemies come rushing along to attack his abode. Without having been informed in so many words of their identity Baʿlu knows already they are the forces of the god of death who have come to fetch him (KTU 1.4:VI-VII).

Now it is very peculiar that at this particular moment the poet makes

Baʿlu say:

> "I alone am the one who can be king over the gods!"
>
> (KTU 1.4:VII.49f., cf. IV.43f.).

This pronouncement implies a definite henotheistic pretension. It is phrased in terms reminiscent of the henotheistic claims that were made on behalf of Amun-Re, Marduk and Assur. However, whereas in those cases the speakers were in dead earnest it looks as if the Ugaritic poet subtly ridicules the pretensions of Ba‘lu. In his case it sounds like the brave language of a coward on the verge of the precipice.

Indeed soon afterwards Ba‘lu disgracefully surrenders himself to the god of death Motu. He descends into the nether world where he experiences weakness like all the other dead. The god of life has been swallowed by Death and even Ilu himself perfunctorily mourns for Ba‘lu (KTU 1.5). The poet has not the slightest hesitation in telling us that Ba‘lu was terribly afraid of Motu (KTU 1.5:II.6f.). As a matter of fact it is remarkable how often he describes the great gods as outright frightened[30]).

It has been stated that in a polytheistic religion a deliberately expressed lack of respect for certain gods may be an indication that new gods are going to take the place of the old ones[31]). If that is true the whole pantheon of Ugarit was ready to be replaced at the end of the Late Bronze Age. For not only to Ba‘lu moments of appaling weakness are attributed, the same is true of Ilu. Time and again he allows himself to be bullied by the women in his entourage[32]). At a dinner party given by their father Ilu the goddesses ‘Anatu and ‘Athtartu demonstratively feed the best pieces of meat to the dogs under the table (KTU 1.114). Ilu himself becomes so inebriated that it looks as if he is under the influence of the hallucinatory drug henbane[33]). Finally he slumps down into his own dung and two younger gods have to carry him off home. It admits of no question that the poet of this baffling text wanted to ventilate his disdain for Ilu and his family, because he makes the lower personnel of the court of Ilu protest vigorously against the behaviour of their masters[34]). Heavy drinking was acceptable in Ugarit provided one did not lose his self-control. Therefore it was decidedly a point in favour of the younger Ba‘lu that he could drink no less than 10.000 jars of wine without showing the slightest sign of drunkenness (KTU 1.3:I.9ff.).

Nowhere in the religious literature of the Ancient Near East wine and sexuality play such a prominent role as in the myths of Ugarit. The texts describe even the most intimate details of the erotic adventures of Ilu and Ba‘lu, including bestiality and cohabitation with more than one partner at the same occasion[35]).

We have no reason to suppose that the inhabitants of Ugarit approved of such behaviour. As far as we know they did not tolerate it in normal life[36]). They merely describe the world of the gods such as they felt it had to be. A world full of hate, violence, treason, weakness, greed, partiality, rashness, blunders, drinking-bouts and orgies. This is the pantheon of disillusion. This is at least *one* side of the crisis of polytheism in Canaan.

In the Ugaritic concept of the divine world a great tension makes itself felt. Doubtlessly this tension reflects the concrete religious experience of the people of that time. Perhaps we do best to describe it as follows: the gods of Ugarit had become too human. None of them really held supreme power, they feared each other and most of all they feared death. When they did not fight they indulged in heavy drinking and debauchery. The world of the gods of Ugarit is a world that looks suspiciously like that of the bickering Canaanite kings at the end of the Late Bronze Age. If there does exist a certain correspondence between the absolute kingship of Egypt, Babylonia and Assyria on the one hand and the absolute hegemony of the national gods Amun-Re, Marduk and Assur on the other, one would have to say that the pantheon of Ugarit reflects the torn political reality of Canaan.

The fundamental questions that were raised in contemporary Egypt and Mesopotamia did not leave the Canaanites untouched. However, the pluralism of the Canaanite society and religion made it impossible to overcome this crisis of polytheism.

3. *Ineffectual foreknowledge*

I now invite your attention to another relevant aspect of the myth of Ba'lu, *viz.* the circumstance that the great gods, though clearly prescient, often appear to be unable to turn their knowledge to good advantage. The poet has picked up this theme several times, so it seems to have fascinated him. Unfortunately some of the passages involved are very fragmentary and this was probably the reason why hitherto they did not draw the attention they deserve[37]).

Very early in the myth of Ba'lu Ilu foresees the misfortunes that will befall Ba'lu. His son-in-law will have to bow down at the feet of the messengers of Yammu, and Motu is already threatening in the background (KTU 1.3:V.10-18). Later on, when Ilu has appointed his own son Yammu to replace Ba'lu as viceroy, Ilu warns Yammu that if he fails to chase Ba'lu away from his mountain, the latter will certainly beat him (KTU 1.1:IV.26f.). Apparently Ilu is unable or unwilling to give his son proper protection.

Soon afterwards Ba'lu senses that Ilu is planning his downfall even though nobody has told him so (KTU 1.1:V). However, Ba'lu is unable to stop his father-in-law. In KTU 1.2:I.21 he is standing meekly beside Ilu in the assembly of the gods. Meanwhile, however, he has uttered a threat revealing that he knows beforehand that the magical axe of

Kotharu will knock down Yammu in the end (KTU 1.2:I.5f.). This does
not, however, prevent Yammu from sending his messengers nor does it
incite him to think out effective counter-measures.

One of the best-known examples of clairvoyancy is the passage where
Ilu foresees in a dream that Baʿlu is still alive and will fill the wadies with
his rains again (KTU 1.6:III.10ff.). Strangely enough, however, Ilu
himself appears to be unable to bring Baʿlu back. Also it does not seem to
bother him in the least that the return of Baʿlu will inevitably involve the
demise of his own beloved son Motu. Soon afterwards an unknown
speaker predicts exactly what will happen: Baʿlu will make a great
massacre of the sons of Ilu before he returns to occupy the throne that is
rightfully his (KTU 1.6:V.1-6). But even this dire message does not pro-
voke any reaction from the side of Ilu. He seems to acquiesce in the in-
evitable as if his foreknowledge is of no avail whatsoever when it comes to
influencing the future course of events.

One of the well-preserved passages dealing with foreknowledge is
KTU 1.4:VII.35ff. Certain unidentified enemies attack the slopes of the
mountain of Baʿlu. The latter surprisingly enough seems to know
beforehand that they are the lackeys of the god of death Motu. He also
correctly surmises that Motu will soon invite him to descend into his
gullet. Because the preceding narrative does not contain even the
slightest hint that such an invitation might be forthcoming this is a sure
sign of Baʿlu's ability to read the future. Although he tries to forestall his
opponent by sending messengers with an invitation of his own, he knows
he does not stand a chance. All auguries are unfavourable:

> "Look, Gupanu-and-Ugaru[38])!
>   The sons of darkness[39]) obscure the day,
>   the sons of deep darkness (obscure) the exalted Princess[40])!
>   The wings of Fate[41]) are dust-coloured,
>   flocks are circling round in the clouds,
>   birds are circling round in the sky[42]).
>   Surely I must bind the snow in [the storehouses],
>   the lightning [in] its [storehouses][43])!"
>   (KTU 1.4:VII.53-60).

Dust was a characteristic attribute of the god of death who was also held
responsible for the sirocco, a hot desert wind frequently obscuring the sun
with dust in spring[44]). To Baʿlu the dusty colour of the sun heralds the
summer when snow and lightning, and also rain, clouds and storms[45]),
disappear completely at the coast of Syria[46]). Soon afterwards Baʿlu surrenders to Motu without offering any resistance (KTU 1.5:II). If my
translation of the expression "the wings of Fate" is correct it offers an ex-

planation for the ineffectiveness of the foreknowledge of the gods in the myth of Baʿlu[47]), because in that case even the gods were subjected to the inexorable course of fate. However, even if a different translation would prove to be preferable it is clear that foreknowledge is of no avail to the gods simply because the myth of Baʿlu describes a deterministic process, *viz.* the mythological prototype of the eternal cycle of the seasons.

4. *The invincible evil*

The great myth of Baʿlu that formed the central piece of the religious traditions of Ugarit can hardly be called a joyful message of salvation to all mankind. On the contrary, this myth was never intended as testimony of any final victory over the forces of evil and was never understood as a closed chapter of primordial history. Surely Baʿlu did defeat Yammu, but in contrast to Marduk who annihilated Tiamat Baʿlu did not destroy Yammu (KTU 1.2:IV.28ff.). As a consequence man still had to fear the god of the sea whose satellites might come along any time to take away not only a daring sailor, but also unsuspecting others, even pregnant women[48]).

Who were these satellites of Yammu? According to KTU 1.2 they were fearsome flying monsters:

> "With jubilant cries they flew heavenwards,
> [   ],
>   a span the jaws of their beaks."
>
> (KTU 1.2:I.12f.).

> "A fire, two fires they appeared,
>   a sharpened sword their tongues."
>
> (KTU 1.2:I.32f.).

Are these monsters related to the monsters ʿAnatu claims to have defeated in KTU 1.3:III.39ff.? It seems so, because among them is "the bitch of Ilu, Fire"[49]). Elsewhere Yammu and his monstrous helpers are more or less identified:

> "Break the neck of Yammu-with-the-forked-tongue
>   which is licking the sky!
> Break the neck of Yammu-with-the-fish-tail,
>   put Tunnanu to the muzzle,
>   bind (them) to the heights of the Lebanon!"
>
> (KTU 1.83:5ff.).

It is illogical to assume that when Yammu was defeated by Baʿlu in KTU
1.2:IV his arrogant satellites would have been spared. Recently John
Day has put forward the theory that there had been an earlier struggle in
connection with God's work of creation. In this primordial struggle not
only Yammu, but also his monsters would have been punished[50]).

At the present state of our knowledge this certainly is a possibility. On
the other hand it has to be observed that about ten to twenty long lines of
the lower part of the column describing the victory over Yammu are
missing (KTU 1.2:IV). In the Babylonian Epic of Creation the description of the punishment of the helpers of Tiamat takes only seventeen
relatively short lines (En.el. IV.105-122). So it is by no means excluded
that also the helpers of Yammu were punished within the context of the
myth of Baʿlu.

However, even if Day is right it has to be observed that in any case the
victory of Baʿlu and ʿAnatu over the monsters of the Sea was only a Pyr-
rhic one. Eventually the god of death Motu exploits this fact to his advantage in his famous speech at the beginning of Tablet V (KTU 1.5:I.1ff.).
Obviously he could not have done so if Yammu and his helpers had been
eliminated completely. Maliciously he reminds Baʿlu of the present
status of Yammu: he is a cup-bearer of Death (KTU 1.5:I.21f.). A further hint of the continuing threat posed by the god of the sea is found in
KTU 1.3:III.32ff. ʿAnatu's explosive reaction to the mere arrival of
messengers of Baʿlu would seem to betray a disproportionate apprehen-
sion that Yammu and his monsters might have mounted another attack
on Baʿlu. Among the monsters she enumerates are Tunnanu (the
Hebrew Tannin) and Lotanu (the Hebrew Leviathan[51]).

Later on Baʿlu refuses to let Kotharu put a window in his palace lest
Yammu might insult his daughters again (KTU 1.4:VI.7ff.). And finally
at the end of the myth of Baʿlu the pious pray that Kotharu will assist
(again!) in defeating the monsters Tunnanu and Arishu (KTU
1.6:VI.51f.).

Recently it has been established beyond any doubt that the people of
Ugarit continued to regard the monsters of Yammu as a demoniacal
threat. There is an incantation against the monstrous flies causing
madness in spite of ʿAnatu's boast to have defeated this particular kind of
monster[52]). In a collection of incantations against evil demons Baʿlu and
ʿAnatu are prayed to smite Tunnanu and the evil serpents once again[53]).
In a third incantation the Sun is prayed to collect the poisonous fog from
the mountains[54]). We know from the Babylonian Epic of Creation that in
the mist the poison of Tiamat was thought to be present (En.el. V.51)[55]).
Presumably the people of Ugarit attributed the ''poisonous'' fog also to
the Sea because at the Syrian coast fog and mist invariably drift in from
the sea[56]).

We now understand why exactly the same evil powers are warded off again and again in the Jewish Aramaic incantation bowls of a much later date. The Sea, the Leviathan, the Tannin, the Fog, we meet them all again here[57]. This folk-religion apparently was a remnant of the ancient Canaanite belief that Yammu and his monsters had never been defeated in a really conclusive way.

Of course the same was true of the other archenemy of Baᶜlu, the god of death Motu. Even though ᶜAnatu did destroy him as effectively as she could (KTU 1.6:II.30ff.) after seven years Motu rose to challenge Baᶜlu again (KTU 1.6:V.7ff.). The god of life and the god of death appear to be equally strong (KTU 1.6:VI.16ff.). To human beings, however, it sometimes looked as if Motu was the stronger (KTU 2.10:12f.).

It should be noted that at the end of the myth the god of death does not succumb to Baᶜlu. It is expressly stated that he only gives in because he fears the wrath of Ilu (KTU 1.6:VI.22ff.). Neither in this case nor in the earlier episode describing the victory over Yammu it is Baᶜlu himself who overpowers his opponent. Yammu is defeated only with the help of the magical axe of Kotharu. Motu is forced to give up as a result of the intervention of the sun-goddess. With such an unreliable champion man had to fear that one time Baᶜlu might fail again, leaving the earth to the god of death for seven or more consecutive years (KTU 1.19:I.40ff.).

All the data provided up to this point prove that the equilibrium between life and death attained in the myth of Baᶜlu can hardly be called stable. People could derive very little reassurance from it. The hymn at the end as well as several other episodes[58] indicate that the myth was actualized in the cult of Ugarit year after year. It is for this reason that the end of the myth links up with its beginning. On a microcosmic scale the vicissitudes of Baᶜlu repeated themselves in the cycle of the seasons. It is this cyclic concept of opposing divine forces governing the laws of nature that lends a decidedly deterministic flavour to the Ugaritic religion at the end of the Late Bronze Age. However, since the forces of evil had never been defeated convincingly man was left with a great deal of incertitude. Who could guarantee that the scale would remain microcosmic for ever?

5. *Man, a puppet on strings*

As I said, man could derive very little hope from a religion so basically pessimistic in its outlook. This is underscored heavily by two Ugaritic legends which might rightfully be called early precursors of the Greek tragedies.

5.1 Kirtu

In the first of these legends we are told how king Kirtu marries no less than seven times only to lose all his wives before they are able to bear him a child. Because in the Ancient Near East only a father of a large family was held in high esteem, Kirtu falls deeply in the public estimation.

One night when he lies brooding over his misfortune his personal patron Ilu appears in his dream. It is noteworthy that at first Ilu thinks that Kirtu is weeping because he wants to be king of the gods, like Ilu himself. Apparently the divinity of kings was a topic that preoccupied the mind of many a Canaanite ruler. We know that the kings of Ugarit were supposed to become minor gods after their death.

The kingship of the gods not being available to man, Ilu offers Kirtu gold, silver and other valuables as a consolation prize. Kirtu, however, declines. His only wish is a large number of sons. This is something Ilu can promise him. He explains down to the minutest detail how Kirtu must act to obtain a suitable and handsome bride.

When Kirtu awakes he punctiliously carries out everything Ilu had ordered him to do. With a huge army of dedicated subjects he starts on his way. However, on the third day something unexpected happens which had not been predicted by Ilu. Kirtu passes a temple of Athiratu, the wife of Ilu. In his understandable enthusiasm he makes a vow there. If he succeeds in bringing home his bride, he will donate twice her weight in silver and thrice her weight in gold to Athiratu.

In every other respect the mission goes off exactly as planned and Kirtu does take his bride home. For the wedding he also invites the gods because he wants them to consecrate his marriage. It is very remarkable that Kirtu does allow the gods to enter his palace, but prevents them from leaving. Baʿlu is the first to understand Kirtu's objective. Mockingly he addresses Ilu as follows:

> "[How] do you think you can leave, o Benevolent,
>   Ilu the Merciful?
> Surely you will have to bless Kirtu, the nobleman,
>   surely you will have to strengthen the gracious lad of Ilu!
>   (KTU 1.15:II.13-16)

We note three interesting points:
1) The poet has a rather low opinion of the power of the gods. An earthly king is able to detain them.
2) Baʿlu takes the liberty to mock at the head of the pantheon.
3) Yet he is unable to bless the newly wed couple himself.
So the tension between Ilu and Baʿlu we noticed in the myths is also expressed in this legend. However, a new element has been added. A human being appears to be able to defy the gods.

Ilu pronounces his blessing on the marriage and promises Kirtu two sons and six daughters which was, incidentally, not exactly what Kirtu had wanted. Nevertheless this large family will elevate him in the public estimation. So everything looks well until Ilu adds, seemingly as an afterthought:

> "The youngest of them—her I will make a firstborn!"
> (KTU 1.15:III.16).

This underdeveloped verse, actually a unicolon, forms the joint on which the whole story is hinged. It is possible to read it as a promise. Even the youngest girl will obtain a position comparable to that of a first-born. Probably Kirtu understood it that way at first. It was not, however, what Ilu meant to say. Being prescient he foresees that eventually Kirtu will lose all his children again except for the youngest girl.

From this moment on everything goes wrong. As soon as the eight children have been born Kirtu is seized by a mortal illness because he is unable to redeem his rashly pronounced vow to Athiratu.

When he lies dying his pretended friends and allies appear to be hardly impressed by his ill luck. They have forgotten him even before he is dead and buried. Thus the poet forces us to concede that the public esteem Kirtu had sought actually means nothing at all.

Kirtu's wife says to the assembled friends and vassals: "Kirtu is going to join Ilu", indicating that he will attain the divine status which, as we remember, Kirtu himself did not aspire. But as I said, the kings of Ugarit derived some consolation from the thought that after their death they would take a place in the lower ranks of the pantheon. It is highly significant that the children of Kirtu do not seem to gain any comfort from this idea which was a cornerstone of the Ugaritic cult of the royal dead:

> "In your life, our father, we rejoiced,
>   in your immortality we exulted.
> (Now), like dogs we prowl through your house,
>   like puppies—ah!—through your basement.
> Ah father! Should you die like mortal men?
>   Alas! Should moaning pass through your basement?
>   Dirges of father's wife on the heights?
> How can they say: Kirtu is a son of Ilu,
>   a child of the Benevolent and Qudshu?
> Alas! Do gods die?
>   Does not a child of the Benevolent live?"
> (KTU 1.16:I.14-23).

What these children are protesting against is part of the official royal ideology of the ancient Canaanite world. We are witnessing here an overt rebellion against the prevailing theology of that time.

Through the personal intervention of Ilu Kirtu does recover miraculously but immediately afterwards he comes into conflict with his eldest son who had expected to succeed his father real soon. Kirtu is compelled to curse his son with a terrible curse amounting to nothing less than a death-sentence.

Unfortunately the last tablet of the series is lost, but the end of the story is all too predictable. Kirtu will loose all his children in succession but for the youngest girl who in this way becomes the firstborn.

The Legend of Kirtu is a protest against the current concepts of divine rule. Kirtu is the righteous sufferer, the tragic victim of the whims of the gods. Having been childless for a long time already because evil deities took away every one of his wives, he is understandably glad when at last Ilu himself promises him a happy family. All his subjects enthusiastically support their king in obtaining his bride. One ill-considered vow in a situation for which Ilu incomprehensibly did not give him any guidance became his undoing, so that in the end Kirtu is almost as destitute as he was in the beginning. He has only one girl left. What Ilu had given was taken away by his spouse Athiratu. Kirtu refused to accept the gold of Ilu, but in the end he did not have the gold to pay Athiratu her due. Kirtu was a favourite of Ilu and was even called his son in accordance with the royal ideology. But what do such big words mean in reality? Ilu uses his power as a creator to give Kirtu the children he wants. Later on he creates a good genius to heal Kirtu. Did he lack the power then to protect his servant effectively? Why did Kirtu recover? We have reason to suspect that it was only to witness the destruction of his family all over again.

5.2. Aqhatu

The second epic text affording us an insight into the relationship between god and man in Ugarit is the Legend of Aqhatu. In this case too the story opens with a king who is inconsolable because he has no son. This king named Dani'ilu or Dan'ilu wants a son *inter alia* because he hopes that after his death this son will raise him as a protective spirit from the nether world[59]). At the intercession of his personal patron Baꜥlu Ilu gives Dani'ilu a son who receives the name of Aqhatu. When Aqhatu is a young man Kotharu, the technician among the gods, comes to pay a visit to Dani'ilu. Because Dani'ilu receives him hospitably Kotharu makes him a present of a wonderful composite bow with which the son Aqhatu goes out hunting.

The beautiful bow arouses the envy of ʿAnatu who is a huntress herself. She first offers Aqhatu silver and gold for the bow, but the young man replies rather tartly that she can have one made for herself. ʿAnatu is not to be daunted, however, and she promises him nothing less than eternal life. Aqhatu turns his offer down too. In doing so he accuses the goddess in plain terms of lying. Again we meet a human being here who dares to defy a deity. It has often been observed that the closest parallel to the insolent behaviour of Aqhatu can be found in the Epic of Gilgamesh. Gilgamesh shows similar contempt for the goddess Ishtar (Gilg.Ep. VI.i.22ff.). It is worth noting that the Kassite ''canonical'' version of the Epic of Gilgamesh is roughly contemporary with the Legend of Aqhatu.

ʿAnatu rushes to her father Ilu and by threatening to kill him she obtains his permission to murder Aqhatu. ʿAnatu returns to her victim and pretends to make him a final offer. She proposes to marry him so that he will automatically become a member of the pantheon. Aqhatu walks into this trap and is murdered during the wedding-dinner. His death is as meaningless as his life, for ʿAnatu does not obtain the bow she had coveted either (KTU 1.19:I.3f., 16f.).

Dani'ilu does know nothing of what has happened. He only notices that the grain on the fields is suddenly withering. The listeners to the story, however, understand perfectly well that this is a consequence of the death of prince Aqhatu. All nature is mourning, but the father suspects nothing. In breathtaking verses the poet describes how the terrible truth slowly dawns upon Dani'ilu.

At last, when he has learnt how Aqhatu has been murdered, he appeals for help to his patron Baʿlu. However, even this great god is unable to bring the son of Dani'ilu back to life. He can only assist him in finding the sorry remains of the body so that Aqhatu gets a more or less decent burial.

In the end we find Dani'ilu busy invoking the spirits of the dead because he hopes to embrace his son once again. So it is not the son who raises the protective spirit of his father from the nether world, as Dani'ilu had hoped, it is the other way round. A pathetic ending indeed.

As in the Legend of Kirtu death and the impossibility to become the equal of the great gods preoccupies the mind of the poet of the story of Aqhatu. At the same time there is the scarcely veiled resentment over the caprices of the gods. Aqhatu owed his existence to the intercession of Baʿlu, the wife of Baʿlu takes his life away. At first Ilu lets himself be convinced that Aqhatu should live, but then he is easily scared into signing his death-warrant. The poet stresses the righteousness of Dani'ilu. He was a king who stood up for the widow and the orphan. Yet he must suffer undeservedly. In the end he has gained nothing. Aqhatu may serve as

a model for a younger generation no longer willing to accept that man
was no more than a puppet on the strings of the unaccountable and conflicting powers in the divine world.

6. *Conclusions*

The vexing religious questions that were raised throughout the Ancient
Near East at the end of the Late Bronze Age did not pass Canaan unnoticed. The inconsistency of polytheism, the problem of undeserved suffering and divine justice, the balance between good and evil—all these
questions did occupy the minds of the people of Ugarit as much as they
did elsewhere. A growing self-consciousness of man, bordering on
disregard for the gods of the old venerated polytheistic pantheons is the
attitude which unites such seemingly disparate phenomena as the reformation of Akhenaten, the revolution of Osarsef, the contemporary
wisdom literature of Egypt and Mesopotamia, the Kassite redaction of
the Epic of Gilgamesh, the Ugaritic Legends of Kirtu and Aqhatu.

However, whereas in Egypt and Mesopotamia polytheism was
ultimately saved by henotheism, *i.e.* by the concentration on one god who
was thought to manifest himself in all other deities, this was never a
realistic option in the factious world of Canaan. In Ugarit the struggle for
power between Ilu and Baʿlu rendered any claim for the supremacy of
either of them totally pointless. So the people of Ugarit did remain true
polytheists, but with how many misgivings in their hearts!

In Egypt and Mesopotamia there was a noticeable increase in personal
piety as an expression of a direct and responsable relationship between
god and man. The Ugaritic version of the crisis of polytheism, however,
resulted in deep scepticism and resignation. True, we find the same spirit
in the wisdom literature of the time, in the Egyptian Song of the Harper
and in the Epic of Gilgamesh. The big difference, however, is that
nowhere but in Ugarit such a fatalistic world view was incorporated into
the myth that formed the very core of its religion, the great myth of baʿlu.

We have seen that not only the legends of Kirtu and Aqhatu, but also
the myth of baʿlu returns to its point of departure. The same artistic
device has been employed in the Kassite version of the Epic of Gilgamesh
to underscore the utter meaninglessness of the quest of its hero (Gilg.Ep.
I.i.16-19; XI.303-305). In Late Bronze Ugarit the crisis of polytheism led
to the conviction that not only human beings but even the gods
themselves were bound to move in the vicious circle of fate. On the one
hand the cyclic concept of time this way of thinking involved led to a great
intellectual achievement, *i.e.* the first conscious effort to explain both the
mechanism and the irregularities of climate in one comprehensive theory.

On the other hand it engendered a pessimism so deep that it left man little hope to lead a meaningful life. Or to say it with the words of a Babylonian wisdom text found in a private library at Ugarit itself:

"Human beings do not know what they are doing,
the meaning of their days and nights lies with the gods"[60]).

APPENDIX

One final observation. It is remarkable that all the major texts reflecting the religious scepticism described in this study were written by the same scribe, Ilimilku the Shubanite. It is characteristic of the personality and theology of this high priest of Ugarit that in the colophon appended to the great myth of Ba'lu he wants himself to be known as the master of gods:

KTU 1.6:VI.54-58
The scribe is Ilimilku, the Shubanite,
pupil of Attanu[61]), majordomo,
high priest, high shepherd[62]),
officiant of Niqmaddu[63]), king of Ugarit,
lord of Yaraggib, master of Tharrumannu[64]).

NOTES

[1]) This paper is a revised and expanded version of Chapter 2 of the writer's Dutch publication: *Uw God is mijn God. Over de oorsprong van het geloof in de ene God* (Kamper Cahiers, 51), Kampen 1983.

[2]) J. ASSMANN, *Re und Amun. Die Krise des polytheistischen Weltbildes im Ägypten der 18.-20. Dynastie*, Freiburg/Göttingen 1983. See also his: *Ägyptische Hymnen und Gebete*, Zürich/München 1975; *Sonnenhymnen in thebanischen Gräbern*, Mainz am Rhein 1983.

[3]) Cf. H. BRUNNER, *Universitas* 17 (1962) 149ff.; C. ALDRED, *Akhenaten, Pharaoh of Egypt. A New Study*, London 1968; *Akhenaten and Nefertari*, New York 1973; E. HORNUNG, *Der Eine und die Vielen. Ägyptische Gottesvorstellungen*, Darmstadt 1971, 239ff.; in: O. KEEL (ed.), *Monotheismus im Alten Israel und seiner Umwelt*, Fribourg/Stuttgart 1980, 83ff.; J. ASSMANN, *Saeculum* 23 (1972) 109ff.; *Lex.d.Ägypt.*, Bd.1, 526ff.; J. A. WILSON, *JNES* 32 (1973) 235ff.; S. WENIG, *Lex.d.Ägypt*, Bd.1, 210ff.; H. SCHLÖGL, *Echnaton-Tutanchamun. Fakten und Texte*, Wiesbaden 1983; D. B. REDFORD, *Akenaten. The Heretic King*, Princeton 1984; B. H. STRICKER, *Het Oude Verbond*, Amsterdam 1984, 5-10.

[4]) W. F. ALBRIGHT, *From the Stone Age to Christianity*, 2nd ed., Baltimore 1946, 150ff.

[5]) With regard to Marduk: W. G. LAMBERT, in: W. S. McCULLOUGH (ed.), *The Seed of Wisdom. Essays ... T. J. Meek*, Toronto 1964, 7ff.; in: H. GOEDICKE, J. J. M. ROBERTS (eds.), *Unity and Diversity*, London/Baltimore 1975, 191ff.; B. HARTMANN, in: O. KEEL (ed.), *Monotheismus* (n. 3), 49ff.; R. BORGER, *BiOr* 28 (1971) 3ff.; M. J. GELLER, *Iraq* 42 (1980) 23ff.; W. SOMMERFELD, *Der Aufstieg Marduks* (AOAT, 213), Neukirchen-Vluyn 1982, cf. W. G. LAMBERT, *BSOAS* 47 (1984) 1-9.

With regard to Assur a prayer of Tukulti-Ninurta I (ca. 1243-1207 B.C.) is most significant, cf. M.-J. SEUX, *Hymnes et prières aux dieux de Babylonie et d'Assyrie*, Paris 1976, 493ff.

   [6]) For the terminological problem see G. E. WRIGHT, *The Old Testament Against its Environment*, London 1950, 36ff.; T. P. VAN BAAREN, *Nederlands Theologisch Tijdschrift* 20 (1965-66) 321ff.; G. WIDENGREN, *Religionsphänomenologie*, Berlin 1969, 127ff.; M. ROSE, *Der Ausschliesslichkeitsanspruch Jahwes*, Stuttgart 1975, 9ff.; H. WILDBERGER, *Gesammelte Aufsätze zum A.T.*, München 1979, 249ff.; B. HARTMANN, art. cit., 67ff., but above all the brilliant book of HORNUNG, *Der Eine* (n. 3), which opens the eyes to the problems involved in the use of terms like "oneness" and "uniqueness" in a polytheistic context.

   [7]) So Celsus as early as *ca.* 130 A.D., cf. C. ANDRESEN, *Logos und Nomos. Die Polemik des Kelsos wider das Christentum*, Berlin 1955, 210ff. See also R. PETTAZONI, *RHR* 88 (1923) 200; *Der allwissende Gott. Zur Geschichte der Gottesidee*, Frankfurt 1960, 117; HORNUNG, *Der Eine* (n. 3), 91; O. KEEL, *Monotheismus* (n. 3), 20.

   [8]) For Egypt, the Wisdom of Amenemope, XIX.10ff. (ch. 18), cf. M. LICHTHEIM, *Ancient Egyptian Literature*, vol. 2, Berkeley 1976, 157f.; for Mesopotamia, Ludlul bēl nēmeqi, esp. II.33-38 (cf. W. G. LAMBERT, *Babylonian Wisdom Literature*, Oxford 1960, 40f.), the Babylonian Theodicy, esp. lines 70f., 135-139, 251f., 254-257, 264, 276-279 (LAMBERT, *Bab. Wisdom*, 74fff.) and the wisdom texts read in Ugarit, J. NOUGAYROL, *Ugaritica V*, Paris 1968, 265ff., 273ff., 291ff.

   [9]) Nergal and Ereshkigal, cf. E. VON WEIHER, *AOAT* 11 (1971) 48ff.; W. G. LAMBERT, in: B. ALSTER (ed.), *Death in Mesopotamia*, Copenhagen 1980, 62ff.; M. HUTTER, *Altorientalische Vorstellungen von der Unterwelt*, Fribourg 1985. Adapa, cf. F. M. Th. DE LIAGRE BÖHL, *WO* 2 (1959) 416ff.; B. R. FOSTER, *Or* 43 (1974) 344ff.; W. VON SODEN, *AOAT* 25 (1976) 427ff. Possibly the Epic of Erra, cf. with regard to the dating problem L. CAGNI, *The Poem of Erra*, Malibu 1977, 20f. And the Epic of Gilgamesh of course.

   [10]) Ink marks prove that the Egyptian scribes were able to read the tablets, cf. J. A. KNUDTZON, *Die El-Amarna-Tafeln*, Bd.1, Leipzig 1915, 25.

   [11]) Although the text of the sceptic Song of the Harper possibly dates from the Middle Kingdom, the only copies that have been preserved are from the New Kingdom. From the circumstance that other Harper-songs contradict this sceptic one, sometimes even in the same grave, it may be concluded that it was regarded as more or less heretic. Cf. M. LICHTHEIM, *Ancient Egyptian Literature*, vol. 1, Berkeley 1973, 193ff.; vol. 2, Berkeley 1976, 115f.; J. ASSMANN, *Lex.d.Ägypt.*, Bd.2, 972ff.

   With regard to the Epic of Gilgamesh see B. LANDSBERGER, in: P. GARELLI (ed.), *Gilgameš et sa légende*, Paris 1960, 34: "Die Geringschätzung des Dichters für die Götter ist ... auffallend".

   [12]) W. G. WADDELL, *Manetho* (Loeb Classical Library), London 1940, 124ff. There is insufficient reason to accept the assertion of Manetho's interpolator to the effect that this Osarseph would have been identical with the biblical Moses (against STRICKER, op. cit., 11f.). Cf. R. KRAUSS, *Das Ende der Amarnazeit*, Hildesheim 1978, 204-217.

   [13]) In O. KEEL (ed.), *Monotheismus* (n. 3), 95f.

   [14]) W. HELCK, *Die Beziehungen Ägyptens zu Vorderasien im 3. und 2. Jahrtausend v.Chr.*, 2.Aufl., Wiesbaden 1971, 107ff.; J. M. WEINSTEIN, *BASOR* 241 (1981) 1ff.; R. HACHMANN, *ZDPV* 98 (1982) 17ff.

   [15]) Cf. HELCK, *Beziehungen* (n. 14), 577; E. VON NORDHEIM, *SAK* 7 (1979) 227ff.; P. AUFFRET, *Hymnes d'Égypte et d'Israel*, Freiburg/Göttingen 1981, 137ff.; ASSMANN, *Re und Amun*, 122, 128ff., 142.

   [16]) KTU 2.23:17-24, see O. EISSFELDT, *Kleine Schriften*, Bd.4, Tübingen 1968, 53ff.

   [17]) H. GOEDICKE, *The Report of Wenamun*, Baltimore/London 1975, 87.

   [18]) As claimed in the hymns to Amun-Re: "On the mountain range Asiatics (= Canaanites) fall down in adoration", cf. ASSMANN, *Sonnenhymnen*, 261 (no. 287:12).

   [19]) In a forthcoming monograph K. SPRONK will demonstrate Egyptian influence on the Ugarit conceptions of afterlife.

   [20]) In order not to burden the presentation of the main argument with a large number of questions of detail the explanatory notes have been kept to the barest minimum. Specific problems with regard to the philological and religious interpretation of the Ugaritic texts have been discussed by the author in his *The Seasonal Pattern in the Ugaritic Myth of Ba^clu* (*AOAT*, 16), Neukirchen-Vluyn 1971; *New Year With Canaanites and Israelites*

(Kamper Cahiers, 21-22), Kampen 1972, as well as in many contributions to periodicals, notably *Ugarit-Forschungen.*

[21]) References with ASSMANN, *Sonnenhymnen*, 396.

[22]) See on all this: *The Bible World. Essays ... C. H. Gordon*, New York 1980, 203ff. as well as A. S. KAPELRUD, *ibid.*, 79ff.

[23]) *UF* 11 (1979) 643.

[24]) KTU 1.4:V.5, cf. M. DIJKSTRA, *Gods Voorstelling*, Kampen 1980, 208, as well as *UF* 14 (1982) 160. Compare Ex. 34:6.

[25]) R. STADELMANN, *Syrisch-palästinensische Gottheiten in Ägypten*, Leiden 1967.

[26]) HELCK, *Beziehungen* (n. 14), 461, 466 (ᶜAnatu was a daughter of Ilu).

[27]) I agree with GIBSON's interpretation of KTU 1.3:III.26, par., cf. J. C. L. GIBSON, *Canaanite Myths and Legends*, Edinburgh 1978, 49, with his note 6. Cf. M. S. SMITH, *UF* 16 (1984) 295-298.

[28]) KTU 1.4:VII.50ff., cf. 1.5:VI.23f.; 1.6:IV.12ff.; 1.16:III.4ff.; 1.19:I.38ff.

[29]) According to the Ugaritic tablets three parties, cf. *UF* 14 (1982) 174.

[30]) KTU 1.2:I.21ff.; 1.3:III.32ff., V.25ff.; 1.4:II.12ff.; 1.6:VI.30.

[31]) HORNUNG, *Der Eine* (n. 3), 143ff.

[32]) KTU 1.3:V.1ff., par.; 1.4:IV.40ff., V.1ff.; 1.6:I.43ff.

[33]) Cf. *UF* 16 (1984) 355f.

[34]) A burlesque text like KTU 1.114 can only be understood as a critique of the prevailing religion, cf. M. P. NILSSON, *Geschichte der griechischen Religion*, Bd.1, 2.Aufl., München 1955, 742, 767ff., 779ff.; Bd.2, 2.Aufl., München 1961, 192ff.

[35]) For references see *Uw God is mijn God* (n. 1), 36, n. 134.

[36]) Debauchery during cultic meals was forbidden, cf. *Loven en geloven. Opstellen ... Nic. H. Ridderbos*, Amsterdam 1975, 217f. Adultery may have been tolerated on the level of myth and legend (KTU 1.18 as well as H. OTTEN, *MDOG* 85 (1953) 30ff.; *MIO* 1 (1953) 125ff.), but it was punished severely in everyday life, cf. L. R. FISHER, *The Claremont Ras Shamra Tablets*, Roma 1971, 11ff. (with older literature) as well as J. NOUGAYROL, *RA* 66 (1972) 88ff.

[37]) Several of the passages in question have been restored in the forthcoming *Cuneiform Anthology of Religious Texts of Ugarit* (J. C. DE MOOR and K. SPRONK).

[38]) Personal attendants of Baᶜlu.

[39]) Lackeys of the god of death Motu.

[40]) Probably the sun. Cf. Am. 5:18,20; 8:9; Zeph. 1:15.

[41]) The word *mnt*, here translated by "Fate", actually means "portion(s)", just like the Greek μοῖρα and αἶσα. Sometimes the Moira were represented as winged goddesses, cf. S. EITREM, *PRE* XV, Stuttgart 1932, 2472. Manat was also a pre-islamic goddess, cf. T. FAHD, *Le panthéon de l'Arabie Centrale à la veille de l'Hégire*, Paris 1968, 123ff.

[42]) A reference to the migration of birds in spring. Because the spirits of the privileged dead were thought to be "with Baᶜlu" in the hereafter in the form of birds, bird migration heralded the revival of Baᶜlu in autumn as well as his journey to the nether world in spring.

[43]) Cf. Job 38:22 (tautological parallelism, as in the Ugaritic passage!) and KTU 1.101:3f. Compare also Job 26:8 and Prov. 30:4, as well as Baᶜlu's "ship" with snow in KTU 1.4:V.7. Towards the end of April snow disappeared from even the highest mountains. Thunderstorms are a rarity in the Syrian summer.

[44]) Cf. KTU 1.4:VIII.21ff.; 6:II.24f. and *AOAT* 16, 114f., 173ff., 187ff.

[45]) KTU 1.5:V.6ff.

[46]) Cf. *AOAT* 16, 187-189.

[47]) It is worth noting that whereas the mythopoet describes Ilu and Baᶜlu as prescient he sometimes seems to emphasize the total ignorance of their wives. Cf. KTU 1.3:III.32ff.; 1.4:II.12ff.; 1.5:VI.

[48]) KTU 1.14:I.14f., cf. *UF* 11 (1979) 643f.

[49]) KTU 1.3:III.45, cf. Maqlû VI.121f.; Ps. 104:4.

[50]) J. DAY, *God's Conflict With the Dragon and the Sea*, Cambridge 1985, 7-18.

⁵¹) With regard to the etymology of Lotanu see *BiOr* 31 (1974) 5, overlooked by J. A. EMERTON, *VT* 32 (1982) 328f. whose case was certainly not strengthened by S. V. UDD, *VT* 33 (1983) 509f. who mixed up different stems of *ḥwy*.

⁵²) KTU 1.3:III.46, cf. *JEOL* 27 (1981-82) 114f.

⁵³) KTU 1.82:1, 6, 26f., 35, 38, see *UF* 16 (1984) 237-250.

⁵⁴) KTU 1.107 *passim*, cf. *UF* 9 (1977) 366f.

⁵⁵) See also Hesiod, *Work and Days*, 125, 255.

⁵⁶) G. DALMAN, *Arbeit und Sitte in Palästina*, Bd.1, Gütersloh 1928, 309ff.; *Air Ministry, Meteorological Office (Naval Division)*, *Weather in the Mediterranean*, Vol. 2, Part 11, 51; E. WIRTH, *Syrien. Eine geographische Landeskunde*, Darmstadt 1971, 77f.

⁵⁷) C. D. ISBELL, *Corpus of the Aramaic Incantation Bowls*, Missoula 1975, glossary.

⁵⁸) Compare KTU 1.3:I with 1.23:1-29; 1.3:II with 1.13:5ff.; 1.17:VI.26ff. with 1.3:I and 1.6:III-VI.

⁵⁹) This is the correct interpretation of KTU 1.17:I.26-28, par., see *UF* 17 (1986), 407ff.

⁶⁰) J. NOUGAYROL, *Ugaritica V* (n. 8), 294:24-26.

⁶¹) Apparently Ilimilku wants to claim the authority of Attanu for the correctness of his account. This may mean that hitherto the myth of Ba‘lu had been handed down orally. In itself it is significant that no less a person than a high-priest was able and willing to write down this extensive religious document.

Because his title "officiant" (see note 63 below) is attested elsewhere in Ugarit it is impossible to regard Attanu as the high-priest.

⁶²) Probably a metaphor for spiritual leadership. Cf. Am. 1:1, but also 7:14f.

⁶³) Niqmaddu II, king of Ugarit ca. 1365-1335 B.C. The king was the pivot of the Ugaritic ritual. Because the king was unable to attend every ceremony in person, the high-priest acted as his stand-in.

⁶⁴) Yaraggib and Tharrumannu were minor deities or spirits of deified heroes who were under the control of the medium Ilimilku. Compare 1 Sam. 28:7 *b‘lt ’wb* "mistress of an ancestral spirit". Tharrumannu is mentioned quite often in the cultic texts of Ugarit. Yaraggib is probably a hypocoristic name. Possible candidates for the full name are the attested Ugaritic divine names *Yrgb-Hd, Yrgb-B‘l* and *Yrgb-L’im.*

TIME AND PLACE IN GENESIS V

BY

N. POULSSEN
Den Bosch

James JOYCE's *magnum opus* Ulysses has done justice to the classical literary canon concerning the unity of time and place in an exemplary and extremely concise manner: sixteen hours in Dublin. The pen of the writer of the register-like Gen. v has not succeeded in producing a similar composition by a long way. In the small compass of this chapter of Genesis no real coordination of time and place materializes. Concretely speaking this discrepancy comes to a head in the shortcut of verse 29 with respect to the remainder of the chapter. Verse 29 is, as a monad, clearly determined by place, whereas independent of it the bulk of the remaining verses measures the successive duration of ten generations and thus receives a special chronological articulation.

The present lecture wants to trace the mutual sensitivities of that spatial-temporal disjunction, while also taking the support of the wider context into account. Given the structuring forces of the categories of time and place in any piece of literature, such a search would illuminate from inside the complexity of an outstanding tradition from the ever intriguing biblical primeval history. It seems to me that the individuality and imagination of vs 29 do not only invite us to use this concise verse as our point of departure, but also to choose it as an observation post from where the rest of the chapter can be inspected.

The individuality of vs 29 is—to begin with—of a formal nature in as far as the verse is structured poetically. After the brief rhyme at the outset—*wayyiqrā ʾèt šᵉmô nōah*—the text follows in rhythmical scansion with a whole sequence of assonances: *zè yᵉnahămēnû mimmaʿăśēnû ûmēʿiṣṣᵉbôn yādēnû min hāʾădāmâ ʾăšèr ʾērᵉrāh YHWH*. The second half of the verse takes up a positive expectation regarding the future. It stands in particular contrast to the gloomy retrospect at the end of the verse. The subjects of the contrary verbs *niḥḥam* and *ʾārar* form the perhaps even audible poles of Lamech's utterance: *zè* and *YHWH*. The determination of place, a preposition *cum* noun: *min hāʾădāmâ*, takes—in the whole of the explanation of the name—if not a central then certainly a pronounced position. According to the Massoretic accent system it is marked by two *zaqqef* signs. Nevertheless the clause introduced by *min hāʾădāmâ* is again

and again considered as just a closer determination of the preceding
nominal phrase *ma⁽ăśēnû ûmēⱱiṣṣᵉbôn yādēnû*. Is this the tenor of the King
James Version: "This *same* shall comfort us concerning our work and toil
of our hands, because of the ground which the LORD hath cursed"? I
understand this English at least in the light of the Targumic New English
Bible: "This boy will bring us relief from our work, and from the hard
labour that has come upon us because of the LORD's curse upon the
ground". Indeed, it seems that the Vulgate already had in mind nothing
else: "Iste consolabitur nos ab operibus et laboribus manuum
nostrarum, in terra cui maledixit Dominus". Ronald KNOX renders this
as follows: "He will console us, that have toiled and laboured with our
hands so long on ground which the LORD has cursed". Compare the
Luther Bible: "Der wird uns trösten in unser mühe und erbeit auff Erden
die der HERR verflucht hat", and its echo in the more recent German
translation by V. Hamp c.s.: "Dieser wird uns trösten bei der
mühevollen Arbeit unserer Hände am Ackerboden, den der HERR
verflucht hat". Finally a corresponding French sound from the *Bible de la
Pléiade*: "Celui-ci nous consolera de notre tâche et de la souffrance de nos
mains provoquée par le sol qu'a maudit Jahvé". The Septuagint pays
more attention to the relative independence of *min hā⁾ădāmâ* but tampers
with the structure of the original text. Moreover it levels the dynamics of
the text by translating the various meanings of the triple preposition *min*
in the same way: Οὗτος διαναπαύσει ἡμᾶς ἀπὸ τῶν ἔργων ἡμῶν καὶ ἀπὸ τῶν
λυπῶν τῶν χειρῶν ἡμῶν καὶ ἀπὸ τῆς γῆς, ἧς κατηράσατο κύριος ὁ θεός. The
versions, however, we have just quoted, recognised at least the variety of
significance of *min*.

All in all it seems better, as is often understood, to lift *min hā⁾ădāmâ*
over the preceding nominal phrase and to relate it with the verbal form
yᵉnaḥămēnû. In this case we have a somewhat floating closer determination
in the rear, in which the preposition *min* has to be interpreted locally, expressing the idea of separation. For instance in the style of the Revised
Standard Version: "Out of the ground which the LORD has cursed this
one shall bring us relief from our work and from the toil of our hands".
An interpretation as this one does not only take into account the mentioned Massoretic caesurae, but joins in also with earlier *min hā⁾ădāmâ* texts,
in particular Gen. ii 7, 8, 19; cf. iii 19. Then it follows quite naturally to
establish another connection, *scilicet* to Gen. ix 20 and to see the announcement of comfort fulfilled in the vineyard planted by Noah, the *⁾íš
hā⁾ădāmâ*. This way one honours the generating power of the *⁾ădāmâ*,
which is obvious from the quotations from Genesis mentioned before. As
a matter of fact the *⁾ădāmâ* can hold good as a substratum and may even
count as the middle, the centre of Israel's primeval history[1]). Besides,

Noah's initiative in Gen. ix 20 tallies with the function of the subject *zè* opposing *YHWH* in Gen. v 29. Therefore it will not do to identify the comfort with the salvation of men and animals from the flood in Gen. vi-viii[2]) or—even less—with the covenant offered to Noah by Elohim according to Gen. ix 8-17[3]). How could one let come up these proportionally rather ideal data in concreto *min hā'ădāmâ*? The world, rather the microcosm of Gen. v 29 does not lose itself in abstracto, but has been described very closely and tangibly. This appears from plastic props such as "toil" and "curse", emphatic words and realities which refer at close range to the homonymous *'iṣṣābôn* and *'ārar* of Gen. iii 17 (c.q. also to the enervating of the *'ădāmâ* in Gen. iv 12: *hā'ădāmâ lō' tōsēf tēt kōḥāh*) and have to compete with the comfort of Gen. v 29, as in its turn this word of comfort itself alternates with Lamech's earlier boasting (Gen. iv 23f.).

More clearly than it was established by way of *status quaestionis* at the onset of the present paper, it now becomes manifest how the smallscale, closed scenery of vs 29, based on the *'ădāmâ* bumps up against the thin, wide atmosphere and the whole structure of Gen. v. For the older literary criticism this incongruity was self-evident. The verse in question—*minus* perhaps the beginning vs 29a—was attributed to the Jahwistic source, also because of the tetragrammaton, whereas the remainder of the chapter (with the name of God Elohim) was considered to be a P-tradition. According to more detailed theories vs 29 would have been the end of the list of the Setites beginning in Gen. iv 25-26 and running parallel with Gen. v[4]), or it may have belonged to an earlier version of the Cainite family tree in Gen. iv 17-18[5]). Whatever the value of such reconstruction attempts, they confirm the signalized isolation of Gen. v 29. Rather than being an island the verse lies vertically in the chapter as a dam and disturbs a strictly calculated horizontal rhythm that develops in solemn monotony. The keyword, the impulse of this rhythm appears promptly in the opening verse: the substantive *tôlᵉdōt*—if you like: a beloved word of P. As far as its meaning is concerned, *tôledōt* can vary from "begettings", which applies here (possibly passive: "generations")[6]) to what in fact can be called "history"[7]), even—as in Gen ii 4a—"story of the origins". Practically speaking, these two meanings are not far apart for the reason that genealogical lists are very apt for filling the gaps of historiograÛhy. Just as 1 Chron. i-ix synthesizes the time of Adam till David and Gen. xi 10-32 loops the flood and Abram together, so Gen. v bridges the period between the creation and the flood. The first pier of that bridge is made up mainly by recapitulating verbally the culminating point of the six days' work (vss 1b-2; cf. Gen. i 26-28 *incipit*). But there is also the starting point, the impulse of our chapter—the noun *tôlᵉdōt* (vs 1a), figuring in the first account of creation as an epilogue

or colophon (Gen. ii 4a). In this manner two parts of the Bible are tuned
very closely to one another. If one attaches Gen. v *de facto* to Gen. i 1-ii
4a[8]), which is equally considered to be part of the priestly tradition, then
the creation story, partitioned according to the schedule of a week,
receives a fitting continuation: after the six days' work the ten predelu-
vian patriarchs appear. As they are mentioned by name and age, they
constitute as many articulations in the ongoing history which is ostensibly
linked with the source of the primeval beginning, more specifically with
Gen. i 28 and hence lead on stereotyped salvific values as blessing, fertility and vitality[9]). Do not we have to say—on the other hand—that such
an intended nearness of the genealogy, measured out in time, with con-
sistency makes the hieratic Gen. i 1-ii 4a take part in the dynamism and
progression of the divine salvific plan culminating in Abram (cf. the
quoted Gen. xi 10-32)? This planned linear "historicizing"[10]) figure
would snatch the biblical creation process away from a metahistoric cyclic
natural event[11]). This evokes the judgment that the Bible obviously does
not start off with the immortal opening words of Thomas MANN's legend
about Joseph: "Tief ist der Brunnen der Vergangenheit. Sollte man ihn
nicht unergründlich nennen?"[12]).

   For the time being staying with the basic figures of line and circle one
can wonder if their divergence does not illustrate the noticeable friction
between Gen v 29 and the remainder of the chapter. The stream of blessings given by a merciful God moves with a designed scansion through
time and seems to make up a point-to-point journey for the ten generations: each time new names, each time different numbers, each time unique realisations. The comfort of the vineyard implied in vs 29, on the
contrary, is not so specific, but rather general and typical, precisely
because it is guaranteed and is ever returning, by availing oneself in a
primeval human way of what already has been called "the generating
power" of the *'ădāmâ*. The registered fertility of man, of these men,
making history across the borders of ever recurring death reports, is
obstructed and stopped in vs 29 by the cycle of earthly fertility which is
timeless or reveals itself even "behind the time". Man, present in
Lamech's anonymous clan, wants to dwell thereupon. The circle pro-
duces quiet (which one should have heard also in the name of
Noah[13]))—and security. Perhaps these words do not have too much of a
grand manner. They befit the intimacy, the already mentioned snugness
of vs 29. The comfort, only indicated in this single verse, looks according-
ly like just a handful, a breathing-spell, in spite of the relaxed and
euphoric way the fruit of the vineyard is spoken about elsewhere[14]). This
comfort does not have the wings of a continued fan-wise unfolding blessing that carries itself through freely and without difficulty. Labour and

toil are there to stay. It is not even certain that after the initiative of Noah the *status quo* of YHWH's curse is lifted, however polar its position within the sentence may be. We have already shown above that tonifying and depressing forces are "competing" in our verse. In this connection the present verb wants to put emphasis on the coexistence of light and shadow. Comfort may alleviate pain, it is also relativized by the same. To specify here another characteristic of vs 29: the island offers shelter only, the dam is a refuge. The hopeful announcement of Lamech, now gradually becoming "a wiser and a sadder man", does anticipate relief, but retrojected on its rustic contours and limitations, its contains something of a sedate melancholy[15]).

Are we not, little by little, burdening a verse, which at the first glance and in its own way can be called plain, with complicated sentiments going against the grain and partially far-fetched, whilst we are searching only for the difference between the local Gen. v 29 and the uncomplicated rectilinear rest of the chapter? The memory of a well known analogon may provide some clarification. If the clear stretch of the creation week, day after day, has evoked the sum-total of a harmonious cosmic universe, ranging from good till very good, the story of paradise follows, being in many respects much more static, not rushing but developing cautiously and considerately in a relatively small agrarian setting with the *ʾǎdāmâ* as the tangible basis, the already so called "centre" of the whole stage. The historicity of man belongs to the dynamics of the chronological creation narrative. Man is equipped with an administrative task *vis-à-vis* the world (Gen. i 26, 28, i.c. the verbs *rādâ* and *kābaš*) and is open towards the future, whereas God Himself withdraws in quiet. The reduction of creation to the dominion, the reach of hand and foot of a self-assured emancipated man is *au fond* unimaginable for the author of Gen. ii-iii. This way Gen. ii 7-8 is already in the constellation of God's handiwork, of his almost feudal command: YHWH God made (*wayyîṣèr*) *hāʾādām* from the dust of the *ʾǎdāmâ*, he planted (*wayyittaʿ*) a garden in Eden and put (*wayyāśèm*) there the *ʾādām* he had made. Hereafter according to vs 9 YHWH let spring all kinds of trees from the *ʾǎdāmâ*, particularly the tree of life and the tree of knowledge of good and evil. The intertexture of man with soil shows also in the fact that his most primary and constitutive needs and aspirations can be externalized and projected in archetypical attributes of landscape like the trees just mentioned. Priestly man goes out into the earth, Jahwistic man is "only" of the earth, it is his destiny, c.q. his fate to form part of it. To typify the energetic attitude of the first figure as "western" needs not sound too forced considering the lines drawn from demythologized Gen. i even towards the ethos of modern science and technology[16]). On the other hand the introspective, oniric

and fairy-like atmosphere of Gen. ii-iii may be called ''oriental''. Not so
much to substantiate this coarse labeling as to notice a striking reflection
of the relationship of—say—P and J, one can point out that the vision on
landscape and in particular on the lay-out of parks in distant Asia are
meant as an integration into mysterious nature. European landscape-
gardening, however, often tends towards real interference, regulating
and transforming[17]). In view of such an efficiency the secular priestly
author withdraws as much energy as possibly from the cosmos in order to
be able to concentrate it in man whom he presents—as befits a
vicegerent—created according to God's image and likeness (Gen. i 27). It
is true J does not want to empty man but he sees him as existing by the
grace and in the grip of his environment. Obviously J is aware of an
organic, almost holistic system, of one big ''animated context''. Such
words as ''grace'' and ''grip'' and in proportion also the equally used
terms ''destiny'' and ''fate'' do not directly guarantee an unmixed naive
Arcadia. They insinuate the ambiguous condition of man in paradise:
safe and cast. Both the primeval force of life and the ecstasy of
knowledge, but besides that also a pressure and constraint which border
upon the myth of Prometheus or the medieval legend of Dr Faustus are
present. A divine aureole may float around the urge to know, breaking
through the original taboo and explaining it (Gen. ii 17; iii 5, 22a), it also
is defaced and frustrated by a very elementary sensation of shame and
vulnerability (Gen. iii 7). Tension and contrast cling even to something
so absolutely substantial and existential as the tree of life, the way to
which is barred by an offended, jealous YHWH (Gen. iii 22b). For the
rest, is not here an eternal universal feeling at stake? Gilgamesh experiences an identical paradox and reserve. He may find the herb, life
itself never falls to his share[18]). The expulsion from the garden of Eden
symbolizes this getting lost of mankind, which, however, does not stop
dreaming time and again about an identical paradise within the wheel of
Gen. ii-iii.

The analogous moments between Gen. i 1-ii 4a *iuncto* Gen. ii 4b-iii 24
on the one hand and the complexity of Gen. v on the other hand may by
now be clearer indeed. Besides, it has been given to understand sufficiently beforehand that the dynamic of the creation week tallies with the
progress of genealogy. In spite of their disproportion the parallelism of
Gen. ii-iii and of Gen. v 29 may by now be manifest too,—their correspondence in physiognomy, horizon and perspective: a mutually comparable intimacy, a being rooted in the *ʾadama* and a circular pattern.
Does consequently the precarious dialectica of the paradise trees not
reconcile us with the established ''coexistence of light and shadow'' in
Gen. v 29, resulting in an ironic awareness concerning the brokenness of

our existence, in a resigned sense of reality? Man dreaming and reaching, but yet not too expansively, yet not too highly. *Allegro ma non troppo.* By what measure we should measure here, one could deduce from the fact that the disproportion of Gen. ii-iii with respect to Gen. v 29 is not only quantitative. For it looks as if the intensity within a certain strand in Genesis gradually diminishes, at least to a certain extent. If man recovers after the decline of the paradise story (Gen. iv 1f.), this revival is disturbed rather quickly by fratricide (vs 8), the announcement of Cain's curse (vs 11) and his exile (vs 16). No sooner have inventive Cain and his family managed to create an existence, variegated and colourful to a certain degree, even outside the *ʾădāmâ* (Gen. iv 17-22), then a new display of power is threatening: the violent song of Lamech (vs 23f.). In vs 25, the third clear articulation of Gen iv, again a birth takes place. Gen. iv 17-24, to be considered as a pendant of Gen. iv 1-16 fell short of its counterpart, not only qua extent. The renaissance of Gen. iv 25 is still shorter of breath, even if vs 26 mentions the invocation of the name of YHWH. The succinct Gen. v 29 is then just a snapshot. Its clear obscure may be grafted upon an innate almost instinctive feeling for ambiguity, as Gen. ii-iii was able to voice this adequately, but via the interjacent Gen. iv this dialectica is sifted in the bottleneck of our verse and tempered in order to manifest itself yet even more strongly after that. In close connection with Gen. v 29 it happens in Gen. ix 20-27, where Noah's joy because of the wine[19]) rivals with the outrage of Cham. But significant, penetrating text fragments like Gen. vi 1-4; viii 20-22 and last but not least Gen. xi 1-9 also bear witness to similar mixed feelings. Verse 29—true enough an island in Gen. v—still constitutes a link in a mobile pliable chain of traditions, which goes on circling regularly around the "faits primitifs" of man, fed as it is by authentic fundamental intuitions. A real development does in fact not show, at the most a spiraloid exploration within the mysterious sheath of life.

One experiences now the more how unadapted and alienating it is to identify the comfort of Gen. v 29 precisely with the covenant offered to Noah by God (Gen. ix 8-17). Sometimes this identification is seen as a "relecture", urged by the context of the originally rural verse—and generally speaking by what is seen as the biblical "proprium"[20]). The greatest attribute of the biblical creed is—thus it is stated decidedly and sometimes almost apologetically—the candid conviction that God, whose word is a vertically directed apostrophe, does not reveal himself in the cycle of seasons or in the rhythm of nature but by his acting on behalf of his people, with whom he had made a covenant[21]). Even after the twelve tribes have settled in Canaan, the classical *magnalia* of exodus and occupation of the land guarantee that YHWH will lead Israel on through

history. Whether here the idea of the traveller-god is still working on
from the desert, we do not know for sure, but the fact is that the faith of
Israel wants to be characterized in a very original manner as a "religion
of the way"[22]). Therefore in the notorious dilemma, order of creation or
of salvation, a choice will be made in favour of the latter[23]). That is the
implication of a re-read, transposed Gen. v 29.

The purport of this implication becomes more transparent against a
wider background. For almost the whole of Gen. i-xi is sometimes con-
fiscated by interpreting it as the doorway of salvific history, giving entrance to Gen. xii, where the traditions of the Israelite patriarchs start.
These traditions are henceforth based upon primeval history, in particular in as far as the vocation of Israel is preluded upon there[24]). Even if
the editorial structure of the present Book of Genesis would justify such
an accolade theology, it sacrifices the mythic content of a great deal in
Gen. i-xi to certain soteriological pragmatics, the sucking-power of which
is not to be underestimated[25]). What was meant to hold a lasting mirror
up to mankind, is reduced to an overture[26]). The beginnings these
chapters deal with, are in danger of introducing themselves again willy-
nilly as a date, a given chronology instead of as a pointer to the natural
bent and quality of man[27]). In order to illustrate this *tour de force* with the
aid of the figures applied above: one has the impression that a circle is
aligned, that is to say that it is used as a phase, still better: as an opening
entry of what henceforth is strikingly called the *oeconomia salutis*. At first
sight the profit of this operation does not look small, the more so because
its wording is able to revert to a firm, acquired terminology, partially
referred to above. The closure is forced open to the future. Man does not
need to stoop any longer or to go down into the labyrinth of his soul. He
is allowed to live as a historical being, he follows the track of time and is
aware of his vocation to engagement, responsibility and fidelity to the
covenant, there in the midst of creation, in fact experienced as "a gift and
a task". The insoluble coherence of "law" and "history" holds good
subsequently as essential for the biblical doctrine of existence[28]). Man of
Gen. i and v, as we have come to know him—going out into the world
and propagating himself in time—is likely to be able to conform to that
radically tense, floating line, with the utmost ease. As a matter of fact it
was stated above in almost as many words that both chapters found and
confirmed each other under the denominator of that objective arrangement. But will the so-called "static" withdrawn space of Gen. ii-iii be
able to bear such a reduction of a circle to a line or to salvific theologizing
without damage? I am referring to the space which can familiarize the
reader with scores of eternally sensitive things: trees as "icons" or
metaphors, the luxury of water, the chtonic serpent, mother earth, the

benevolence and the hardness of the soil. The answer probably is after all: yes. For the paradise story has at its disposal an abundance of content and substance, so much so as to rule out being forced by a total vision, which adjusts and globalizes everything, actually showing no real respect for our "faits primitifs", nor awareness of its incapacity of imposing the male factor "time" upon such a female category as "landscape", so dominantly present in Eden[29]).

Would we not, particularly from this last consideration, at one stroke hit upon the deepest reason why Gen. v 29 with its concise landscape cannot really be open to the proposed "relecture", but why it will continue to press itself upon the chronological text-tissue as a *corpus alienum* by its individuality? From the wider background we are back again at the smaller compound of Gen. v in which we want to reflect further on the position and significance of vs 29, with among others the question just asked at the back of our minds. The verse may intrude itself in an already mentioned respect, its impact is, in comparison with the intensity within the ideal framework of Gen. ii-iii not so strong. Precisely in connection with the trees of paradise we could speak about quantities as the "primeval force of life" and the "ecstasy of knowledge". However much assailed and trapped, better perhaps: precisely because of that, these quantities tend towards an earnest, close interpretation and a sounding in depth of the *condition humaine*. They dó honour Thomas MANN's words without reserve, while the explanation of the name by Noah's father nevertheless irradiates a certain pathos. As far as the narrowness of a sluice, of a bottleneck, permits, a landscape is evoked here—however impressionistically—that remains striking enough in order to profile itself against vineyard texts furtheron in the Bible. In Gen. v there is more than the moralizing parable of Jes. v 1-7 or the political contestation around Nabot's property in 1 Kings xxi 1-16. Besides, more than the comfortable security and the prosperity of Judeans and Israelites, sitting free from care under their vines and fig-trees from Dan to Beersheba (i Kings v 5; cf. Mi. iv 4; Zech. iii 10). Whereas this feeling of security even in its messianic perspective is limited specifically between the borders of the promised land and without any more ado appears as an ideal or an idyll, Gen. v 29 is characterized by universality, by a general interest and besides that also by an awareness of "brokenness", by the vision of "roses on ruins". The imagery appeals to a hazardous but indestructible faith in the ʾădāmâ, which in Gen. iv 17-24 was still present, be it negatively, as a starting point of Cain's exile but is not suspected at all any longer in Gen. iv 25-26. Moreover, otherwise than in Gen. ii 9, where the verb *nāṭaʿ* occurred as well, man arranges the landscape in Gen. v 29, still better: he "creates" himself a space. The mere last verb would be able to remind of the inventive atmosphere of Gen. iv 17-24 for a moment. If, however, our verse appeals to the "faith" in the earth, then it refers to an attitude different from the satisfied joy of the *homo faber* because of urban and "technical" achievements. Living space is only created by the patient combined action of man and of the recalcitrant *ʾădāmâ*. Via the preposition *min* justice is done to this co-causality of the *ʾădāmâ*, the "generating power" of which was pointed out more than once above, be it naturally in a different spirit than the causal "because of" in the quoted English translations. The "faith" in the *ʾădāmâ* according to letter and spirit does not reach out towards God who has after all cursed the soil. He is not considered as the giver of fertility (as e.g. in Ps. lxxxv 12) and his presence is no longer associated with the *ʾădāmâ*, as the numinous paradise garden and even Gen. iv 14, 16 make us aware of. There is no question any longer of a "religiosité c.q. mystique agraire" or of a "sainteté tellurique"[30]). In spite of all "Erdgeruch" and all bonds with the earth, it means a certain desintegration of the original Jahwistic landscape. Also in this respect one could speak, concerning our verse, of "brokenness". The exegesis of vs 29 is apparently in itself already a "spiraloid exploration", it develops by way of an in more than one respect dialectical giving and taking. The amount of content the microtext is in a position, after all concessions, to attract, is impressed by the volume, the aura of words as "pathos" and "faith". The verse takes part in the splendour of primeval stories, immersed in prehistoric times. It has a primordial quality by which the figure of Noah obtains something of a mythic flavour about it as elsewhere the gift c.q. the invention of cereals or wine are attributed to Demeter, Osiris and Dionysos, and surely not only in the shape of aetiological anecdotes either. If this means—specifying our statement more pointedly—that in Gen. v 29 the figure of a saviour appears[31]), then our verse complies suddenly with a soteriological perspective, but a completely different one from that presented by the "relecture". Gen. v 29 has great confidence in the "relief" (I have dropped the word before) of a cosmogonic, natural and sensuous salvation. Almost every word in this sentence formulated thus breathes the calm of depth—one could be reminded of Thomas MANN again. After the six days' work culminating in the *ʾădām*, the genealogy of Gen. v may assert itself with emphasis, activating the male potency repeatedly, reaching out to the times of Abram and his seed, but our stray verse has learned sufficiently from the paradise story: that man related to the *ʾădāmâ* recognizes himself and reads himself in the light and shadow of the trees. If the landscape of Gen. v 29 is animated by these connotative, archetypical values, if in that manner its space is experienced, wholly "primitive", without ever being occupied and dominated, and not annexed by secondary preoccupations as "gift and task", then the verse is far from being shaped on a small scale and adds up to far more than a "microcosm". It is nothing less than a baiting-place and a stop along the way, where we can come to ourselves on the ground which is the commonplace for all of us. The verb *śîm* in Gen. ii 8b, quoted above, conveys a well considered massive meaning: *wayyāśem šām ʾèt hāʾādām ʾăšèr yāṣār*. It is significant that the adherence to the soil of human existence has ever been taxed as insufficient and that under the propelling force of the divine blessing one wants to drive creation forward irreversibly through the centuries[32]). "To get there" is then the parole becoming engaged to all that is called history. It wants to pass by the "to be here", which dwells upon and is rotating continually. In the fact that these two paroles—to strive and to dwell upon—are considered to point to a male and female attitude respectively, we would like to see, in retrospect of an earlier question, that the still landscape of Gen. v 29 too discriminates itself in a happy and expressive way concerning the genealogy moved by time. Referring to the opening sentence of the present lecture, one could describe the lack of spatial-temporal logic within Gen. v after all as follows: as distinct from JOYCE's sixteen hours in Dublin, the amply counted generations of the genealogy do not directly evoke "ages gliding in a psychic universe", whereas on the contrary the considerate vs 29 leans closely against a maxim of Shakespeare: "Enclose the universe in a nutshell"[33]). Speaking of the divergent "sensitivities" of our Genesis chapter which are to be traced from the outset: I treasure the inspired vs 29 and let the register of begettings take its own course. No doubt the family tree will get there, the veiled wisdom of Lamech's statement is here.

NOTES

[1]) See also Gen. i 25; ii 5-6; iii 17, 23; iv 2-3, 10-12, 14; vi 1, 7, 20; vii 4, 8, 23; viii 8, 13, 21; ix 2, 20. Cf. E. VAN WOLDE, "Il legame tra dām, ʾādām e ʾadāmāh in Genesi 2-4", *Sangue e Antropologia nella liturgia* 1 (1983) 219-227.

[2]) F. M. Th. BÖHL, *Genesis* I, Groningen-Den Haag 1923, 76.

[3]) *Partim* J. DE FRAINE, *Genesis*, Roermond-Maaseik 1963, 76.

[4]) Among others H. GUNKEL, *Genesis*, Göttingen 1966[7], 54.

[5]) Cl. WESTERMANN, *Genesis*, Neukirchen-Vluyn 1971f., 487.

[6]) Gen. x 1; xi 10, 27; xxv 12; xxxvi 1, 9.

[7]) Gen. vi 9; xxv 19; xxxvii 2.

[8]) R. DE VAUX, *La Genèse*, Paris 1953, 53 d): "La liste (sc. Gen. v) ... se rattache au chap. 1".

[9]) About this meaning of Gen. v, see E. A. SPEISER, *Genesis*, Garden City-New York 1964, 41: "One need not look far for an explanation of (the) persistent interest in genealogies. To dedicated guardians of cherished traditions, unbroken lineage meant a secure link with the remotest past, and hence also a firm basis from which to face the future. Thus to P these were vital statistics in more ways than one". Still more explicitly

Cl. Westermann, *o.c.*, 471: "P bringt in ihr (sc. the genealogy of Gen. v) zum Ausdruck, dass das in der Erschaffung des Menschen durch Gott (Gen. 1 26-31) Gemeinte in dieser Genealogie weitergeht. Dem Geschöpf Mensch wurde die Segenskraft verliehen. Eben dies, was in den Imperativen "Seid fruchtbar und mehret euch und füllet die Erde!" gemeint war, geschieht in der Genealogie von Kap. 5. Die dem Menschen verliehene Segenskraft wird wirksam in dem nun einsetzenden mächtigen Rhythmus der Generationen, die sich in stetiger Folge in die Zeit hinein erstrecken. Was eigentlich mit der Menschenschöpfung Gen. 1 26-31 gemeint ist, kann erst deutlich werden zusammen mit der nun wirklich sich vollziehenden Geschlechterfolge, wie sie im 5. Kap. im Rhythmus von Zeugung und Geburt, Lebenserstreckung und Tod dargestellt ist".

[10]) L. Köhler, *Theologie des Alten Testaments*, Tübingen 1936, 71: "Der Schöpfungsbericht ist Bestandteil eines Geschichtsaufrisses, der durch Zahlen und Daten gekennzeichnet wird".

[11]) G. von Rad, *Theologie des Alten Testaments* I, München 1958: "Besonders der priesterschriftliche Schöpfungsbericht betont (das) Stehen in der Zeit, denn er hat die Schöpfung in das Toledotschema, das grosse genealogische Gerüst der Priesterschrift einbezogen ... Steht die Schöpfungsgeschichte aber in der Zeit, so hat sie endgültig aufgehört, ein Mythus zu sein, eine zeitlose, sich im Kreislauf der Natur ereignende Offenbarung". Cf. id., *Das erste Buch Mose, Genesis*, Göttingen 1972⁹, 110: "Israel hat nicht einfach von einem urzeitlichen Mythus her eine gerade Linie auf sich in die Zeitlichkeit herabgezogen" and 46: "Aus Gen. 5 ist das Bestreben zu entnehmen, die Welt- und Menschheitszeiten theologisch zu gliedern. Dem atl. Jahweglauben ist (im Unterschied zu dem mythischen Kreislaufdenken der altorientalischen Religionen!) ein auffallend stark ausgeprägtes Zeitdenken eigen; er weiss um eine Geschichte Gottes mit den Menschen und mit seinem Volk Israel, um Abläufe, die einmalig sind und nicht umkehrbar. Diese Abgrenzung von heilsgeschichtlichen Epochen ist ein markantes Charakteristikum der Priesterschrift".

[12]) Th. Mann, *Joseph und seine Brüder* I, Frankfurt/M-Hamburg 1971, 5.

[13]) Cf. the Septuagint version, quoted above.

[14]) Judges ix 13; Am. ix 13; Zach. x 7; Ps. civ 15; Prov. xxxi 6f.; Qoh. x 19; Sir. xxxi 27f.

[15]) Cf. J. Skinner, *Genesis*, Edinburgh 1930², 133: "The utterance (of Lamech sc.) seems to breathe the same melancholy and sombre view of life which we recognise in the Paradise narrative".

[16]) O. Procksch, *Theologie des Alten Testaments*, Gütersloh 1950, 490; H. Cox, *The Secular City*, New York 1966, 17, 24.

[17]) Cf. T. Lemaire, *Filosofie van het landschap*, Bilthoven 1970², 75f.; R. Nicolai-Haas, "Die Landschaft auf der Insel Felsenburg", in: A. Ritter (ed.), *Landschaft und Raum in der Erzählkunst*, Darmstadt 1975, 273f., 278.

[18]) The Epic of Gilgamesh xi 256-300: ANET 96f.

[19]) According to B. Jacob, *Das erste buch der Tora*, Genesis, New York 1974 (reprint) 260, Gen. ix 21a hints at a vintage feast.

[20]) A. van Selms, *Genesis* I, Nijkerk 1967, 100.

[21]) W. Eichrodt, *Theologie des Alten Testaments*, II-III, Stuttgart-Göttingen 1961⁴, 76: "Wie Gott selber nicht eine Naturkraft ist, sondern der lebendige Herr, der nur mit dem Menschen durch die Gemeinschaft des Wortes sich verbindet, so sieht sich auch der Mensch der Menge der natürlichen Dinge und Kräfte gegenübergestellt als Andersartiger, dessen Wesen und Bestand nur in Gott seine Bürgschaft hat". Cf. A. Weiser, *Glaube und Geschichte im Alten Testament*, Göttingen 1961, 64: "Die Verbindung zwischen Jahwe und Volk ist nicht durch die Bande der Natur ...., sondern durch eine geschichtliche Tat Jahwes geworden. Dadurch ragt der Gottesbegriff von Anfang an über die Nation hinaus und besitzt eine Beweglichkeit und Lebendigkeit, wie sie bei Natur-und reinen Nationalgöttern nicht zu finden ist".

[22]) The expression is borrowed from J. Hempel, *Geschichten und Geschichte im Alten Testament bis zur persischen Zeit*, Gütersloh 1964, 47.

²³) Th. C. Vriezen, *Hoofdlijnen der theologie van het Oude Testament*, Wageningen 1974⁴, 306f.

²⁴) G. von Rad, *Theologie*, 142f.: "Weder bei J noch bei P ist ... das Schöpfungswerk Jahwes um seiner selbst willen betrachtet, sondern es ist in einen Geschichtslauf einbezogen, der zur Berufung Abrahams führt und mit der Landnahme Israels endet. Bei beiden Quellenschriften liegt also der Standort des "Verfassers" im innersten Kreis des Heilsverhältnisses, das Jahwe Israel gewährt hat. Aber um dieses Heilsverhältnis theologisch zu legitimieren setzen beide Geschichtsdarstellungen bei der Schöpfung ein und führen von da die Linie auf sich zu, auf Israel, auf die Stiftshütte, auf das verheissene Land. So anmassend es klingt—die Schöpfung gehört zur Ätiologie Israels!''. Cf. Id., *Genesis*, 9f. about "der theologischen Verbindung von Urgeschichte und Heilsgeschichte": "In dieser Verklammerung der Urgeschichte und Heilsgeschichte gibt der Jahwist Rechenschaft von dem Sinn und Zweck des Heilsverhältnisses, das Jahwe Israel gewährt hat. Er gibt die Ätiologie aller Ätiologieen des Alten Testaments und wird an dieser Stelle zum wahren Propheten''.

²⁵) Cf. above n. 11.

²⁶) According to Th. H. Gaster, *Myth. Legend and Custom in the Old Testament*, New York-Evanston 1969, xxxiv, the concern of myth "is with experience, not with categorization; it articulates a present, existential situation in general, continuous terms, translating the punctual into the durative, the real into the ideal''. It seems that the "accolade theology" is doing just the reverse: translating the durative into the punctual.

²⁷) Cf. G. von Rad, *Theologie*, 143: "Der Beginn dieser Gottesgeschichte (sc. from Abram till Joshua) wurde ... bis zur Schöpfung vordatiert. Diese Hinausverlegung des Beginns der Heilsgeschichte war aber nur möglich, weil eben auch die Schöpfung als ein Heilswerk Jahwes verstanden wurde''.

²⁸) W. Eichrodt, *l.c.*, writes on the "aus Gesetz und Geschichte genährte Erfahrung des Menschen in der Welt''. The Law here dealt with is perceptibly another one than the cosmic Law in Judaism about which speculates G. Scholem, *Zur Kabbala und ihre Symbolik*, Frankfurt/M 1973, 114f.

²⁹) About the "male" and "female" character of resp. time and space: W. Barnard, *Tussen twee stoelen*, Amsterdam 1959, 127.

³⁰) According to the terminology of M. Eliade, *Traité d'Histoire des Religions*, Paris 1959, 228 and 307.

³¹) So J. Hempel, "Glaube, Mythos und Geschichte im Alten Testament'', *ZAW* 65 (1953) 135, referring to W. Staerk, *Die Erlösererwartung in den östlichen Religionen*, Stuttgart 1938, 44ff.

³²) So Cl. Westermann, *o.c.*, 471: "Der Mensch, den Gott geschaffen hat, ... ist nicht ein durch die Erschaffung hergestelltes Wesen, das dann vorhanden ist; der Mensch ist das sich kraft des Segens in die Zeit erstreckende Geschöpf''.

³³) With regard to the characterization of Joyce's opus and the reference to Shakespeaere see R. Karst, "Franz Kafka: Wort–Raum–Zeit'', in: H. Politzer, *Franz Kafka*, Darmstadt 1980, resp. 552 and 547.

MEGIDDO IN THE PERIOD OF THE JUDGES

G. I. DAVIES
Cambridge

The biblical references to Megiddo in the period of the Judges are meagre and I have no intention of trying to construct a paper around them[1]). It would require much exercise of the creative imagination to do so. Fortunately the excavations at Tell el-Mutesellim are much more informative about the history of the city at this and other periods, for all the problems attaching to the interpretation of archaeological evidence in general and that from Megiddo in particular. The difficulties in evaluating the evidence from Megiddo are well-known to archaeologists. They arise in part from the fact that some important discoveries were made at the beginning of the century, when Palestinian archaeology was in its infancy, and partly from the much-criticised methods and final report of the Chicago expedition which worked at the site between 1925 and 1939. Mortimer WHEELER, who visited Palestine in 1936, was exceptionally severe in his comments, and probably excessively so: "It will suffice to say this: that from the Sinai border to Megiddo and on to Byblos and northern Syria, I encountered such technical standards as had not been tolerated in Great Britain for a quarter of a century. With rare and partial exceptions, the methods of discovery and record were of a kind which, at home, the Office of Works would have stopped by telegram. The scientific analysis of *stratification*, upon which modern excavation is largely based, was almost non-existent. And the work was being carried out upon a lavish and proportionately destructive scale''[2]). The warning needs to be heeded, but the situation is not so bad for the period with which we are concerned as it is for some others and in any case the study of the Megiddo reports in the light of other excavations elsewhere in Palestine is increasingly making it possible to utilise the vast amount of information in them with confidence for more general studies. The possibility of also salvaging useful data from the reports of Gottlieb SCHUMACHER and Carl WATZINGER on the German excavations at the beginning of the century is less often recognised, but despite the even greater uncertainties here they also provide some contributions to our theme which we shall be able to incorporate[3]).

Archaeological evidence has recently not been as thoroughly exploited for the period of the Judges as it has for the preceding period of the Israelite settlement/conquest or the following period of the United Monarchy, though two Dutch scholars, H. J. FRANKEN and C. H. J. DE GEUS, are notable exceptions to this generalisation[4]). Where it has been considered in detail, the interest has tended to be in either the arrival of the Philistines in south-west Palestine or the new "Israelite" settlements in the hill-country rather than in the old Canaanite cities such as Megiddo. This tendency is likely to be encouraged further by the recent announcements about a hill-top site where a bronze image of a bull was found and a platform on Mount Ebal which is surrounded by an enclosed area, both firmly dated to the Judges period[5]). But the lowland sites like Megiddo are of at least equal interest, for two reasons: they enable us to see the complex development that was taking place in Canaanite areas at the same time as these other processes—a development which is understandably barely touched on in the Old Testament—and they were later to make an important positive contribution to the culture of the Israelite monarchy. As I have written elsewhere, "Here Canaanite civilisation survived as both an inspiration and an enticement to the Israelite tribes and, while the pre-eminent position of Jerusalem as a transmitter of Canaanite culture is not to be denied, it is likely that the contribution of Megiddo and its neighbours to the development of the northern tribes was no less important"[6]).

By the standards of much current "biblical archaeology" this paper will seem a very traditional treatment of its topic, for it will be concerned with destruction levels, pottery, palaces and so on. It will offer very little by way of answers to the intriguing questions about economics and organisation of the means of production which have been raised by N. K. GOTTWALD[7]). This is partly due to my own interests but it is also conditioned by a doubt as to whether some of his questions *can* be answered in a convincing way from archaeological evidence alone, particularly when that evidence comes from an excavation in which little or no effort was made to collect materials such as bone, pollen and seeds. As always the assumptions and interests with which an excavation was conducted place severe limits on the kinds of question which its results can be used to answer. Regrettable this may be, but avoidable it is not, except to a very limited extent.

The beginning of the Judges period is conventionally placed around 1200 B.C., and I am for the purpose of this paper following that convention, despite the uncertainties that must attach themselves to that or any other date which one might select. Certain of the episodes in the book of Judges presuppose the arrival of the Philistines in Palestine, which took place about this time, but the loose-knit structure of the book in no way guarantees that the different episodes are in chronological order and, as far as I can see, we have no sure way of knowing when the earliest of them took place. Possibly some of them did not take place at all. If we do take 1200 as our starting-point we are in archaeological terms at the turning-point from the Late Bronze Age to the Iron Age—another convention, which obscures considerable continuity in a site like Megiddo. There is an interruption about this time in the history of Megiddo, but while it to some extent presaged the approaching end of a long period of stability it brought few immediate changes[7a]).

The Chicago expedition reached levels of the Judges period in four areas: AA, BB, CC, DD (see fig. 1). In Area AA the palatial building of Stratum VIIB was rebuilt c. 1200 in substantially the same form, but with its floors now raised by between one and two metres[8]). The upper floor level was not preserved (or not observed), but its position could be

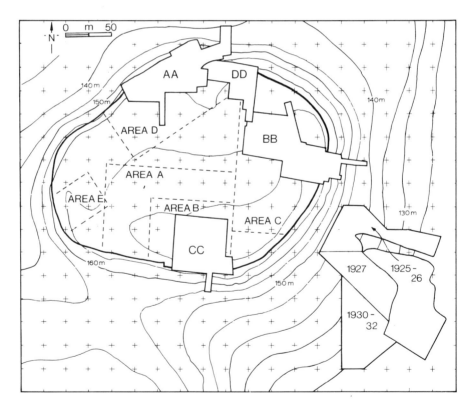

Fig. 1. Plan of areas excavated at Megiddo by the Chicago expedition, 1925-1939 (A. Brown: based on *Megiddo II*, fig. 377, and *Megiddo Tombs*, fig. 1, with the permission of the Oriental Institute, Chicago)

deduced from the level of the base of the wall-plaster of the Stratum VIIA palace[9]). One important change was made in the layout of the palace, in the west, where an underground cellar-block of three rooms was added (the "treasury"). The city-gate in the north-east of the area continued virtually unchanged. A similar situation is indicated by the finds in Area DD, where another large building with a courtyard existed and had its floor level raised by nearly a metre between Strata VIIB and VIIA[10]). In a third area, BB, it is possible that the transition from the "Stratum VIIB" phase of Temple 2048 to the "Stratum VIIA" phase also took place about this time, with a raising of the floor-level, but no major change in the layout: the entrance continued to be in the north and a raised platform, enlarged in "VIIA", lay along the opposite wall[11]). In the fourth area which was excavated to this depth, CC in the south, the remains appear to be of private houses[12]). A distinction between VIIB and VIIA was not made throughout the area: this may be due to the lack of any systematic rebuilding here, or it may be that the excavation did not everywhere reach the earlier phase of Stratum VII.

The fact that there is scarcely any change in the plans of the major buildings probably indicates that there was no serious disturbance to the population of Megiddo or its internal organisation and hierarchy at this time, and it is possible in the light of this that the end of Stratum VIIB should be attributed to a natural disaster such as an earthquake, or even simply to a ruler who had the resources and the will to replace dilapidated buildings with new ones, rather than to destruction by an enemy attack.

The city represented by Stratum VIIA continued to exist well into the second half of the twelfth century B.C. before falling victim to a much more catastrophic destruction which resulted in the abandonment of all its major public buildings. A comparison of the plans of this and the following stratum (VIB) makes this very clear. In Area AA the palace and the city gate are built over with small, rather poorly preserved buildings which reflect the transfer of these plots of land into the hands of the common population[13]). A further sign of a hasty departure by the occupants of the palace is a hoard of gold and ivory which they left in the "treasury"[14]). The story is the same in Area DD, though rather little evidence of Stratum VIB survives here; and in Area BB the temple seems likewise to have gone out of use and the area to have been given over to small houses[15]). An upper limit (*terminus post quem*) for this major break in the history of the city is provided by two Egyptian inscribed objects which inject a welcome element of precision into the archaeological chronology of the period. One is an ivory pen-case 35 cm long which was found among the treasure in the underground cellar (locus 3073) of Stratum VIIA[16]). At the top a king is portrayed kneeling before, and presumably making an offering to, the god "Amon-Re, Lord of Heaven". Below are two royal cartouches bearing the names of Ramesses III who, according to recent views about Egyptian chronology, ruled c. 1184-1153 B.C.[17]) The other object is a bronze statue-base bearing several inscriptions which associate it with Ramesses VI[18]). This was actually found buried, without the statue which once stood upon it, under a wall of a house in the southern part of the city which was attributed to Stratum VIIB (Area CC: locus 1832 in square R9). It must be intrusive here and was apparently buried by whoever was responsible for taking down the statue from its place of honour elsewhere in the city. Such treatment can only reflect a determination to be rid of Egyptian hegemony and it is most likely that it coincided with the end of Stratum VIIA, which marked the end of a long period of contact with and subjection to the Egyptian court. Since Ramesses VI ruled c. 1142-1135[19]) the end of Stratum VIIA may be placed at the earliest c. 1140 B.C.

Something of the prosperity and cultural and economic relationships of Megiddo in the early to mid-twelfth century B.C. can be inferred from the pottery and other small finds of Stratum VIIA. The pottery as published includes a large number of pieces, local and imported, which suggest a continuation of the styles of Stratum VIIB and the end of Late Bronze Age Palestine generally[20]). In her magisterial work on the Philistines T. DOTHAN has re-examined the find-places of much of this pottery and concluded that it in fact derives from Stratum VIIB[21]). She may be guilty of now drawing too hard and fast a line between the pottery assemblages of Strata VIIB and VIIA, but as far as the imported pottery at least is concerned she seems to be on firm ground, and her work enables the new features of VIIA to stand out the more clearly. These include a cessation of Mycenaean and Cypriote imports and the presence of Philistine pottery. One Philistine bowl was published in *Megiddo II*, but DOTHAN has detected another sixteen sherds, most of them in the Oriental Museum in Chicago and previously unpublished, which on grounds of typology or find-place or both should belong to Stratum VIIA[22]). She deduces that: "From the large quantity of pottery found it can be inferred that a garrison of Sea Peoples was stationed at Megiddo."[23]) That may be to read too much into the evidence, but it certainly shows that already at this time the Philistines had close contacts with this inland Canaanite city of northern Palestine.

Secondly, the hoard of gold and ivory from the palace cellar in Area AA. From the way in which the precious objects were deposited in the chamber, with related pieces often separated by some distance, it has been deduced that they lay where they had been abandoned by looters who had no use for them. Alternatively it may be that they were no

longer valued in their own right as *objets d'art* or for their original func-
tional purpose, but as resources for barter in an age when money did not
yet exist[24]). This is fully compatible with the suggestion of DOTHAN that
they (or most of them) had previously been kept in a similar tripartite
chamber in the palace of the preceding period[25]). The hoard includes
jewellery of both gold and precious stones: there are gold beads, a gold
pendant, and necklaces of beads and lotus pendants made from carnelian
stone[26]). But it is the ivory pieces which predominate, both in number
and in splendour. A total of 382 separate pieces was recorded[27]). An ex-
cellent and well-illustrated treatment of these pieces and their wide
ramifications has recently been given by R. D. BARNETT, and I shall here
be content with a few examples to illustrate the variety of the material[28]).
Returning to the theme of women's adornment, we may mention nine
combs, of which one is decorated with a scene of a lion crouching among
trees[29]). BARNETT finds this group typical of "the finest Late Mycenaean
style" and regards them as imports either from the Aegean or, in the
light of recent discoveries at Kition, from Cyprus[30]). A different tradition
is represented by a remarkable box, carved from a single piece of ivory,
with lions and sphinxes portrayed prowling around the sides: there are
analogies with Syrian art and particularly with the gateway figures from
the Hittite capital of Hattuša[31]). A number of pieces were designed to
decorate household furniture such as chairs or beds, such as a plaque
showing a sphinx holding a cup and another of a robed female figure,
whom BARNETT refers to as typical of the "pious donor"—she has an in-
laid glass eye. These are both in low-relief open work and have (or had)
tenons at top and bottom which will have fitted into the wooden frame at
the side of a chair or the foot of a bed[32]). Two other pieces of the same
type show the Egyptian god Bes running, and the discovery of a related
ivory carving in a contemporary temple at Kition, but with a Cypro-
Minoan inscription on the base, has led to the suggestion that this whole
group may have been made in the same Cypriote workshop[33]). Boards
for two popular games were found among the ivories: one board for what
is referred to as the "Game of Twenty Squares" has a naturalistic
decoration showing a lion chasing its prey in one corner, which may give
a clue to the nature of this game, and there were several boards for the
"Game of Fifty-Eight Holes" or "Dogs and Jackals", as the Egyptians
called it—it was apparently similar in conception to Ludo. In one case a
single board provided for the playing of one of these games on each
side[34]).

There is also some evidence of religious practices at this time. The
finds from Temple 2048 clearly reflect its cultic function[35]). They include, in addition to a range of jugs, bowls, flasks and lamps, several

figurines of both bronze and clay. One of the bronze figurines, which was found in the destruction debris of the temple, had been coated with gold[36]). It represents a seated figure with an oval crown, holding in its left hand a "standard" which is embossed with a four-pointed star. There is little doubt that the metal figurines represent the deity worshipped in the temple, but there is no clear evidence of his identity. The seated or enthroned position probably indicates that he was conceived of as a king, which would (in the light of our other knowledge of Canaanite religion) suggest an identification with either Ilu or Baᶜalu. Two clay models of animal livers found near the temple point to the practice of extispicy, the examination of the entrails of sacrificed animals, particularly the liver, in order to predict the future. This practice is best known in the Near East from texts found in Mesopotamia and the fact that a similar but earlier liver model from Hazor is inscribed with cuneiform omens shows that some Canaanite priests were familiar with this kind of Mesopotamian "science"[37]). Other objects presumably used in the cult are crescent pendants in both gold and bronze and four small bronze cymbals[38]). A collection of bronze objects buried beneath the floor may be a foundation-offering[39]). Further evidence of religious beliefs and practices of a different kind comes from the amulets which begin to be numerous about this time. Small figurines of certain deities, animals, symbols such as the sacred eye and even parts of the human body had long been used in Egypt as a protection against evil, but they are found at Megiddo predominantly in the strata which mark the transition from Canaanite to Israelite rule in the twelfth to the tenth centuries (Strata VIIA-VA)[40]). The initial impulse must have come from contacts with Egypt, but their continued popularity (even after such contacts had ceased) points to the uncertainties of life at this time and, perhaps, to the same "crisis of belief" in traditional polytheism which is described by J. C. DE MOOR elsewhere in this volume.

Around 1140 B.C., perhaps, the prosperous, pro-Egyptian city of Megiddo VIIA came to an end. As we have already seen, there is a complete change in the plan and character of the city in its next stage, Stratum VIB. But was there also a period of abandonment at the site, a gap in occupation, at this point? This is commonly asserted, particularly in connection with attempts to date the Song of Deborah: it has been suggested that the location of the battle btᶜnk ᶜl my mgdw (Jud. v 19) rather than ᶜl mgdw fits best a time when Megiddo was uninhabited. There are several problems with this argument, but we have here only to consider whether the archaeological evidence supports or does not support the view that there was a gap in occupation at Megiddo in the late twelfth century. It seems to be W. F. ALBRIGHT who was the first to speak of such

a ''gap in occupation'' at Megiddo[41]). The excavators'' report says
nothing about any such gap and their summary chart implies that the
Stratum VI(B) occupation followed immediately on that of Stratum
VII(A)[42]). This is consistent with a photograph which shows the walls of a
VIB house resting directly on the ruined walls of the VIIA palace, and
one of the excavators in a separate article says explicitly that there was no
sign at this stage of a period of abandonment at the site[43]).

Perhaps, then, after no great interval the re-occupation of the mound
represented by Stratum VIB took place. It was clearly defined only in
Areas AA and DD in the north of the mound and even here there are no
complete building plans. The site of the earlier palace in AA was occupied by much smaller buildings, although they are well-built for their
size[44]). There are no signs of any fortifications or a gate from this period.
In several buildings rows of pillars are used instead of solid walls between
some rooms: this is a characteristic found in later levels at Megiddo and
at many other sites from the early Iron Age on. Stone-lined pits and
ovens are also present in considerable numbers, confirming the domestic
character of the buildings. In Areas BB and CC this stratum was not
distinguished from Stratum VIA which followed it. Some structures
belonging to VIB may be discernible there by the isolation of walls that
belong to different overlapping building plans, but it is possible that the
new occupation did not extend over the whole surface of the mound or
even over a large part of it. In SCHUMACHER's report there is a reference
to some slight buildings over the ruins of an older palace in the centre of
the mound (the so-called *Nordburg*) which from their stratigraphical position might belong here. They include two installations designed for pro-
cessing olive-oil[45]). The pottery and small finds ascribed to this phase are
meagre and undistinguished for the most part, even when one allows for
the possibility that some objects from the undivided Stratum VI in Areas
BB and CC may belong to Stratum VIB. There is a growing tendency to
decorate jugs and jars with groups of narrow horizontal bands of paint,
and a very few Philistine pieces also appear[46]). DOTHAN has argued that a
number of other Philistine pieces—a jug and five sherds—ought also to
be ascribed to this stratum, although they were attributed by the excavators to Stratum VIA, on the grounds that they ''are typologically inconsistent with the pottery of that stratum'' (i.e. VIA)[47]). The argument
is that Stratum VIA is characterised by what DOTHAN refers to as the
debased third phase of Philistine pottery—the pieces in question belong
to the second phase—therefore they belong not to Stratum VIA but to the
earlier Stratum VIB[48]). I hesitate to disagree with an expert in this field
such as DOTHAN is, but it does seem to me that her argument here is un-
sound, for three kinds of reason. The first is its chronological implica-

tions: it leads her to an improbable chronology for the site. She dates
VIB c. 1150-1050 and VIA c. 1050-1000, believing that it was destroyed
by David[49]). The outer limits raise no particular difficulty (though, as we
have seen, 1150 is a little early for the transition from VIIA to VIB), but
the date c. 1050 for the VIB/VIA transition is problematic, because it attributes twice as long to the occupation represented by the meagre remains of VIB as to the much more substantial occupation implied by
Stratum VIA. Yet DOTHAN's date for the transition follows directly from
her view that VIA corresponds only to the third phase of Philistine pottery (which belongs to the latter part of the eleventh century): if it were
allowed that it also overlapped with part of the second phase, its beginning could be placed near the beginning of the eleventh century, which
would fit the excavated remains much better. Secondly, it is based on an
unproven assumption: it assumes a tidy correspondence of pottery phases
to excavated strata, and reallocates pieces that are "inconsistent" with
this assumption. Thirdly, the logic of the argument does not stand up to
scrutiny in the individual cases: 1) The so-called "Orpheus jug"[50]) is
described by DOTHAN as "an outstanding example of the debased
Philistine pottery of Megiddo VIA"[51]). It is difficult to see why, after
stating this, she continues by constructing two ingenious arguments for
its having possibly originated in Stratum VIB, as it is, from her own ad-
mission, anything but "typologically inconsistent" with Stratum VIA. 2)
Two of the sherds in question come from loci with a well-preserved floor
(5224 and 3021 respectively)[52]). A mistaken allocation by the excavators
is much less likely in such cases than where no floor was preserved or
none was observed. 3) In a footnote DOTHAN reports that in Yigael
YADIN's excavations at Megiddo in 1972 he found a white-slipped
Philistine bowl in Stratum VIA[53]). This shows that white-slipped pottery
is not "typologically inconsistent with Stratum VIA", yet in the three remaining cases it appears to be solely the white slip which is regarded as
an argument for attribution of the sherd to Stratum VIB.

Even if DOTHAN's argument were accepted, it would be doubtful if the
evidence were sufficient to make Megiddo VIB a Philistine settlement. If
it is rejected, there can certainly be no question of it. Who the inhabitants
of Megiddo were at that time is a rather tantalising question, to which we
shall return. At any rate, their occupation seems to be a short-lived in-
terlude between the much more impressive cities of Strata VIIA and
VIA. Around 1100, I would estimate, large buildings were once again
constructed in Areas AA and DD—the contrast is again very clear in the
plans[54]). In AA there is once again a large palatial building and beside it
what seems to be a small city gate. To the west of the "palace" a continuous block of slighter rooms extends to the edge of the excavated area,

serving apparently to enclose the top of the mound. In DD also there are more massive structures, as well as what are probably ordinary houses. In both areas the major buildings and parts of others are constructed out of an unusual kind of reddish, partially-baked bricks on stone foundations[55]). These distinctive building materials help to identify buildings of the same period in Areas BB and CC where, as I have said, the excavators did not distinguish between the two stages of Stratum VI. In the south-east of the plan of CC it is also possible to recognise a structure excavated by SCHUMACHER and called by him "the southern castlegate" (*Südliches Burgtor*) and its plan can be completed from SCHUMACHER's drawings[56]). It was a rectangular structure 17m × 10m with walls a metre thick and openings in the south-east and north-west (the latter with an impressive stone threshold 2.50m wide). Carl WATZINGER, in his valuable second volume of the report on SCHUMACHER's work, dismissed the idea that this structure could be a gate, but the similarity of conception to the Israelite outer gate a century later at Beersheba makes this still a possibility[57]). Another find of SCHUMACHER's which probably belongs here is the vaulted chamber "f", probably a grave, above the so-called *Mittelburg* in his Stratum IV[58]).

Much of this city remains to be excavated. When it is, I venture to suggest that it will be found to have had a protected access to a water-supply. The American excavators attributed the artificial approaches to the cave which they discovered in the south-west of the city to the twelfth century B.C., but YADIN has shown conclusively that they in fact belong to the period of the Israelite monarchy[59]). Some pottery in the cave does suggest that this spring was being used in the Judges period, but this will have been by access from the outside, without any protection[60]). There was however, I believe, an approach to a safe water-supply in the north of the city at this time, with its opening close to the palace in Area AA. Three pieces of evidence point to this: two were recognised by one of the American excavators, R. S. LAMON, at the beginning of his report *The Megiddo Water-System*, but have subsequently been forgotten, while the third, which is crucial for the dating of the presumed system, has not been noticed before, as far as I am aware. LAMON noticed that on the surface of the mound there was a shallow depression near the northern gate area and conjectured that it was the top of a deep shaft reaching down to the water table[61]). It was a very similar depression on the south side of the tell at Hazor which led YADIN to look for and in due course to find the ninth-century water-system there[62]). It is still possible to see what LAMON was referring to today, as in the aerial photograph (pl.1). Second, LAMON drew attention to a stone-built channel at the spring Ain el-Kubbi north of the tell which had been found by SCHUMACHER and was traced by him

Pl. 1. Aerial view of Megiddo from the north-east. The trench in Area AA is at the far right and the depression referred to in the text is the darker area a little to the left of it (Photograph courtesy of Richard Cleave, Pictorial Archive Inc., Jerusalem)

for a distance of some 40m to the south-west of the spring, exactly in the direction of the depression on the surface of the tell[63]). It was from this channel that the spring-water emerged. The local inhabitants told SCHUMACHER that an underground channel led all the way from here to the spring of Ain es-Sitt at Lejjun nearly 2 km to the south-west, and SCHUMACHER believed them because he observed small fish of the same type swimming in the waters of both springs. "Der Lauf der *ain el-ḳubbi* mag unter der alten Ortslage von *tell el-mutesellim* gefasst und zur Speisung der Bewohner des Tell mittelst Senkbrunnen ausgenützt worden sein." The local tale and SCHUMACHER's reason for believing it are obviously fanciful, but it is likely that both springs have their origin in the water-table under the ridge at the north end of which Megiddo lies, so that his conjecture that the ancient inhabitants of the mound sank shafts to draw water is not unreasonable. The third clue, which offers some evidence about the date, comes in the exploratory trench dug in Area AA by the Americans in late 1935 and early 1936, when LAMON was still a member of the excavation staff. At the southern end of the trench, the excavators were puzzled by the fact that below remains of Strata IV, V and VIA they found nothing but "sterile earth". Even when they deepened the trench at this point by another eight metres they found no structures, while a little to the north the regular succession of strata was found[64]).

The southern part of the trench is adjacent to the depression observed by LAMON, and it is tempting to suppose that they are connected. The sterile earth is difficult to explain in this position except as the filling of some kind of pit or shaft, and it could well have been part of the approach to a subterranean water supply. Because of the overlying structures, the pit or shaft must have been dug (and filled in) not later than Stratum VIA. Further excavation here might well uncover a pre-Israelite protected access to water. The water-systems at Gezer and Jerusalem (Warren's Shaft) which have in the past been thought by many to be of Canaanite origin have recently been claimed to be from the period of the Israelite monarchy, by analogy with the securely dated Iron Age II systems at Megiddo and Hazor, but there appears to be no new evidence from Gezer and Jerusalem which supports this and the argument from analogy may be misleading[65]). There is good reason to believe that the older system at Gibeon (the cylindrical "tank") is from the early Iron Age (cf. 2 Sam. ii 13)[66]), so that there can be no objection in principle to the suggestion that Megiddo was furnished with a similar arrangement at the same time, if not earlier. The existence of such a system in the fifteenth century B.C. could help to explain how Megiddo was able to hold out against Tuthmosis III for seven months after it had been encircled by a siege wall[67]).

In the rooms of the palace in Area AA a variety of bronze objects were found and, just outside it on the west, three bundles of silver pieces wrapped in cloth. The silver is a mixture of earrings, pendants and such like with flat pieces, some of them bearing incised decoration, which have been cut from larger objects, perhaps cups or dishes. The excavators suggest that the silver had been prepared for melting down in a workshop: this is a possibility, but it could also represent a payment of some kind made to the ruler of Megiddo or a merchant[68]). The most impressive metalwork came from the southern part of the city where (along with the more common axeheads and spearheads) an unprecedented quantity of bronze jugs, bowls and strainers were found in a single locus (1739), constituting a fine example of a type of "wine service" also known from Egypt[69]). It is interesting that SCHUMACHER found a quantity of bronze objects in almost the same place. Evidently he penetrated the destruction debris of Stratum VI(A)—which is what he referred to as the *Brandschicht* or "burnt layer"—and in it he reports finding a double axehead, two hoes, a javelin, four iron knife-blades and five bronze stands. The latter had tripod supports (in one case four legs) mounted on a ring base and stood about 35 cm high. A flat bronze dish was placed on top and in some cases this had clearly been used for burning some substance. The vertical part of one stand was cast in the form of a naked female figure playing a double flute and decorative motifs are also evident elsewhere[70]).

The pottery of this period shows considerable Philistine influence, perhaps enough to establish that Megiddo had now become a Philistine outpost[71]). One Philistine jug that is particularly noteworthy is the so-called "Orpheus jug" mentioned above: the main frieze of its decoration depicts a scene of animals surrounding a lyre-player, a most unusual case of the portrayal of the human form by a Philistine painter. Similar scenes are known on seals from south-eastern Turkey of a slightly earlier date[72]). It is not certain that the Orpheus legend (or a similar one) is being referred to: B. MAZAR suggested, alternatively, that the animals might be the subject of the musician's song[73]). Also of interest is a White-Painted Cypriote bowl, which points to the beginnings of a recovery of wider trading relations[74]). In Area CC eight large storage jars (pithoi) of a type which is characteristic of this period ("collared-rim storage jars") were found in Stratum VI, and SCHUMACHER found two more a little to the east[75]). These have often been regarded as distinctively Israelite in origin, because they are generally found at sites in the hill-country, where the Israelite tribes first settled[76]). Chiefly on the basis of this evidence Y. AHARONI (following a suggestion first made, but later withdrawn, by W. F. ALBRIGHT) argued that Megiddo Stratum VI was an Israelite settlement[77]). There are, however, difficulties with this argument. First, the presence of these storage jars may be due to trade rather than the local population of Megiddo. Second, these ten jars seem rather insignificant alongside a great mass of pottery of a character quite different from what is usually found at Israelite sites. We have mentioned the Philistine influence, and note also needs to be taken of the increasing popularity of decoration with groups of narrow horizontal bands of paint[78]). Thirdly, it is by no means certain that this type of jar is distinctively Israelite. Archaeologists are now much more wary than was formerly the case of the "pots equal people" assumption, and in the present case examples of the "collared-rim storage jar" have been found in areas well outside the limits of early Israelite settlement, for instance in Transjordan, at other sites in the Jezreel plain and even in the northern coastal plain[79]). It is unfortunately not clear whether the loci in which the jars were found belong to Stratum VIA or VIB, and it is on that distinction that any reconstruction of the history of Megiddo in this period must rest.

As we have seen, the destruction of the city of Stratum VIIA was followed by a short-lived settlement of a village character, which in its turn was replaced by the flourishing city of Stratum VIA, with its palace and foreign contacts and highly developed metal industry. The settlement of Stratum VIB could conceivably be Israelite, though this cannot be proved. On the other hand, it is most improbable that this can be said of Stratum VIA, which has a much stronger claim to be regarded as

Philistine. A telling argument is that Stratum VIA ends with a massive destruction, which was noted both by SCHUMACHER and by more recent excavators[80]). It is very likely that this reflects campaigns of David against the Philistines, about which we are only imperfectly informed in the Bible (2 Sam. v 17-25; viii 1). Megiddo was certainly in Israelite hands by the time of Solomon (1 Kings iv 12; ix 15). We are nowhere told how or when it was captured, but since it evidently did not form part of the territory claimed by the Israelites at the time of Saul's death (2 Sam. ii 8-9: Jezreel here as elsewhere refers only to the city of that name, not the whole region), it can only have been conquered under David.

If Megiddo VIB were a short-lived Israelite settlement at the site, we could conjecture that it was a group from the tribe of Issachar that occupied it, for it was to Issachar that Megiddo and the other cities of the Jezreel plain and valley were originally assigned, according to Joshua xvii 11. It appears from Gen. xlix 14-15 that Issachar was forced to accept subjection to a Canaanite (or was it a Philistine?) overlord, a situation which might easily be reflected in the transition from Stratum VIB to VIA at Megiddo. The majority of the tribe seems subsequently to have been restricted to a more easterly region (Joshua xix 17-23—cf. 1 Kings iv 17), so that when the need still to conquer Megiddo is mentioned in Judges i 27 (a document of the time of David at the earliest) it is the powerful tribe of Manasseh which is said to be responsible for it.

To conclude, I will make a few observations on this period of history as a whole, first with reference to Megiddo itself and then with reference to the northern lowlands (i.e. the Jezreel valley, the plain of Jezreel or Esdraelon and the northern coastal plain) as a whole. Historians have, since the American excavations were completed in 1939, occupied themselves with a search for the *caesura* in the history of Megiddo in the early Iron Age: the term itself was introduced into the discussion by J. SIMONS[81]). ALBRIGHT, followed much later by AHARONI, located the *caesura* after Stratum VII, while R. M. ENGBERG, one of the excavators, placed it at the end of Stratum VI, as did in their turn SIMONS and Albrecht ALT[82]). The above account of the archaeological evidence should make it clear that, if by a *caesura* we mean a gap in occupation of any length, there was probably none at either of these points. The destruction of Stratum VIIA was quickly followed by the reoccupation represented by Stratum VIB; while the destruction of Stratum VIA should probably be attributed to David and was followed, within his reign, by the domestic dwellings of Stratum VB, which in their turn gave way to the monumental architecture of the Solomonic city. If, on the other hand, we mean by a *caesura* a major upheaval in the life of the city in architectural and political terms, there were no less than three during the two centuries which we have considered, with a change in the population or at least of its leadership being a possibility at each point:

       VIIA   Pro-Egyptian city-state

(1)   ————————————————

       VIB   Village of ??

(2)   ————————————————

       VIA   Pro-Philistine city-state

(3)   ————————————————

       VB   Village in David's kingdom

Our understanding of these historical and political developments can only be advanced further when Megiddo is considered in the context of the whole region of the northern lowlands, as attested in both textual and archaeological sources. As with several other topics in the history of Palestine, such an attempt at synthesis is to be found in the writings of Albrecht ALT, in three articles which have never been superseded[83]). They are now out of date from the archaeological point of view at least, but ALT's ability to draw together a mass of disparate evidence into a coherent historical account remains a challenge to scholars today. Future research will need to direct attention, on the textual side, to such issues as:

(a) Who was Shamgar ben Anat (cf. Jud. iii 31, v 6)?[84])

(b) What, more generally, is the Canaanite/Philistine background to Judges iv-v?[85])

(c) What, if anything, has the early history of the tribe of Issachar to do with this region?[86])

(d) What are we to make of the enigmatic statement in 1 Sam. xxxi 7 about "the men of Israel who dwelt *on the other side of the plain*" and "abandoned their cities and fled" after the battle of Mount Gilboa, with the result that "the Philistines came and dwelt in them"?

On the archaeological side, finds at neighbouring sites have already contributed to our argument at one point—the collared-rim storage jars—but a more thorough review of their historical implications is needed. Evidence from the neighbouring sites of Taanach and Afula has long been available, as well as from Beth-shean at the eastern end of the lowland area and Dor in the coastal plain[87]). More recently the Yoqneam project directed by A. BEN-TOR has begun to produce further evidence, as have excavations in the adjacent coastal plain at Tell Keisan, and various surface surveys[88]). The picture created by preliminary reports of these new investigations is much more complex than that implied by the brief biblical accounts to which I referred at the beginning of this paper. It was not simply a matter of initial resistance to the Israelite tribes followed by capitulation ''when Israel grew strong''—the case of Megiddo has shown this. But initial comparisons suggest that *each* of the major cities listed in Jud. i 27 may have had its own distinctive history during this period, as is only to be expected given their independent status and their different geographical positions.

Beth-shean apparently remained pro-Egyptian to the end of the Judges period, without any period of domination by the Philistines, except possibly a very brief one after the battle of Mount Gilboa. Some of the well-known anthropoid clay coffins may point to the use of mercenary troops of ''Sea-People'' origin, but the city seems to have remained respectful toward Egypt until the end of the Judges period[89]). Excavations conducted by Yigael YADIN shortly before his death have introduced new complications and suggest that here too there may have been an interval of ''village'' life which was not noticed in the earlier excavations[90]).

Taanach was destroyed c. 1125 B.C. and was not reoccupied until the end of the eleventh century[91]).

The city of *Ibleam* awaits excavation. It is probably situated at Tell (or Khirbet) Bel‘ame 2 km south of Jenin in the West Bank region of Jordan[92]). This is a large site, with surface pottery attesting a long period of occupation in antiquity, and it is already clear that at some stage of its history it had a sloping tunnel leading down towards a spring on the east side of the tell. It will no doubt offer rich rewards to archaeologist and historian alike when a just settlement of the political problems of the region makes its excavation a possibility.

NOTES

[1]) Cf. Jos. xvii 11-13; Jud. i 27; v 19.

[2]) R. E. M. WHEELER, *Still Digging* (London, 1955), p. 112. Cf. Jacquetta HAWKES, *Mortimer Wheeler: Adventurer in Archaeology* (London, 1982), p. 133.

[3]) On the identification of Tell el-Mutesellim with Megiddo and the various archaeological expeditions which have worked there see chapters 1 and 2 of my forthcoming book *Megiddo*, to be published in 1986 in the series ''Cities of the Biblical World''. The present article is an amplified version of part of chapter 4 of that book.

4) The discussions of (e.g.) A. D. H. MAYES, in J. H. HAYES and J. M. MILLER (eds.), *Israelite and Judaean History* (London, 1977), pp. 285-331, and J. A. SOGGIN, *A History of Israel* (London, 1984), pp. 172-85, are based almost exclusively on their evaluation of the literary evidence. Contrast FRANKEN, in *The Cambridge Ancient History*, 3rd ed., II/2 (Cambridge, 1975), pp. 331-38, and DE GEUS, ''The Importance of Archaeological Research into the Palestinian Agricultural Terraces'', *PEQ* 107 (1975), 65-74, and *The Tribes of Israel* (Assen, 1976).

⁵) A. Mazar, "The 'Bull Site'—An Iron Age I Open Cult Place", *BASOR* 247 (1982), 27-42; A. Zertal, "Has Joshua's Altar been found on Mount Ebal?", *Biblical Archaeology Review*, Jan/Feb 1985, 26-43.

⁶) *Megiddo* (above, n. 3), p. 37.

⁷) *The Tribes of Yahweh* (London, 1980), pp. 650-63.

⁷ᵃ) Recently D. Ussishkin has proposed to date the transition from the Late Bronze Age to the Iron Age c. 1150 B.C.: see "Levels VII and VI at Tel Lachish and the End of the Late Bronze Age in Canaan", in *Palestine in the Bronze and Iron Ages*, Papers in honour of Olga Tufnell, ed. J. N. Tubb (London, 1985), pp. 213-230.

⁸) G. Loud, *Megiddo II. Seasons of 1935-39*, Oriental Institute Publications, 62 (Chicago, 1948), figs. 383 and 384.

⁹) *Megiddo II*, p. 29 (cf. fig. 21).

¹⁰) *Megiddo II*, figs. 411 and 412.

¹¹) *Megiddo II*, figs. 403 and 404.

¹²) *Megiddo II*, fig. 409.

¹³) *Megiddo II*, fig. 385.

¹⁴) *Megiddo II*, p. 31: see also below, pp. 38f.

¹⁵) *Megiddo II*, figs. 405 and 412. It is just possible that the temple continued in use, as the pottery in its debris included several pieces which are otherwise characteristic of Stratum VI (*Megiddo II*, pl. 71.7, 9, 19; pl. 72.1, 7, 9) and the first buildings to be built over it belong to Stratum VB.

¹⁶) G. Loud, *The Megiddo Ivories*, Oriental Institute Publications, 52 (Chicago, 1939), no. 377 (cf. pp. 11-12).

¹⁷) E. Hornung, *Grundzügen der aegyptischen Geschichte*, 2nd ed. (Darmstadt, 1978), p. 163; K. A. Kitchen, *Pharaoh Triumphant. The Life and Times of Ramesses II, King of Egypt* (Warminster, 1982), p. 239.

¹⁸) *Megiddo II*, pp. 135-6, figs. 374-5.

¹⁹) Hornung, loc. cit.

²⁰) *Megiddo II*, pl. 67-70, 139-140.

²¹) T. Dothan, *The Philistines and their Material Culture* (Jerusalem, 1982), pp. 71-4.

²²) *Megiddo II*, pl. 69.7; Dothan, *Philistines*, pp. 74-6.

²³) P. 76.

²⁴) See, respectively, *Megiddo Ivories*, pp. 7-9, and Barnett (below, n. 28), p. 25.

²⁵) *Philistines*, p. 71.

²⁶) *Megiddo II*, pl. 215. For the full list of finds in the "treasury" see p. 171 of the text volume.

²⁷) In *Megiddo Ivories*. Another piece (*Megiddo II*, pl. 204.2) was found in a locus in Area CC attributed to Stratum VIIA. *Pace* Barnett (see the next note), p. 25 the ivory flask with gold bands (*Megiddo II*, pl. 202) is not from the VIIA hoard but from an earlier one belonging to Stratum VIII. It should also be noted that the two pieces which he attributes to "a tomb ... of Level VIA" (p. 28) come respectively from Stratum VIII (*Megiddo II*, pl. 203.1) and a *room* of VIA (pl. 204.3).

²⁸) R. D. Barnett, *Ancient Ivories in the Middle East*, Qedem Monographs, 14 (Jerusalem, 1982), esp. pp. 25-8. Cf. H. Kantor, "Syro-Palestinian Ivories", *JNES* 15 (1956), 153-74.

²⁹) *Megiddo Ivories*, nos. 107-115.

³⁰) Op. cit., p. 26.

³¹) *Megiddo Ivories*, no. 1; Barnett, loc. cit.

³²) *Megiddo Ivories*, nos. 21 and 173.

³³) *Megiddo Ivories*, nos. 24 and 25; Barnett, p. 27.

³⁴) *Megiddo Ivories*, nos. 220-25; Barnett, pp. 26-7.

³⁵) For a full list see *Megiddo II*, p. 159.

³⁶) *Megiddo II*, pl. 237-8; cf. O. Negbi, *Canaanite Gods in Metal*, (Tel Aviv, 1976), pp. 50-53, 139, 172 (no. 1453).

³⁷) *Megiddo II*, pl. 255.1-2; Y. Yadin, *Hazor*, Schweich Lectures 1970 (London, 1972), pp. 82-3 and pl. 10a.

[38]) *Megiddo II*, pl. 185.4-5; pl. 214.81-3,85.

[39]) *Megiddo II*, pl. 180.38; pl. 184.12; pl. 283.3 and bowl a1261.

[40]) *Megiddo II*, pl. 205-6; cf. W. M. F. Petrie, *Amulets* (London, 1914: repr. with an introduction by G. T. Martin, Warminster, 1972), and K. Galling (ed.), *Biblisches Reallexikon*, 2nd ed. (Tübingen, 1977), pp. 10-11.

[41]) First in *BASOR* 62 (1936), 29, 68 (1937), 25; cf. *The Archaeology of Palestine* (Harmondsworth, 1949), pp. 117-8, and J. Bright, *A History of Israel* (London, 1960), p. 157 n. 70.

[42]) *Megiddo II*, p. 5.

[43]) *Megiddo II*, fig. 80 (cf. the section drawing of Area AA in fig. 416); R. M. Engberg, *BASOR* 78 (1940), 5.

[44]) *Megiddo II*, fig. 385.

[45]) G. Schumacher, *Tell el-Mutesellim I* (Leipzig, 1908), pp. 72-4 and Tafel 19.

[46]) *Megiddo II*, pl. 74.9, pl. 142.12; Dothan, *Philistines*, pl. 19.3 (p. 77).

[47]) *Philistines*, p. 78.

[48]) For the important distinction of three phases in this pottery see the summary in *Philistines*, pp. 94-6.

[49]) *Philistines*, p. 291 (cf. pp. 76, 80).

[50]) *Megiddo II*, pl. 76.1: cf. below, p. 46.

[51]) *Philistines*, p. 78.

[52]) *Megiddo II*, pl. 143.17; Dothan, *Philistines*, pl. 19.4 (p. 77).

[53]) *Philistines*, p. 78 n. 300.

[54]) *Megiddo II*, figs. 386 and 413.

[55]) *Megiddo II*, pp. 33, 37.

[56]) *Megiddo II*, fig. 410 (squares S10-11); Schumacher, *Tell el-Mutesellim I*, Tafel 21 and fig. 108. The brick-on-stone construction is described on p. 80.

[57]) C. Watzinger, *Tell el-Mutesellim II* (Leipzig, 1929), p. 42; Y. Aharoni, "Excavations at Tel Beersheba. Preliminary Report of the Fifth and Sixth Seasons, 1973-1974", *Tel Aviv* 2 (1975), 146-68 (see pp. 147-8).

[58]) *Tell el-Mutesellim I*, pp. 75-7 and Tafel 20.

[59]) R. S. Lamon, *The Megiddo Water-System*, Oriental Institute Publications, 32 (Chicago, 1935), pp. 36-7; Yadin, *Hazor*, pp. 161-5.

[60]) *Megiddo Water-System*, pp. 12 and 26.

[61]) Op. cit., p. 1.

[62]) Yadin, *Hazor*, p. 172.

[63]) Lamon, loc. cit.; *Tell el-Mutesellim I*, p. 161 and fig. 233.

[64]) *Megiddo II*, p. 6 and figs. 1, 5, 386 and the section of Area AA on fig. 416.

[65]) For the suggestion that they are Israelite cf. W. G. Dever, in M. Avi-Yonah and M. Stern (eds.), *Encyclopaedia of Archaeological Excavations in the Holy Land* (Jerusalem and London, 1975-8), p. 439 (Gezer); Y. Shiloh, *Excavations at the City of David I (1978-82)*, Qedem Monographs, 19 (Jerusalem, 1984), pp. 21-4 (Jerusalem).

[66]) J. B. Pritchard, *The Water System at Gibeon* (Philadelphia, 1961), pp. 22-3.

[67]) Lamon, *Megiddo Water-System*, p. 36; cf. J. B. Pritchard (ed.), *Ancient Near Eastern Texts Relating to the Old Testament*, 3rd ed. (Princeton, 1969), p. 238.

[68]) *Megiddo II*, pl. 176.60, 177.5, 183.19, 20, 22, 184.21, 187.21-2 (bronze); pl. 229 (silver). A further quantity of gold, silver and bronze, some of it also wrapped in cloth, was found in Area DD (pl. 228.4-6). This evidence of wrapping "money" in cloth, with which a similar hoard from Arad Stratum XI should be compared (M. Aharoni, *Qadmoniot* 13 (1980), 39-40), is relevant to discussion of Heb. ḥārîṭ (2 Kings v 23, Is. iii 22; according to M. Noth, *VT* 9 (1959), 421, also in Exod. xxxii 4, on which Rashi held a similar view (cf. *VT* 10 (1960), 74)). The context in Isaiah suggests that a garment is meant, and the archaeological evidence shows that such a meaning would not be inappropriate in 2 Kings v, where the "tying up" of a large quantity of silver is referred to.

[69]) *Megiddo II*, pl. 173.11-13, 183.15-17, 189-90.4-12. On the "wine-service" cf. O. Negbi, "The Continuity of the Canaanite Bronzework of the Late Bronze Age into the Early Iron Age", *Tel Aviv* 1 (1974), 159-72 (esp. pp. 163-7).

⁷⁰) *Tell el-Mutesellim I*, pp. 85-7; cf. Watzinger, *Tell el-Mutesellim II*, pp. 26-31. This evidence is overlooked by Negbi in the article just referred to. A very similar stand, but better preserved, was found in Tomb 911A1, ascribed to Late Bronze Age II (cf. P. L. O. Guy and R. M. Engberg, *Megiddo Tombs*, Oriental Institute Publications, 33 (Chicago, 1938), pl. 119.1).

⁷¹) Dothan, *Philistines*, pp. 79-80.

⁷²) *Megiddo II*, pl. 76.1: cf. Dothan, *Philistines*, pp. 150-3.

⁷³) "The 'Orpheus' Jug from Megiddo", in F. M. Cross et al. (eds.), *Magnalia Dei*: *The Mighty Acts of God*, G. E. Wright Memorial Volume (Garden City, 1976), pp. 187-92.

⁷⁴) *Megiddo II*, pl. 78.20.

⁷⁵) *Megiddo II*, pl. 83.1, 4; *Tell el-Mutesellim I*, p. 143.

⁷⁶) E.g. R. Amiran, *Ancient Pottery of the Holy Land* (New Brunswick, 1970), pp. 232-3.

⁷⁷) "New Aspects of the Israelite Occupation in the North", in J. A. Sanders (ed.), *Near Eastern Archaeology in the Twentieth Century*, Glueck Festschrift (Garden City, 1968), pp. 254-267 (esp. pp. 263-5); cf. Albright, *BASOR* 68 (1937), 25, 74 (1939), 23 n. 49, 78 (1940), 8.

⁷⁸) E.g. *Megiddo II*, pl. 75.7-8, 10-11, 20-1. The best parallels for this seem to come from Tell Keisan in the coastal plain: cf. J. Briend and J. B. Humbert, *Tell Keisan* (*1971-1976*): *une cité phénicienne en Galilée*, Orbis Biblicus et Orientalis, Series Archaeologica, 1 (Fribourg, 1980), pl. 57.9, 61.10-11, 13, 69.4, 6, 70.1-4, 71.1-2, 8c, 79.4-6, 11.

⁷⁹) For Transjordan see M. M. Ibrahim, "The Collared-Rim Jar of the Early Iron Age", in P. R. S. Moorey and P. J. Parr (eds.), *Archaeology in the Levant*, Kenyon Volume (Warminster, 1978), pp. 116-26; for the Jezreel Plain, W. E. Rast, *Taanach I. Studies in the Iron Age Pottery* (Cambridge, Mass., 1978), pp. 9-10 (Taanach and Afula), A. Ben-Tor, *IEJ* 28 (1978), 81 (Yoqneam), *BA* 42 (1979), 109 (Tell Qiri); for the coastal plain, Briend and Humbert, *Tell Keisan* (*1971-1976*), p. 206, *RB* 88 (1981), 388, 399 (Tell Keisan). Three jars of this type were attributed to Stratum VIIB at Megiddo (*Megiddo II*, pl. 64.8, pl. 65 (jars P6468 and P6460)) and seemed to Engberg (*BASOR* 78 (1940), 5) and others to attest Canaanite use of such jars. According to Rast, *Taanach I*, pp. 9-10, they may belong to Stratum VIIA (or later).

⁸⁰) The frequent references to the *Brandschicht* in the German reports can be correlated with the end of Stratum VI of the American excavations in the area of the "*Südliches Burgtor*"; for more recent work see D. Ussishkin, *BASOR* 239 (1980), 5-6, and G. J. Wightman, *Levant* 17 (1985), 117, 125.

⁸¹) "Caesurae in the History of Megiddo", *Oudtestamentische Studien* 1 (1942), 17-54.

⁸²) Engberg, *BASOR* 78 (1940), 4-7; Simons, art. cit., 51-2; Alt, "Megiddo im Übergang vom kanaanäischen zum israelitischen Zeitalter", *ZAW* N.F. 19 (1944), 67-85 (= *Kleine Schriften I* (Munich, 1953), pp. 256-73), esp. p. 75 (= p. 264).

⁸³) See, in addition to the article just referred to, "Zur Geschichte von Beth-Sean 1500-1000 v. Chr.", *PJB* 22 (1926), 108-120 (= *Kleine Schriften I*, pp. 246-55); "Meros", *ZAW* N.F. 17 (1941), 244-7 (= *Kleine Schriften I*, pp. 274-7).

⁸⁴) Compare the views of Alt, "Megiddo..", pp. 73-5 (= 261-3), and Aharoni, art. cit., pp. 255-60.

⁸⁵) For one view see A. D. H. Mayes, "The Historical Context of the Battle against Sisera", *VT* 19 (1969), 353-60. See also A. F. Rainey, "The Military Camp Ground at Taanach by the Waters of Megiddo", *Eretz-Israel* 15 (1981), 61*-66*, and "Toponymic Problems (cont.): Harosheth-Hagoiim", *Tel Aviv* 10 (1983), 46-8.

⁸⁶) Cf. Z. Gal, "The Settlement of Issachar: some new observations", *Tel Aviv* 9 (1982), 79-86.

⁸⁷) See the summary accounts (with bibliographies) in Avi-Yonah and Stern (eds.), *Encyclopaedia* (n. 65), and now Rast, *Taanach I*. A new series of excavations was begun at Dor in 1980.

⁸⁸) Ben-Tor, *IEJ* 28 (1978), 57-82, 29 (1979), 65-83; *BA* 42 (1979), 105-13; *IEJ* 31 (1981), 137-67, 33 (1983), 30-54; Y. Portugali, *Tel Aviv* 9 (1982), 170-88; Briend and Humbert, *Tell Keisan* (*1971-1976*) (n. 78), and *RB* 88 (1981), 373-400; Z. Gal, art. cit.

[89]) Note the reappearance of Egyptian stelae in "Lower Level V", which probably corresponds approximately to the eleventh century. The evidence of the coffins (on which see DOTHAN, *Philistines*, pp. 268-76) must be interpreted against this general background and the paucity of Philistine pottery at Beth-Shean.

[90]) Y. YADIN and S. GEVA, *IEJ* 34 (1984), 187-9.

[91]) RAST, *Taanach I*, pp. 55-6.

[92]) F.-M. ABEL, *Géographie de la Palestine*, II, 2nd ed. (Paris, 1938), p. 357; AHARONI, *The Land of the Bible*, 2nd ed. (London, 1979), p. 436; M. KOCHAVI (ed.), *Judaea, Samaria and the Golan. Archaeological Survey 1967-1968* (Jerusalem, 1972), pp. 201, 210.

COVENANT IN A CENTURY OF STUDY
SINCE WELLHAUSEN

BY

E. W. NICHOLSON
Oxford

Not so long ago covenant was among the least controversial issues in Old Testament study. Arguably, indeed, it was the least controversial of all. There was virtual unanimity among scholars that God's covenant with Israel was among the most ancient features of Israelite religion and was fundamentally constitutive of its distinctiveness from the outset. Those of you who were my contemporaries as students in the 1950s will recall how we were familiarized with this in the prescribed textbooks and other recommended reading of the time, in, for example, the widely used histories of Israel by John BRIGHT and Martin NOTH, or Bernhard ANDERSON's popular *The Living World of the Old Testament*, in those well-known monographs by G. Ernest WRIGHT as well as in standard works from influential British scholars, most notably H. H. ROWLEY. It came to us from our teachers and from books such as these as something of an "assured result" of Old Testament research long since established and accepted among scholars internationally. Indeed, you will recall that exactly at that time, in the mid-1950s, a new phase in covenant-study was launched by G. E. MENDENHALL's famous essay in the *Biblical Archaeologist* which seemed to offer remarkable proof from a quite unexpected source—Hittite treaties of the Late Bronze Age—of just how assured we could be about that "assured result". There followed, into the 1960s, a seemingly endless flow of monographs, articles and notes on "treaty and covenant" further buttressing the well-established consensus. At the same time there began to appear in ever increasing numbers translations of important German works, both old and new, by such internationally renowned figures as A. ALT, A. WEISER, W. EICHRODT, G. VON RAD, W. ZIMMERLI which we could now as teachers introduce to our students and which further illustrated, if that were needed, just how universally accepted was this view of the antiquity and fundamental importance of the covenant.

But the 1960s, though they saw the appearance of still further works in support of the received view, saw also a new challenge to it, and the decade ended with the publication of L. PERLITT's remarkably vigorous

and impressively detailed *Bundestheologie im Alten Testament* which incisive-
ly shook confidence in it and argued that the notion of a covenant between God and Israel was after all a theologoumenon coined in the late
pre-exilic period, just as WELLHAUSEN had maintained in his *Geschichte
Israels I* in 1878. Thus a century or so of study had brought us back to
where it began, and there is now renewed controversy about an issue
which had seemed long settled, just as there was in the years which
followed the publication of WELLHAUSEN's momentous work.

My purpose in this paper is to outline the history of research which
has led full circle back to WELLHAUSEN, first because it may help to explain why we are where we are currently on this subject, and second
because it may also help to point the way forward. My introductory
remarks have already indicated four main phases in the study of covenant
since WELLHAUSEN: the debate which followed his work, a second phase
which brought about the consensus to which I have referred, a third
phase which endeavoured to consolidate this on the basis of ancient Near
Eastern suzerainty treaties, and, finally, the current situation in the wake
of Perlitt's work.

(I)

The controversy which WELLHAUSEN's work generated and which
yielded a variety of conflicting views on the origin and nature of the covenant is of some interest in itself, and I shall briefly mention some of these
views. But my main purpose in taking you back to that period of controversy, which persisted from the publication of his *Geschichte Israels I* to
the end of the First World War, is that it sets in sharp relief the
remarkable unanimity of opinion on the subject which very quickly came
about in the immediately following years, and raises the question how
such unanimity suddenly appeared where hitherto there had been marked division of opinion. Further, that division of opinion was not simply
between critical scholarship in adherence to WELLHAUSEN on the one
side, and conservative, church apologists on the other. Critical scholarship itself was divided on the issue, and scholars who shared
WELLHAUSEN's methods and conclusions on other important matters
were opposed to each other on this one.

I mention but a few who came down on his side of the debate. He had
the weighty support of B. STADE in his monumental *Geschichte des Volkes
Israel* and other works, and notable, detailed studies of the covenant texts
in the Old Testaments by, for example, R. KRAETZSCHMAR and J. J. P.

VALETON likewise supported him or at least substantially so. Or again, though scholars such as K. BUDDE and H. GUNKEL argued against him that a covenant was made at Sinai, it was merely to conclude that this was a covenant between the Israelites and the Kenites or Midianites, not between God and Israel; the notion of this latter covenant, they agreed with WELLHAUSEN, arose only as a much later development.

On the other side, however, there was no shortage of disagreement with WELLHAUSEN's view. STADE's history of Israel in support of it was matched by R. KITTEL's influential *Geschichte der Hebräer* opposing it. Within the ranks of the "history-of-religions movement" H. GRESSMANN differed from his close colleague GUNKEL on this issue, finding, for example, that the short narrative in Exodus xxiv 9-11—the eating of a meal in the presence of God on the holy mountain—is a covenant-making tradition of very great antiquity. Similarly, in an article which has remained influential to this day, C. STEUERNAGEL, who identified himself with many of WELLHAUSEN's critical views, argued that the covenant blood-ritual in Exodus xxiv 3-8 is also of great antiquity, possibly even reflecting a covenant ceremony of the pre-settlement period. Others attacked WELLHAUSEN's view at its heart, rejecting his understanding of early Israelite religion as a "natural bond" between God and the people. Rather, it was a religion grounded in historical events which, interpreted by Moses, pointed to the divine election of Israel which was consolidated by the making of a covenant between Yahweh and his newly appropriated people (so, for example, F. GIESEBRECHT in his influential monograph *Die Geschichtlichkeit des Sinaibundes*). Here in England, W. ROBERTSON SMITH too, for all his admiration of WELLHAUSEN's work, opposed him on the matter of the covenant. He argued that from the time of Moses onwards Yahweh was no mere natural clan deity but the God of a confederation for which a covenant religion was entirely appropriate. That is, the covenant was no mere "theological idea" of a late period but performed an ancient religio-sociological function, as we may describe it, uniting diverse groups with each other and with their common God Yahweh—an understanding of the origin and nature of the covenant in the earliest period of Israel's history which, as we shall see, was later to become widely favoured.

This is a sufficient, though far from exhaustive, description of the debate which WELLHAUSEN's work generated during the period to which I refer. Very remarkably, however, as I have already indicated, the controversy rapidly disappeared in the years immediately following the First World War, and within little more than a decade the consensus which I mentioned earlier had established itself.

(II)

A striking illustration of the shift which now took place from controversy to widespread agreement is provided by GUNKEL's article on "Moses" for the second edition of *Die Religion in Geschichte und Gegenwart* in 1930. In the first edition of this article in 1913 he had written: "Um Sinai hat M(ose) dann die Stämme gesammelt und einen Bund mit den Midianitern geschlossen." ("Moses then assembled the tribes at Sinai and made a covenant between them and the Midianites.") In the second edition, however, this same sentence was changed to read: "Um Sinai hat M(ose) dann die Stämme gesammelt und durch einen "Bund" Jahves mit ihnen sie innerlich geeinigt." ("Moses then assembled the tribes at Sinai and by means of a covenant of Yahweh with them gave them an inner unity.")

The arguments which now so widely prevailed were as follows.

(1) The view already argued in the preceding period that the covenant was from the outset a necessary feature of Israelite religion as a religion founded upon historical events, a religion of "election" and not a "natural bond", now found fresh and widespread emphasis. One thinks especially in this connection of influential works by J. HEMPEL, A. WEISER, K. GALLING, and most notably W. EICHRODT's well known *Theologie des Alten Testaments*.

(2) Crucially significant, and lastingly so, was M. NOTH's famous monograph *Das System der zwölf Stämme Israels* in which he argued that Israel originated as a confederation of tribes founded upon a covenant between them and their common God Yahweh. With this work a point of stability was achieved for understanding the covenant, not as a theological *idea*, but as an *institution* which was formative and normative in Israelite society and religion from the outset.

(3) Contributions from S. MOWINCKEL during the 1920s were also influential, first his *Psalmenstudien I-VI* (especially the second volume *Das Thronbesteigungsfest Jahwäs und der Ursprung der Eschatologie*) and then still more especially his monograph *Le Décalogue*. In these works he argued not only that the covenant was an essential feature of Israelite society and religion but also that a "renewal of the covenant" formed a significant part of an annual cultic festival centring upon Yahweh's kingship as creator of the world and Lord of his people Israel, and he found evidence of the influence of this liturgy upon, for example, the form and contents of the Sinai pericope in Exodus xix-xxiv. The influence of MOWINCKEL's ideas can be seen in works by, for example, A. ALT, A. WEISER, and G. VON RAD which in turn were themselves widely influential.

Why was it that these arguments so effectively dispelled the controversy which had hitherto abounded on the matter of the nature and antiquity of the covenant? After all, as you will have noticed, they were not wholly new. The first was familiar among those who opposed WELLHAUSEN's view in the preceding generation, and the second is clearly akin to W. ROBERTSON SMITH's suggestion made much earlier that the covenant would have performed a necessary religio-sociological function in early Israel as a tribal society.

Due weight must be given to the vigour and fresh detail in which they were now newly argued. For example, whilst it had been suggested much earlier that pre-monarchic Israel took the form of a tribal "amphictyony", it was not until NOTH's epoch-making monograph that it was presented in such detail and so compellingly. But when allowance has been fully made for the powerful advocacy which these views now received, and for the new insights advanced by MOWINCKEL, other important trends contributed significantly, indeed decisively, to the consensus which now emerged and which was to prove so durable concerning the nature and antiquity of the covenant.

A variety of trends converged to focus increasing attention upon the distinctiveness of Israelite religion and of Old Testament faith and piety. For example, though the "history-of-religions movement" now began to go into decline, its well known quest for the individuality (*Eigentümlichkeit*) of Israel, its culture and religion, remained as a legacy which served to emphasise the covenant as a conspicuously distinctive feature of Israelite religion. Still more influential in this connection was the emerging Neo-orthodoxy of those years. Its emphasis upon revelation "von oben nach unten" and its corresponding denigration of "natural theology" created a climate conducive to an emphasis upon Israel's history as the arena of God's self-revelation, and gave increased impetus to discerning the uniqueness of Israel's faith which from now onwards was more and more regarded as having been radically discontinuous with the religious thought-world of its environment. All this led to increased attention upon the "particularist" elements of Israelite faith such as the "saving history", "election", and "covenant". The notion that Israelite religion began as something of a "natural bond" was abandoned; indeed, nothing could have been more alien to the new theological climate of the time than such a view. In addition, darkly ominous during those years after the First World War was the beginning of a new upsurge of anti-semitism in Germany which carried with it a call for the abandonment of the Old Testament as part of the church's scriptures. Reaction to this yielded a corresponding fresh emphasis upon the abiding value of Old Testament faith and piety, including its covenant-theology. To this may be further added that a theology of "the people of God", of which the covenant grounded in that people's confessional choice formed such an important basis, became a subject of increasing interest in a situation which had begun to give rise to racially-based German *Volkstum.*

But much more significant than these various trends, because it was much more direct, was the influence that now came from the sociology of religion which had entered its modern era largely through the work of Emil DURKHEIM and, of special interest for Old Testament research, Max WEBER.

In broad terms, it may be said that whereas hitherto a society's religion had come to be regarded as one feature among others in its life, one social phenomenon among other such phenomena, it was now seen to be a formative and normative force, creative in forms of social life and organization. Religious beliefs and practices with their related institutions were now viewed as belonging to the very "nuts and bolts", so to speak, of a society, creating solidarity among its members and influencing powerfully many aspects of its life. As a result, attention was now increasingly focused upon the *function* of religious beliefs and commitments in the making and development of a society.

I cannot here describe in detail why WEBER devoted himself to a study of ancient Israelite religion in his work *Das antike Judentum* which first appeared as articles in 1917-19 and then as the third volume of his *Gesammelte Aufsätze zur Religionssoziologie* in 1921. His primary interest was in the relation between a society's religion and its economic activity. For our purpose what is important is the predominant role he assigned to the covenant in the foundation of Israelite society and religion and in their subsequent history. From the outset Israel was an "oathbound confederation"; by means of a covenant Yahweh became partner to the ritualistic and social order of the confederation. Thus the covenant was no mere "theoretical construction", but was the basis of the cohesion which existed between the otherwise diverse groups which became known as Israel. For Israel the deliverance from bondage in Egypt was seen as a token of God's power and of the absolute dependability of his promises, and also of Israel's lasting debt of gratitude. The uniqueness of the exodus was constituted by the fact that this miracle was wrought by a god until then unknown by Israel who thereupon accepted him as its God by means of a solemn covenant. This covenant was based upon mutual pledges bilaterally mediated through Moses: Yahweh by this means gave his solemn promises to Israel and accepted Israel's pledges of obedience to his holy enactments. And since Yahweh was a partner to the covenant, all violations of these enactments were violations of the solemn agreement between him and Israel: the confederacy law was thus jealousy guarded

by Yahweh. Further development of the confederacy law was carried out
on a covenantal basis. Weber also argued that already in the pre-
monarchic period the Levites became exponents and teachers, and thus
transmitters, of the divine law. The pre-classical prophets were likewise
custodians of the covenance enactments which at a later time similarly
underlay the preaching of the great prophets.

The decisive role of its religion in the foundation and making of Israel
as a people and a nation had long been a prominent interest among
students of the Old Testament. Not surprisingly, therefore, they were a
receptive audience to this new emphasis in the field of sociology upon just
such a creative role of religion in societies generally. Leading figures such
as KITTEL and GRESSMANN, in programmatic essays in the 1920s on the
future tasks of Old Testament research, urged attention to the insights
which this field was currently offering, and they made special reference to
WEBER's impressive and in so many ways fascinating work. They were
not hammering on closed doors. The scholarly literature in our subject
during those years, and notably that which concerned itself in one way or
another with the origin and significance of the covenant, contains
numerous references to WEBER's work. This can be seen in contributions
by, for example, ALT, WEISER, HEMPEL, GALLING, EICHRODT, and
NOTH. As far as I am aware, the only serious critical dissent came from
W. CASPARI. The view that the covenant originated at the earliest time as
the means whereby the disparate elements of Israel were united and held
together and bound to Yahweh their common God now became widely
approved. In fact the matter can be summed up succinctly as follows:
though other important influences came to bear on the issue, WEBER's
work was crucially decisive in swinging scholarship away from controversy on it to the view that the covenant was of the essence of Israelite
religion and society from the earliest period of its history. From within
the ranks of Old Testament scholars proper NOTH's monograph on pre-
monarchic Israel as a sacral confederation firmly established such a view
and gave it the widest possible currency for a generation to come.

(III)

Time does not permit me to document the widespread reception of this
understanding of the antiquity and significance of the covenant in the
writings of scholars during the inter-war and immediate post-Second
World War years. I must move ahead to the third phase of covenant
research since WELLHAUSEN, that which concerned itself with the
evidence of ancient Near Eastern suzerainty treaties.

As I mentioned earlier, MENDENHALL's essay in the *Biblical Archaeologist* in 1954 launched this new phase. He accepted the dominant view of earlier research of the socio-religious and institutional nature of the covenant in Israelite origins and history. Since Israel did not emerge in the genealogical manner described in the Old Testament, it can only have been the covenant, he maintained, that constituted the basis of the relationship between the tribes. What was lacking in the discussion hitherto, however, was a concept of a covenant which would have bound together the tribes and at the same time would have formed a foundation for their belief that in this event Yahweh became the God of Israel. This difficulty is overcome, Mendenhall argued, once it is seen that the type of covenant which operated was modelled upon the Hittite treaty-form whereby a great king bound his vassals to faithfulness to himself and at the same time ordered relationships between these vassals themselves as subjects of the same overlord. Further and significantly, this particular treaty-form was contemporary with Israelite origins in the Late Bronze Age. He then went on to argue that the decalogue in Exodus xx and other covenant texts in the Old Testament display the influence of that treaty-form.

A spate of monographs and articles by others followed, further developing and elaborating MENDENHALL's tersely stated thesis, and treaty texts from the neo-Assyrian period of the first millennium were now also brought into the discussion. In addition to the influence of the treaty-form upon Old Testament covenant texts, the use of individual words and phrases in these texts was now likewise traced to the treaty literature, for example, the "father-son" relationship as applied to Yahweh and Israel, "to know" Yahweh in the sense of acknowledging his legitimate claims as Israel's suzerain, the command "to love" Yahweh, the description of Israel as Yahweh's *segullāh* "special possession"; it was suggested that even the central demand of the covenant texts for Israel's exclusive allegiance to Yahweh may have been influenced by the demand of suzerains in the treaty texts for the exclusive loyalty of their vassals.

Many were persuaded by all or much of this, and I include myself among them. But further reflection has convinced me that this phase in covenant research is one that in fact has yielded little that is of lasting value.

In his well known study *Treaty and Covenant* D. J. MCCARTHY effectively disposed of the view that the Sinai pericope in Exodus xix-xxiv was influenced by the Hittite treaties. The resemblances are merely superficial; the pericope lacks essential features of the Hittite treaties such as a historical prologue and the curses and blessings formulae. Rather, McCARTHY argued, the pericope witnesses to an ancient ritualistic covenant-making tradition in Israel which was foreign to the treaty tradition. It is

only in late texts such as 1 Samuel xii and Joshua xxiv, which he
classified as "proto-Deuteronomic", and most prominently in
Deuteronomy itself that the influence of the treaties manifests itself,
specifically the form and terminology of the neo-Assyrian treaties. M.
WEINFELD in his full-length study supported MCCARTHY's conclusions in
this respect.

But the same observation which MCCARTHY made about the Sinai
pericope may also be made about Deuteronomy, namely, that the
resemblances between it and the treaty-form as exemplified in the neo-
Assyrian treaties are more apparent than real. The pronounced historical
element in the prologue to Deuteronomy has nothing resembling it in
these treaties, and the laws in Deuteronomy are much broader in their
scope than the treaty stipulations. In the works of both MCCARTHY and
WEINFELD the weight of the analogy in fact rests upon Deuteronomy
xxviii, the long list of curses which resembles the similarly long lists in the
Assyrian treaties and indeed seems to incorporate some formulations
from these treaties.

Yet here too there is a significant difference, for Deuteronomy xxviii-
also includes a list of blessings, a feature lacking in the contemporary
Assyrian treaties. Further, it is only by an uncritical acceptance of the
curse list in Deuteronomy xxviii as the work of a single author, or
substantially so, that it can then be argued that this author in drawing up
such a long list was seeking to emulate the lists in the treaties. Indeed,
there has been something of an argument in a circle in this matter: the
treaty lists are appealed to for proof that the curse list in Deuteronomy
xxviii is a unity, or substantially so, and then Deuteronomy xxviii,
established as a unity on this basis, is appealed to as evidence that its
author was influenced by the treaty lists. But the majority of commentators are agreed that Deuteronomy xxviii developed in several stages,
and if, as seems likely, this is so, then neither the length of the list nor its
heavy emphasis upon curse can be regarded as the planned work of a
single author seeking to emulate the long curse lists in the treaties. The
end result may look like such a treaty list, but neither in origin nor in its
subsequent stage-by-stage expansion was it consciously intended as such.
The heavy emphasis upon curse in this chapter is readily explained by the
historical circumstance that it was developed and expanded during a
period—the late seventh and early sixth centuries B.C.—when curse was
seen to hover more and more ominously over the nation and then fell
catastrophically upon it in the events of 597 and 587 B.C. Thus the threat
which had accompanied the giving of Yahweh's *Torah* was sharply
augmented, in both length and severity; Israel's crime was thus made to
fit the foreordained punishment, and so the punishment fitted the crime.

At another but, I think, no less important level, it has in any case to be asked whether the suzerain-vassal analogy would have had any appeal of an apt or desirable nature in ancient Israel. Notwithstanding all the references in the treaties to the "love" of suzerain for vassal and of vassal for suzerain, to the suzerain as "father" and the vassal as "son", such relationship were surely rarely if ever like that. Vassals did not as a rule "love" those who conquered and dominated them, and the very language of intimate and familial relationships employed in the treaties reflects, not the reality of the relationships, but the politically, strategically and economically motivated endeavour of suzerains to maintain with the least amount of trouble possible the subserviance of subject states. To tell Israelites that Yahweh "loves" them in the same way as Ashurbanipal or Nebuchadrezzar "loves" his vassals, including Israel, and that they are to "love" Yahweh as vassals "love" their suzerains would surely have been a bizarre depiction of Yahweh's love for his people and of the love with which they were called upon to respond to him. The use in Deuteronomy and related texts of such imagery as the "father-son" relationship, the command to "love" Yahweh, "to know" Yahweh, and so forth, need not be seen as a borrowing from treaty texts. Rather, it is more plausibly explained as the result of borrowing on the part of both treaty scribes and the biblical authors from a common and self-evident source: the familiar settings of everyday life.

(IV)

The attempt to relate the Old Testament covenant to suzerainty treaties may be said to represent a dead-end in the social/functional approach; the search for a model that will explain how the covenant functioned in the religious and social life of ancient Israel here overreaches itself. More than this, it is apparent in prominent works of the treaty approach such as those by MCCARTHY and WEINFELD that they themselves have gone some way towards cancelling it. Both of these scholars still insist that there was a covenant in the earliest stages of Israelite history which exercised some sort of socio-religious function. But in their consideration of the influence of the treaties they have begun to understand it as having become a metaphor or analogy for the relationship between God and his people. Thus what began with MENDENHALL as an attempt to buttress the received view of the socio-religious and institutional nature of the covenant, represents in its later stages something of a shift back to understanding it as a theological ideal or analogy. On a different basis a contribution from G. FOHRER in the mid-1960s represents something of the same shift. Already a few years earlier, C. F. WHITLEY

in a brief discussion had restated WELLHAUSEN's main conclusion that the
covenant was a late innovation in Israelite religion. Thus the course of
research since WELLHAUSEN began to turn full circle, and was completed
most notably by PERLITT's work, alongside which may also be mentioned
that of E. KUTSCH. For both of these scholars the notion of a covenant
between Yahweh and Israel was a theological concept of the late pre-
exilic period, a creation of the Deuteronomic movement of the seventh
century B.C. designed to meet specifically theological needs and crises
which confronted Israel at that relatively late time.

KUTSCH's work is the most detailed study of the word *berīt* since
KRAETZSCHMAR's monograph in 1896. I do not think it is successful (see
especially J. BARR's critique in the Zimmerli Festschrift). His intention is
to determine the meaning of the word from its various contexts in the Old
Testament. But in essence he seems to be guided by an etymological approach, a search for a *Grundbedeutung*. This he finds to be "obligation",
and he concludes that a *berīt* consisted of the unilateral imposition or acceptance of an obligation; *Verpflichtung* rather than *Bund* is the proper way
to understand the word.

The discovery of such a "common denominator", however, shows only that it was simply that: one particular feature that was part of what it
meant to make a *berīt*; and it is a mistake to proceed from this, as KUTSCH
does, to the conclusion that *berīt* can then be represented simply by
"obligation", as though a *berīt* necessarily consisted solely of this, and
this exhaused the semantic range of the word. The word itself refrains
from mapping out the various distinctions which KUTSCH wishes to draw
between one kind of a *berīt* and another. It is the context alone which
determines this, and if, with KUTSCH's own stated intention, we are to
ascertain the meaning of the word not from its etymon, whatever that
may be, but from its usage, then it is difficult to see how, as it seems, he
can regard the bilateral connotation of the word in some contexts as a
secondary or exceptional use of it. It seems rather that the semantic range
of the word was such that it could be used indifferently for unilateral and
bilateral arrangements. It seems indeed that this one word in Biblical
Hebrew had to do service for a range of activities which in, say, English
are covered by such terms as "agreement", "treaty", "contract", "promise", "obligation", and the like.

Whilst KUTSCH's study of the word *berīt* is the most detailed since
KRAETZSCHMAR's monograph of 1896, PERLITT's book is the most detailed presentation yet of the view that Israel's covenant traditions are the
product of a late period and arose in response to various theological needs
and crises. He begins where the theological use of the word *berīt* is most
expansively and intensively employed, that is, in the Deuteronomic/Deu-

teronomistic corpus of the seventh and sixth centuries B.C., whence he moves to other texts to determine whether its theological usage is a product of the late period in which it is most in evidence or of earlier origin. He finds that none of these other texts witnesses to a pre-Deuteronomic origin of a covenant-theology, not even the book of Hosea where the one clear reference to a covenant between Yahweh and Israel (viii 1) is a secondary, Deuteronomistic addition (vi 7, he maintains, has nothing to do with such a covenant).

(V)

In the works of both PERLITT and KUTSCH, conspicuously so in KUTSCH's many contributions on the subject, there is a marked scaling-down of the significance usually attached to the covenant in the study of the Old Testament. This, together with other shifts of interest in current research, has contributed to something of an eclipse in the study of covenant recently. And in any case, a century or so of debate which was turned full circle back virtually to where it began may understandably be considered to have run itself into the ground, leavening ''covenant'' as seemingly rather a played-out concept for students of the Old Testament.

In the few minutes that remain to me I can state only very briefly the gains I consider to have been made in the recent stages of the debate together with a proposal which I offer as a way of helping to place the study of the covenant firmly once again on the agenda of Old Testament research[1]).

In two main respects I would align myself with PERLITT's conclusions. First, I welcome the shift away from understanding the covenant as having been originally an institution which operated in the formation of Israel as a tribal society. None of the descriptions of the making of the covenant provides any evidence that any part of its purpose was to unite the diverse tribes into a tribal league. That the tribes already belong together as ''Israel'' is the presupposition of each of these texts. What they concentrate on is Israel's relationship with, and commitment to, God as the people chosen by him for his own. That is, in origin the covenant had to do with an ideal or vision of what it meant to be ''the people of Yahweh''. I shall say something more about this below.

Second, I am persuaded that the notion of such a covenant was a relative latecomer in the history of Israelite religion. Against PERLITT, I believe that the references to it in Hosea are authentic; but on the other

---

[1]) I provide a fuller discussion of this and of the survey in the foregoing pages in my book *God and His People*: *Covenant and Theology in the Old Testament*, Oxford 1986.

hand, I do not believe that we can with any confidence trace its origins
further back than the period of this prophet, and it is in any case clear
that it received its most intensive and expansive treatment at the hands of
Deuteronomic authors of the late pre-exilic and the exilic period.

   In these two respects PERLITT's work has, in my opinion, fully vin-
dicated the position of WELLHAUSEN. Beyond this I find a further insight
of WELLHAUSEN which provides a basis not only for a way forward in the
debate about the covenant but also for a fresh understanding of how
crucial it was in the development of what is distinctive in the faith of ancient Israel. He wrote of the great prophets of the eighth century as having effected a decisive change in Israel's perception of its relationship
with God by breaking the mould of a "natural bond" between them and
transferring the relationship unto the plane of moral response and commitment. My proposal is that in this also WELLHAUSEN was correct and,
further, that the notion of a covenant between Yahweh and Israel arose
as one of the results of the decisive change these prophets brought about.
And here the sociology of religion which in earlier stages of the debate
seemed to offer an attractive but ultimately misleading line of enquiry,
since it diverted scholarship into a wild goose chase after a very early,
socially operative covenant, still has some useful insights to offer.

   I refer to the arguments of such recent writers as Peter BERGER, on the
basis of lines already laid down by thinkers such as DURKHEIM and
WEBER, that religion and religious concepts have as one of their most important roles the legitimation of particular sorts of social order. Now if
such an analysis is applied to ancient Israel (as it has been, at least implicitly, by H. H. SCHMID) one can trace a highly distinctive development, in which a phase where religion legitimates society is succeeded by
one in which a new style of religious thought emerges that challenges and
de-legitimates the apparently stable and divinely ordained social structures. The crucial figures in bringing about this transformation were (as
WELLHAUSEN correctly saw) the classical prophets. But if covenant-
theology was also a creation of this same period, then the conclusion that
the covenant idea itself is intimately bound up with the vast religious
change which these prophets initiated lies close to hand.

   The proposal with which I conclude, therefore, is that covenant-
language served as the focal point for that desacralization of a religious
society of which the prophets were the chief agents. The concept of a
covenant between Yahweh and Israel is, in terms of "cash-value", the
concept that religion is based, not on a natural or ontological equivalence
between the divine realm and the human, but on *choice*: God's choice of
his people and their "choice" of him (cf. for example Deut. xxvi 17-19;
xxvii 9-10; Josh. xxiv 22), that is, their free decision to be obedient and

faithful to him. Thus understood, the covenant is a central expression of the distinctive faith of Israel as "the people of Yahweh", children of God by adoption and free decision rather than by nature or necessity. This has been obscured somewhat by too narrow a concentration on questions of terminology, and lost sight of altogether in the (fruitless) quest to find ancient parallels in the sphere of social institutions. So far from being a social institution, the covenant represents the refusal of prophets and their disciples to encapsulate Yahweh's relationship with his people in institutions, and to insist that it depends on a moral commitment on both sides which needs to be continually reaffirmed in faithful conduct, not taken for granted as though it were part of the order of nature.

Just how dominant was this element of response and freely-given commitment in the covenant concept may be seen from the "new covenant" prophecy in Jeremiah xxxi 31-4, where an insistence on the non-automatic character of the covenant is maintained even in a passage which is precisely concerned to say that God's grace is in the future to be bestowed without the requirement of any human response, and that it is, indeed, guaranteed; so imbued is the author with the idea that the covenant was a two-sided affair with no built-in guarantees that he is constrained to produce a paradoxical theory according to which God himself promises to make possible the very response which he inexorably demands.

So far from being merely one among a wide range of terms and ideas that emerged, flourished, and had their day, the covenant is, therefore, a central theme that served to focus an entirely idiosyncratic way of looking at the relationship between God and his people, and indeed, between God and the world. As such it deserves to be put back squarely on the agenda for students of the Old Testament.

BIBLIOGRAPHY

ALT, A., *Die Ursprünge des Israelitischen Rechts*, Leipzig 1934, reprinted in his *Kleine Schriften*, I, Munich 1953, pp. 278-332; E.trs. "The Origins of Israelite Law", *Essays on Old Testament History and Religion*, Oxford 1966, pp. 79-132.

ANDERSON, B. W., *The Living World of the Old Testament*, Englewood Cliffs 1957 and London 1958.

BARR, J., "Some Semantic Notes on the Covenant", *Beiträge zur Alttestamentlichen Theologie, Festschrift für Walther Zimmerli zum 70. Geburtstag*, ed. H. H. Donner, R. Hanhart, R. Smend, Göttingen 1977, pp. 23-38.

BERGER, P., *The Social Reality of Religion*, London 1969.

BRIGHT, J., *A History of Israel*, London 1960.

BUDDE, K., *The Religion of Israel to the Exile*, New York and London 1899.
Die Religion des Volkes Israel bis zur Verbannung, Giessen 1900.

CASPARI, W., *Die Gottesgemeinde am Sinai und das nachmalige Volk Israel*, BFChrTh 27, Gütersloh 1922.

EICHRODT, E., *Theologie des Alten Testaments*, I, Leipzig 1933, II, 1935, III, 1939. E.trs. *Theology of the Old Testament*, I, London 1961 (from the sixth German edition of vol. I, Stuttgart 1959), II, London 1967 (from the fifth German edition of vols. II and III, Stuttgart 1964).

FOHRER, G., "Altes Testament—'Amphiktyonie' und 'Bund'?", *TLZ* 91, 1966, cols. 801-16 and 894-904.

GALLING, K., *Die Erwählungstraditionen Israels*, BZAW 48, Giessen 1928.

GIESEBRECHT, F., *Die Geschichtlichkeit des Sinaibundes*, Königsberg 1900.

GRESSMANN, H., *Mose und seine Zeit. Ein Kommentar zu den Mose-Sagen*, FRLANT, N.F. 1, Göttingen 1913.
"Die Aufgaben der alttestamentlichen Forschung", *ZAW* 42, 1924, pp. 1-33.

GUNKEL, H., "Mose", *Die Religion in Geschichte und Gegenwart*, first edition, vol. IV, Tübingen 1913, cols. 516-24.
"Mose", *Die Religion in Geschichte und Gegenwart*, second edition, vol. IV, Tübingen 1930, cols. 230-7.

HEMPEL, J., *Gott und Mensch im Alten Testament. Studie zur Geschichte der Frömmigkeit*, BWANT III: 2, Stuttgart 1926.

KITTEL, R., *Geschichte der Hebräer*, I, Gotha 1888. E.trs. *A History of the Hebrews*, I, London and Edinburgh 1895.
"Die Zukunft der alttestamentliche Wissenschaft", *ZAW* 39, 1921, pp. 84-99.

KRAETZSCHMAR, R., *Die Bundesvorstellung im Alten Testament in ihrer geschichtlichen Entwickelung*, Marburg 1896.

KUTSCH, E., *Verheissung und Gesetz. Untersuchungen zum sogenannten "Bund" im Alten Testament*, BZAW 131, Berlin and New York 1973.

McCARTHY, D. J. *Treaty and Covenant*, Analecta Biblica 21, Rome 1963, second revised edition, Analecta Biblica 21A, Rome 1978.

MENDENHALL, G. E., "Covenant Forms in Israelite Tradition", *BA* 17, 1954, pp. 50-76.

MOWINCKEL, S., *Psalmenstudien II. Das Thronbesteigungsfest Jahwäs und der Ursprung der Eschatologie*, Kristiania 1922.
Le Décalogue, Paris 1927.

NOTH, M., *Das System der zwölf Stämme Israels*, BWANT IV: 1, Stuttgart 1930.
Geschichte Israels, Göttingen 1950. E.trs. *The History of Israel*, second revised edition, London 1960.

PERLITT, L., *Bundestheologie im Alten Testament*, WMANT 36, Neukirchen-Vluyn 1969.

RAD, G. VON, *Das formgeschichtliche Problem des Hexateuch*, BWANT IV: 26, Stuttgart 1938, reprinted in his *Gesammelte Studien zum Alten Testament*, Munich 1958, pp. 9-81. E.trs. "The Form-Critical Problem of the Hexateuch", *The Problem of the Hexateuch and Other Essays*, Edinburgh and London 1966, pp. 1-78.

ROWLEY, H. H., *The Biblical Doctrine of Election*, London 1950.
From Joseph to Joshua: Biblical Traditions in the Light of Archaeology, London 1950.

SCHMID, H. H., *Altorientalische Welt in der alttestamentlichen Theologie*, Zürich 1974.

SMITH, W. Robertson, *The Religion of the Semites*, London 1889.

STADE, B., *Geschichte des Volkes Israel*, I, Berlin 1887.

STEUERNAGEL, C., "Der jehovistische Bericht über den Bundesschluss am Sinai", *ThStK* 72, 1899, pp. 319-50.

VALETON, J. J. P., "Bedeutung und Stellung des Wortes ברית im Priestercodex", *ZAW* 12, 1892, pp. 1-22.
"Das Wort ברית in den jehovistischen und deuteronomischen Stücken des Hexateuchs, sowie in den verwandten historischen Büchern", *ZAW* 12, 1892, pp. 224-60.
"Das Wort ברית bei den Propheten und in den Ketubim. Resultat", *ZAW* 13, 1893, pp. 245-79.

WEBER, M., *Das antike Judentum, Gesammelte Aufsätze zur Religionssoziologie*, III, Tübingen 1921. E.trs. *Ancient Judaism*, London 1952.

WEINFELD, M., *Deuteronomy and the Deuteronomic School*, Oxford 1972.

WEISER, A., *Die Bedeutung des Alten Testaments für den Religionsunterricht*, Giessen 1925, reprinted in *Glaube und Geschichte im Alten Testament und andere ausgewählte Schriften*, Göttingen 1961, pp. 19-50.

Glaube und Geschichte im Alten Testament, BWANT IV: 4, Stuttgart 1931, reprinted in *Glaube und Geschichte im Alten Testament und andere ausgewählte Schriften*, pp. 99-182.

WELLHAUSEN, J., *Geschichte Israels I*, Berlin 1878, second edition published as *Prolegomena zur Geschichte Israels*, Berlin 1883. E.trs. *Prolegomena to the History of Israel*, Edinburgh 1885.

WHITLEY, C. F., "Covenant and Commandment in Israel", *JNES* 22, 1963, pp. 37-48.

WRIGHT, G. E., "How did Early Israel differ from her Neighbours?", *BA* 6, 1943, pp. 1-20.

The Old Testament Against Its Environment, London 1950.

God Who Acts, London 1952.

ZIMMERLI, W., *The Law and the Prophets*, London 1965.

DISTORTION OF OLD TESTAMENT PROPHECY

The Purpose of Isaiah xxxvi and xxxvii *

BY

K. A. D. SMELIK

Utrecht

Chapters xxxvi-xxxix constitute a part of the book of Isaiah that was rather neglected until recently. This was mainly because they are almost identical to parts of 2 Kings (2 Kings xviii 13, 17 - xx 19). According to general opinion[1]) the parts in Kings are more original than the chapters in Isaiah. It is assumed that Isaiah xxxvi-xxxix have been extracted from 2 Kings and added to the already complete first part of the book of Isaiah (Is. i-xxxv) in the same way as the concluding chapter of Kings has been added to the book of Jeremiah. The other possibility that these narratives have been borrowed by the editor of Kings from the book of Isaiah and that they have been originally written as part of Isaiah instead of Kings, has been ruled out. In most commentaries on Isaiah these chapters are, therefore, omitted; the reader is referred to a commentary on Kings[2]).

Only of late has the position of Isaiah xxxvi-xxxix attracted the attention of Old Testament scholars: I mention the names of ACKROYD, MELUGIN, RENDTORFF and CLEMENTS[3]). Their conclusions make it useful to reconsider the question as to whether the narratives about Hezekiah and Isaiah have not been composed as part of Isaiah instead of Kings. To this question the first part of this paper will be devoted.

The second point will be a re-appraisal of STADE's interpretation of the narratives published almost one hundred years ago[4]), because his view has dominated the exegesis of these stories up till now. Special attention will be paid to STADE's suggestion that the account of the Assyrian invasion of Judah in 701 B.C.E., which we find in the book of Kings as well as in Isaiah, does not constitute a literary unity. He proposed a division into three strands; although there has been some discussion about details,

*) In 1981 I published an earlier article in Dutch which deals especially with the historical problems concerning the Hezekiah-narratives; cf. K. A. D. SMELIK, "'Zegt toch tot Hizkia'; Een voorbeeld van profetische geschiedschrijving", in *ACEBT* 2 (1981), 50-67. Reacting to this article two other papers were published in *ACEBT*, one by LEENE (see below n. 51) and one by DE JONG (see below n. 109). Their comments have been most useful. I like to thank also my students in Utrecht with whom I discussed the views presented in this paper.

this view is generally accepted[5]). But recent developments in the exegesis of these passages raise the question as to whether STADE's view is still convincing or that it needs modification.

This change in opinion becomes evident when we compare CHILDS' study "Isaiah and the Assyrian Crisis" from 1967[6]) with the commentary on Kings published by WÜRTHWEIN in 1984[7]). CHILDS accepts the division proposed by STADE with only some minor changes[8]). In only a few cases does he distinguish later additions[9]). Althouh he recognizes unhistorical elements in these accounts, he points to their historical reliability in other respects[10]).

Compared to CHILDS, WÜRTHWEIN modifies STADE's literary analysis considerably. He discerns four accounts in 2 Kings xviii 13 - xix 37 where STADE has only three[11]). But he also distinguishes many later additions which he dates to the exilic and Persian period. In this way he divides the text into six strands or even more[12]). The extreme way in which WÜRTHWEIN fragmentates the text is his response to some serious problems which are raised by current interpretation of the narratives. But is it not possible to solve these problems in a less complex way?

At the end of this paper I hope to discuss briefly a third problem regarding Isaiah xxxvi-xxxix. I mean the historical background of the narratives. Some scholars used to regard these chapters as historical reports, and to account for the serious difficulties arising from this approach, they were even prepared to assume that the Assyrian king Sennacherib invaded Judah twice, although the Assyrian sources mention only one attack[13]). The theory of the two Assyrian invasions has now been abandoned by most scholars[14]), but the historical value of these narratives has still not been firmly established.

The primacy of Isaiah xxxvi-xxxix

In 1821 GESENIUS[15]) argued that 2 Kings xviii 13, 17 - xx 19 are an integral part of the book, whereas Isaiah xxxvi-xxxix appear to be an appendage. According to him, the text of Kings was also to be preferred above the text of Isaiah. But, even if this were the case, it would not prove that the position of the accounts in Kings is more original than in Isaiah. During centuries of transmission, the text of Isaiah (though being the original one) could have become more corrupted than the later text of Kings[16]).

Actually, the text of Kings is not better than the text of Isaiah, contrary to what GESENIUS suggested. At times, Kings has the preferred reading, while at other times it is Isaiah[17]). Therefore, the textual argument has no conclusive force. But what about GESENIUS' first argument? At first

sight, Isaiah xxxvi-xxxix seem to be extraordinary compared to the
general nature of the book as a whole, whereas 2 Kings xviii 17 - xx 19
are not very conspicuous in the book of Kings. Therefore it is not surprising that most scholars have followed GESENIUS in this respect. But, at second sight, 2 Kings xviii 17 - xx 19 do not fit that well in the context of
Kings. This is the only place in Kings where a prophet, whose sayings
have been recorded in the books of the Latter Prophets, appears in a narrative. The other prophets, Hosea, Amos, Micah and Jeremiah, are not
mentioned in Kings[18]. Not even in 2 Kings xxv 22-26 does Jeremiah
figure, although this passage is clearly a summary of Jeremiah xl - xliii.
Why would the authors of Kings have made an exception for Isaiah?

On the other hand, the book of Isaiah contains other narratives in
which Isaiah figures prominently and which are not included in Kings.
Especially ch. 7 provides a close parallel[19].

Some parts of the Isaiah-narratives in Kings and Isaiah are written in
poetic language. This is, of course, common in the Latter Prophets, but
not in Kings. Also in this respect are 2 Kings xviii 17 - xx 19 exceptional
in the context of the book as a whole.

Moreover, if one compares the account of Hezekiah's illness in Kings
with the parallel story in Isaiah, it appears that the story in Isaiah is better composed than that in Kings. The Isaiah account does not contain the
disturbing element of Hezekiah's medical treatment, whereas the theme
of the sign given by the Lord is well integrated in the Isaiah-account and
only added in the Kings version[20].

But most important is that Isaiah xxxvi-xxxix are not merely an
addition to the First Isaiah comparable to Jeremiah lii. It has been
established that these chapters serve as an editorial "bridge" between the
First and the Second Isaiah[21]. In ch. xxxv the reader is prepared for the
shift in the book from the period of the historical prophet to the situation
at the end of the Babylonian exile. In this chapter themes of the second
part of the book are already introduced. In ch. xxxvi-xxxix the prepara-
tion is continued. The deliverance from the Assyrian oppression and
from death foreshadows the deliverance preached by the Second
Isaiah[22]. In ch. xxxix this becomes very evident when a link is made
between Hezekiah, Isaiah and the Babylonian exile. Once Isaiah pro-
phesied the Babylonian exile to Hezekiah, it becomes less amazing that
he is also supposed to have announced the return of the exiles in the days
of the Persian king Cyrus.

Seen from this perspective, it is only natural that words and themes of
the Second Isaiah are to be found in the earlier chapters including the ch.
xxxvi-xxxix[23]. If we assume, however, that the version in Kings is the
earlier, these occurrences become rather puzzling. They force

WÜRTHWEIN to separate major parts of 2 Kings xviii 17 - xx 19 as later additions from the exilic and Persian period[24]). For example: the supposed original account of the visit of the Babylonian envoys (now to be found in Isaiah xxxix // 2 Kings xx 12-19) contained according to WÜRTHWEIN only two verses of the present text. It stated that the envoys came to Hezekiah and that he showed them all his treasuries. Since this is a rather short story, WÜRTHWEIN suggests that the original conclusion is missing; it must have described the admiration of the Babylonians[25]). I do not agree with this kind of approach, because it makes no sense to reduce an interesting and meaningful story with a surprising end to an insignificant note and then postulate an equally dull conclusion[26]).

But Isaiah xxxvi-xxxix are not only linked to the second part of the book of Isaiah. They also show some remarkable parallels to the first part. I mention the idea of a remnant, the rôle of Assyria in history and the rejection of Egypt as an ally[27]). As already noted by ACKROYD[28]), the most important parallel is provided by ch. vii.

By means of cross-references[29]) the reader of Isaiah xxxvi-xxxix is invited to compare these chapters with ch. vii. Hezekiah is the counterpart of his father Ahaz. Both kings are confronted with the threat of a siege of Jerusalem, but Hezekiah's reaction is the opposite of that of his father, as we shall see later. Since Isaiah vii is only to be found in the book of Isaiah, it is evident that its counterpart, Isaiah xxxvi-xxxix, must also have been intended for Isaiah and not for Kings.

It is worth noting in this respect that the historical introduction of Isaiah vii (v. 1) bears a close resemblance to 2 Kings xvi 5, in the same way as Isaiah xxxvi 1 is a quotation of 2 Kings xviii 13 (or an earlier source). Therefore, not only Isaiah xxxvi but also Isaiah vii presupposes historical information to be obtained from another source, as these introductions are to be considered as cross-references rather than as sufficient sources of information. The reference can have been to the now lost Chronicles of the Kings of Judah[30]) or to the book of Kings. If the latter is intended, we have to assume that the book of Kings was already in existence, when these narratives were written, albeit not in the present form[31]).

A last argument in favour of the primacy of Isaiah xxxvi-xxxix is the following: in Isaiah xxxviii 6 it is said that YHWH will deliver Hezekiah and Jerusalem out of the hand of the king of Assyria, but such a deliverance has already taken place at the end of the previous chapter. A more logical sequence would, therefore, have been: first the narrative of Hezekiah's illness, and only then the story of Jerusalem's deliverance. In such an arrangement, however, also the account of the Babylonian em-

bassy had to precede the story of Jerusalem's deliverance, as it is the sequel of the narrative concerning Hezekiah's illness. Such a more logical
arrangement would fit in the book of Kings, but not in the book of Isaiah,
because it would destroy the connection between the account of the
Babylonian embassy and Isaiah xl. We have to conclude that the present
arrangement of the Hezekiah-narratives is only understandable from the
perspective of the book of Isaiah, not from that of Kings.

In summary: the general opinion that Isaiah xxxvi-xxxix are borrowed
from Kings has to be reconsidered. In my view these narratives were intended to be inserted between the two parts of Isaiah. Words and themes
from the preceding and following chapters have been introduced because
of the function of these narratives as an editorial bridge. Only some time
afterwards, they were added to the book of Kings because of the prominent part played by king Hezekiah in these narratives.

The division of Isaiah xxxvi and xxxvii

In the second part of this paper I would like to discuss STADE's interpretation of the Isaiah-narratives. I shall concentrate on his proposal to
divide 2 Kings xviii 17 - xix 37 into two separate accounts. 2 Kings xviii
13-16 are left out of consideration because of the different nature of this
account[32]).

STADE draws attention to the fact that 2 Kings xviii 17 - xix 37 contain
three different oracles concerning the fate of the Assyrian king[33]). Each
oracle predicts that the Assyrian king will withdraw to his own country,
but each time without reference to the other oracles. STADE considers this
to be strange; one would expect (in his words) "bei einem auch nur
einigermassen geschickten Schriftsteller" that he would produce a more
coherent story[34]). Consequently, the narrative cannot be considered to be
a literary unity.

STADE's argument is remarkable because it reveals a typical approach
towards biblical narrative. Evidently a 19th century German author
would not write a story in such a way; if he would include more than one
oracle, he would refer to earlier ones. But this argument is not applicable
to a Judaean author of the biblical period any more than to a modern
German writer, as logical arrangements are not typical of biblical or
modern literature.

STADE tried to divide the narrative into two complete, separate accounts, but he only partially succeeded. In his analysis, he found only
one conclusion for the two accounts; the other was lost. He attempted to
explain this loss by supposing that the editor who did not mind the triple
repetition of Isaiah's oracle, did not want to maintain two different con-

clusions[35]). A rather awkward solution, but this weak spot in STADE's argumentation was later smoothed away by dividing the end of 2 Kings xix into two different conclusions. In the analysis of Childs[36]) v. 35 is seen as the conclusion of the second account and vv. 36-37 as the end of the first account. WILDBERGER[37]) adds the first part of v. 36 to the end of the second account, which makes more sense.

STADE assumed that in 2 Kings xix 9 one could detect the seam joining the two accounts. This became the general assumption notwithstanding some slight differences of opinion[38]). The first word of the second account would be *wayyāšobh*, which can be translated as "he returned" or "again"[39]). This is, however, a rather strange opening for an independent account, the more so because in this first sentence the subject is missing. We would have expected the designation "the king of Assyria" to occur, as it is not very probably that a narrative would begin with the phrase "He returned and sent" (or "He sent again"), when it is not stated who "he" is.

Moreover, right at the alleged seam in v. 9 one should note an important textual variant. The text of Isaiah does not read *wayyāšobh* but *wayyišmaᶜ* ("and he heard")[40]). This verb is even less likely to serve as the opening of a separate account. The reader wants to know what was heard that made someone send messengers to Hezekiah. These observations prove that if two narratives have been combined, the beginning of the second must have been deleted by an editor who also altered the concluding parts.

The pattern of the two supposed accounts is very similar: the delivery of a message, the reaction of Hezekiah, the message of the Lord and the final deliverance (if we divide the concluding verses into two strands)[41]) This is, of course, remarkable. But I wonder if the division of the narrative into two different strands really offers a solution to the problem. Does it not create a new problem? According to CHILDS[42]), both writers shared a common body of oral tradition, but the author of the second account did not use the first account directly. If this is the case, how is it possible that the second account is written with the pattern, arrangement and even words of the first account without making use of its text? Therefore, we have to assume that if there were two accounts, the writer of the second reworked the first account which he had before him[43]). CHILDS also provides an historical argument as to why the narrative is to be divided into two strands. Historically speaking the repetition of an occurrence such as that in our narrative is improbable[44]). If the narrative were historically reliable, I would agree with this argument, but it is clearly not so. The military contribution of an angel is not very decisive in actual history, and there was no reason for Sennacherib to send envoys to Hezekiah when they had just concluded an agreement[45]). Moreover, if we follow CHILDS, we get two accounts neither of which is less improbable from a historical point of view. The second account ends with the destruction of an immense army by one angel in one night. The first account concludes with Sennacherib's withdrawal after the message of Tirhakah's arrival. Would the Assyrian king who had defeated the Egyptians at Eltekeh in the same year[46]), have been seized with panic by the appearance of an 18 years old boy?[47]) It is hard to believe.

Consequently, we must not ask if it is historically probable that the Assyrian king first sent Rabshakeh and subsequently a letter to Hezekiah, but rather: is it possible from a literary point of view?

Repetition as a literary device

Repetition is a common phenomenon in biblical narrative, but scholars are inclined to remove repetitions by source analysis. Nevertheless, it is generally agreed that repetition need not indicate a combination of earlier sources. For example: both in 1 Samuel xix 18-21 and in 2 Kings i 9-15 messengers are sent three times, yet these passages are considered to be literary units. We cannot preclude, therefore, that the delivery of two speeches by Rabshakeh and the sending of a letter by the Assyrian king are similarly examples of a threefold repetition used as a literary device[48]).

Accepting this possibility, we can reconsider Isaiah xxxvii 8 and 9.

Let us first translate the Hebrew:

> 8. And Rabshakeh returned
>   and he found the king of Assyria
>   making war against Libnah
>   for he had *heard*
>   that he had departed from Lachish.
> 9. And he *heard*
>   concerning Tirhakah, the king of Ethiopia,
>   saying:
>   He is come forth to make war against thee.
>   And he *heard*[49])
>   and he sent messengers to Hezekiah
>   saying: ...

STADE noted that Sennacherib's reaction to the message concerning Tirhakah is remarkable. In his words: ''Ein sonderbarer Feldherr war doch dieser König von Assyrien, wird man denken, dass er als Gegenmassregel gegen das ihm gemeldete Heranrücken der Meroiten eine zweite Gesandschaft gegen das trotzige Felsennest Jerusalem absandte''[50]).

But the king's reaction is not that surprising from a literary point of view. It refers the reader back to Isaiah's oracle in xxxvii 7:[51])

> 7. Behold I lay in him a spirit
>   and he shall *hear* something to *hear*
>   and he will return to his land
>   and I will cause him to fall by the sword in his land.

To *hear* is a motif word in these verses. But what do we readers hear? A rather obscure oracle about a spirit, about something to hear and about a violent death. It is not yet possible for us to understand what the author is hinting at here. But as soon as we notice the triple repetition of ''and he heard'' in the following two verses, we will suspect that the fulfilment of the oracle is near.

Contrary to our expectations, the narrative continues with the sending of another message to Hezekiah instead of describing Sennacherib's withdrawal and violent death. STADE saw in this surprising turn in the narrative a seam joining two separate accounts. I shall try to prove that another interpretation is possible.

At this point we have to turn to Rabshakeh's remark in Isaiah xxxvi 6 and 9 that Hezekiah is deceiving himself by relying on Egypt, because it will not be able to save Judah from the Assyrian army. Rabshakeh's prediction will prove to be correct and it is also in conformity with Isaiah's prophecies, especially those in ch. xxxi. But is Rabshakeh's opinion also that of the author? When it is reported that Tirhakah is planning to attack Sennacherib, the question arises: Will Rabshakeh's words yet be proven false and will Egypt appear to be a reliable ally after all? The obscure oracle of Isaiah allows for such a conclusion to the story.

In my opinion the author made the oracle deliberately ambiguous, because he wanted to suggest the possibility that the Assyrian king would withdraw before Tirhakah. But instead of withdrawing, Sennacherib continues to taunt the Living God. It is not the Egyptian ally who will silence the Assyrian king, but the Lord Himself, as appears only at the very end of the narrative. By supposing that in the first account the news of Tirhakah's arrival ended Sennacherib's attack, STADE actually walked into the trap the author has set for the reader.

Repetition in biblical narrative is not only a stylistic device; it is meant to clarify the author's intention. What is only indicated on the first two occasions is made explicit by the last repetition where the wording is different[52]). This general rule applies also to Isaiah xxxvi and xxxvii. With

every repetition the purpose of the narrative becomes more evident. In
order to elucidate this we will examine the threefold message of the
Assyrian king.

The threefold message of the Assyrian king

The first two messages are given by Rabshakeh[53]). His first speech is
addressed to the representatives of Hezekiah. Literary analysis shows
that it is carefully structured[54]). Rabshakeh starts with the question:
''What is this trust that thou trustest?''[55]) This will be the main theme of
the first speech, בטח, ''to *trust*'', being the central motif word[56]). In the
speech Rabshakeh examines possible answers to this question, but in
each case only to conclude that Hezekiah has no reason to expect that
Jerusalem will be delivered.

The first possibility is that Hezekiah has put his trust in military aid
from Egypt. With an expression also used in Ezekiel xxix 6 to
characterize Egypt, Rabshakeh explains that Egypt is not a reliable ally.
The other possibility is that Hezekiah is trusting in the Lord. This is, of
course, the right answer, but Rabshakeh is suggesting that the Lord is offended by Hezekiah's cultic reforms and no longer wishes to support
him[57]). The description of the reforms differs from the account in 2 Kings
xviii 4[58])—another indication that the narrative was not originally a part
of the book of Kings. In the eyes of Rabshakeh the Lord suffered a great
loss when Hezekiah removed the high places and altars belonging to
Him. The reader knows, however, that these reforms are in accordance
with God's command. Rabshakeh is distorting the truth[59]).

Having ruled out the two possibilities Rabshakeh discloses Hezekiah's
military weakness by proposing a wager: ''I will give thee two thousand
horses, if thou be able on thy part to give riders upon them!'' (Is. xxxvi
8). As Hezekiah is unable to do this, the futility of his attempt becomes
evident. This being the core of his speech, Rabshakeh continues. He
repeats the two possibilities: Hezekiah relies on Egypt or on the Lord. In
both cases his hope is idle. Egypt cannot help with chariots and horsemen
and it was the Lord who gave the Assyrian king the order to destroy
Judah; the Assyrians wage war with God on their side[60]).

We cannot say that Rabshakeh's words are in complete disagreement
with the theopolitical view of the great prophets. On the contrary, his
characterization of Egypt as a broken reed returns in Ezekiel; the rejection of Egypt as an ally is also typical of Isaiah and Jeremiah[61]). Isaiah
xxxi 1 offers a very close parallel to Rabshakeh's words:

Woe to them who go down to Egypt for help!
On *horses* they do rely
and they *trust* in *chariots*

because they are many
and in *horsemen*
because they are very numerous.
But they do not look to the Holy One of Israel
and the LORD they do not seek.

But what about Rabshakeh's claim that the Lord gave the Assyrian king orders to destroy Judah? Also to these words of Rabshakeh there exists a close parallel in the First Isaiah. In ch. x 6 God says:

I send (the king of Assyria) against a godless nation
and against the people of My wrath I give him order
to ransack and to plunder
and to trample them down
like mud in the streets.

So we have to conclude that Rabshakeh was a diligent pupil of the prophets, especially Isaiah[62]). Only by his misinterpretation of Hezekiah's cultic reforms has he betrayed himself. In the following, however, his real nature will be revealed. After a short intermission Rabshakeh delivers a second speech, this time not directed to Hezekiah's representatives but to the people on the city-wall[63]). The theme of the first speech is continued but the portrayal of the Assyrian king becomes more clear[64]). Rabshakeh tries to make the people distrust Hezekiah in order to win them over to the Assyrian camp. He admonishes the people:

Let Hezekiah not deceive you,
for he will not be able to deliver you! (Is. xxxvi 14)

In this way a new motif word, נצל, "to deliver", has been introduced into the story[65]). In the next verse, a connection to the first speech is established:

Let Hezekiah not make you trust in the Lord!

The earlier motif word, בטח, "to trust", is used here in the causative. The theme of trust in the Lord is retained in the second speech, but the other possibility, trust in Egypt, is not mentioned anymore. This is an indication that in the repetition the story is already more focused on the central theme: the arrogance of the Assyrian king.

Having admonished the people three times not to listen to Hezekiah, Rabshakeh makes a proposal. Unlike the first speech he does not offer them two thousand horses (Is. xxxvi 8), but he holds out the prospect of peace and resettlement in a new land. When the inhabitants of Jerusalem surrender, a peaceful life will be their reward. Instead of eating their own dung and drinking their own urine (Is. xxxvi 12), they will eat the fruit of their own vines and fig-trees, and drink the water of their own cisterns. In short, they will live the life described in the prophecies on Israel's future[66]). In this part of the speech the Assyrian king poses as the new Saviour of Israel, as becomes evident when Rabshakeh continues. After a while, the Assyrian king will arrive and a new era in Israel's history will commence. He will lead them to a new land, a new Promised Land! The description of this new land resembles that of the land of Israel in the book of Deuteronomy (viii 8)[67]). The Assyrian king will act as God: he will give Israel a new land[68]).

When he has made this proposal, Rabshakeh warns the people again. Do not listen to Hezekiah when he assures you saying: the Lord will deliver us! At this point the Assyrian discloses his real nature: his king is a blasphemer and all his words have only been a distortion of Old Testament prophecy. Notwithstanding their resemblance to the words of the prophets, their intention is completely different. Rabshakeh boasts:

> Hath any of the gods of the nations delivered his land
> out of the hand of the king of Assyria? (Is. xxxvi 18)

and he enumerates several gods of Syro-Palestinian states[69]) who were not able to defend their people successfully. If these gods failed, why should the God of Israel be an exception? The reader knows the answer: Because the God of Israel is different from all other gods; He is not the work of men's hands (Is. xxxvii 19).

This passage is clearly inspired by Isaiah x where we also find an enumeration of Syro-Palestinian states in a similar context[70]). There it is revealed that the Lord uses Assyria as the rod of His anger in order to punish His people, although the Assyrian king is not aware of this. He thinks that he has defeated so many adversaries by his own power and he has become haughty. But ''shall the axe boast itself against him that heweth therewith?'' (Is. x 15) Because of his arrogance, the Assyrian king will be punished by the Lord. Seen from this perspective we can consider Isaiah xxxvi and xxxvii as an elaboration of the theme in Isaiah x.

The sacrilegious nature of Rabshakeh's words is underlined in the sequel of the narrative. Isaiah as well as Hezekiah describe them as words intended to taunt the Living God[71]). Because of the blasphemy Hezekiah's representatives and the people on the city wall do not react. In ACKROYD's words: ''There is no answer from men to a blasphemer; the answer comes from God''[72]). But they rend their clothes and Hezekiah follows their example when he hears the sacrilegious words Rabshakeh spoke[73]).

We have noted that the third message of Sennacherib to Hezekiah is considered to be a duplicate of Rabshakeh's speeches; it is assigned to the second account[74]). But is it possible to interpret it as a sequel to Rabshakeh's words in the context of a single narrative? It is important to note that the king does not send Rabshakeh for a second time. He chooses another way to induce Hezekiah to surrender: he writes a letter. A letter has to convince where spoken words have failed. It will be the culmination of Sennacherib's arguments and blasphemy.

The opening-sentence is a tendentious transformation of Isaiah xxxvi 14-15 where Rabshakeh warns the people not to be deceived by Hezekiah, as he is not able to deliver them. In the letter, however, the king warns Hezekiah not to be deceived by his God:

> Let not thy God deceive thee
> in whom thou trustest
> saying:
>> Jerusalem shall not be given
>> in the hand of the king of Assyria! (Is. xxxvii 10)

It is clear that this is even more blasphemous than the words of Rabshakeh. In order to prove Assyria's military superiority a survey of recent conquests follows. The gods of other nations could offer no defense, and their kings met a terrible fate. The list of names is more elaborate than in Rabshakeh's second speech, and special attention is paid to the fate of the kings as the letter is addressed to a king. It is evident that this letter resembles the second speech of Rabshakeh to such a degree that literary dependency has to be assumed. But it is not a mere duplicate: the words have been adapted to the new situation and the blasphemy of the Assyrian king is aggravated[75]).

When we compare the three messages of Sennacherib we arrive at the following: In the first speech Rabshakeh tries to convince Hezekiah that he has no one to rely on. His words resemble those of the prophets Isaiah, Jeremiah and Ezekiel. Only in one instance does it become clear that Rabshakeh is distorting the prophetic message.

In the second speech Rabshakeh tries to separate the people of Judah from their king. He still uses biblical language but the distortion of prophecy is now evident: the Assyrian king tries to replace the Lord.

In his letter Sennacherib tries to separate Hezekiah from his God; the king's blasphemy culminates in calling God a deceiver.

Our conclusion must be that these three messages are not duplicates: each has its own function in the narrative and together they enhance the suspense in the narrative: will the Assyrian king taunt the Living God with impunity?

Hezekiah's reaction and Isaiah's oracles

Hezekiah reacts to the kings' messages twice, but the second reaction is not a mere duplicate of the first. The first time Hezekiah rends his clothes, covers himself with sackcloth and goes into the Temple. At the same time he sends representatives to Isaiah. Thus he behaves as a pious king should. He does not panic notwithstanding the Assyrian threat. He knows that his Redeemer will act and he leaves it to Him to interfere.

This reaction is to be contrasted with that of his father Ahaz in Isaiah vii. There the prophet is sent to reassure Ahaz, but the king does not want to listen to him and to ask for a sign. He refuses to wait for the Lord to deliver Jerusalem, and prefers his own way. From 2 Kings xvi 7 we learn that he begged the Assyrian king to rescue him[76]).

Hezekiah, however, asks Isaiah to pray for "the remnant that is found". He vividly describes the great distress and suggests that the Lord will confute the words of the Assyrian king who taunts the Living God. Compared to Sennacherib's arrogance, Hezekiah's words attest to his modesty. He does not request that the Lord will protect Jerusalem. He only mentions the possibility that God will punish the blasphemy of the Assyrian king.

The second time Hezekiah's reaction is different. Instead of sending a message to Isaiah asking him to pray to the Lord, he addresses God personally. He goes to the Temple, spreads out the letter before the Lord so that He may read it, and then prays to Him directly. The prayer is well structured[77]) and connected with the earlier message to Isaiah by the words "Hear all the words of Sennacherib which he hath sent to taunt the Living God"[78]). Although the author must have known the earlier message from the supposed first account, he does not simply repeat it. On the contrary, the prayer shows that Hezekiah does not need the prophet's intercession, now that he has been reassured by Isaiah that Sennacherib will withdraw. The Lord will punish the blasphemer and deliver Jerusalem. For the Lord is God alone and unlike the other gods who were powerless before the Assyrian king, He will be able to stop the Assyrian arrogance. Hezekiah can ask God to save Judah, because in this way the Lord will reveal Himself to all the kingdoms of the earth as the only God.

By using concepts of the Second Isaiah[79]) the author refutes the argumentation of the Assyrian king that no god will be able to save his or her people from the Assyrians. His blasphemy is now disclosed; he has confused the Lord with the idols who are only the work of men's hands.

Compared with Hezekiah's earlier message to Isaiah the prayer witnesses an important change in the king's attitude. It is possible to account for this change by assuming that the prayer has been written by another author who had read the earlier account[80]). But it seems more probable that the change is due to the internal development of the story: because Hezekiah has been reassured earlier by an oracle, he dares to approach God personally.

In the messages of Sennacherib as well as in Hezekiah's reactions we have noted that repetition is a device used to clarify the author's intentions. Does the same apply to Isaiah's oracles? We remember that the threefold repetition of an oracle, twice apparently without any consequence, induced STADE to divide the narrative into two strands[81]).

As we have noted before, the first oracle is rather obscure. The reader will at first connect it with the message of Tirhakah's arrival, but Sennacherib's reaction precludes this interpretation. The Assyrian king does not show any fear. Why should he? Egypt is but a broken reed. Instead he sends a letter taunting the Living God. Therefore, the "spirit" mentioned in Isaiah's first oracle cannot be a spirit of panic, but rather a spirit of excessive pride, as LEENE has pointed out[82]). God will stimulate the pride of the Assyrian king in order to disclose his real nature. Only when the Assyrian has declared that the Lord will not be able to defend Jerusalem (Is. xxxvii 10), will he hear something to hear. What he will hear is not yet clear. But it will make him return and die.

The second prophecy is rather elaborate compared to the first one. It consists of three parts: a taunt-song (Is. xxxvii 22-29), a sign (30-32) and an oracle (33-35). It has been argued that the taunt-song as well as the sign are later interpolations[83]). Although these passages do not fit neatly into the narrative, it is not necessary to remove them as later additions. Regarding the taunt-song, we can compare its inclusion with the occurrence of a psalm in the account of Hezekiah's illness in Isaiah xxxviii[84]). Both poems have clearly been written for another occasion, but this does not preclude the possibility that they have been introduced into the narrative by the original author. The function of such an insertion has convincingly been described by ACKROYD. It is "an endeavour to draw out the significance of the narrative by the use of poems which point to important elements which it is desired to underline"[85]).

Therefore, I would suggest that the author included an already existing taunt-song written sometime after the conquest of Egypt by Esarhaddon[86]) in his narrative, because it dealt with the Assyrian arrogance of power and announced that the Lord will cause the oppressor to return shamefully to his own land. He reworked it especially at the beginning to create a link to the three messages of the Assyrian king[87]). By including this reworked poem the author underlines that the blasphemous arrogance of Israel's enemy is the central theme of his narrative.

The three verses concerning a sign (Is. xxxvii 30-32) are rather puzzling. They were possibly included because in the counterpart of this narrative, I mean Isaiah vii, the motif of a sign is very important[88]). The idea of a "remnant" which dominates this passage, reminds us of the earlier words of Hezekiah in Isaiah xxxvii 4.

The taunt-song ends in an oracle:

> And I will put My hook in thy nose
> and my bridle in thy lips
> and I will turn thee back by the way
> by which thou camest! (Is. xxxvii 29)

After the announcement of a shameful retreat in the second oracle Sennacherib's defeat is specified more fully in the third prophecy (Is. xxxvii 33-35). He will not be able to lay siege to Jerusalem but return by the way he came. For the Lord will defend Jerusalem[86]). It is not yet disclosed how this will happen and what will happen afterwards.

We can return now to STADE. Is the fact that the narrative contains three oracles instead of one to be ascribed to the clumsiness of an editor? I do not think so. The repetition of the oracles has the function of intensifying the suspense. The readers become eager to know what will happen to the arrogant blasphemer whom they will identify with the foreign oppressor of their own time. Moreover, the first oracle has impact in the development of the story (contrary to what STADE suggested): it reassures Hezekiah whose attitude then changes in the second part of the narrative.

In spite of the fact that the end is announced by way of three oracles, the conclusion will still surprise the reader. The final act of God suits His omnipotence. His angel strikes down a hundred and eighty five thousand men in the Assyrian camp[90]). Explanations in terms of a plague are not to the point, as this destruction is not a historical event but the consequence of the theopolitical view of the author[90]). The news of this disaster forces Sennacherib to leave, and not the arrival of Tirhakah.

He does not return to Judah, but even in his own capital, in the very house of the idol he adores Sennacherib is killed by his sons who manage to escape[92]). A blasphemer is nowhere safe from the power of the omnipotent God.

In this way all the oracles have been fulfilled. Regarding the first oracle we note that Sennacherib was filled with a spirit of arrogance; he had to hear that his army was routed by an angel of the Lord; he returned home and was killed there. Regarding the second oracle we note that Sennacherib had come as a victor, but he had to leave without his army. Regarding the third oracle, we note that Sennacherib did not succeed in laying siege to Jerusalem, because the Lord was defending this city as He had promised; the Assyrian king had to return by the way he came. We see that the three concluding verses of the narrative allude to the three oracles together. Therefore it is impossible to divide these verses into two strands without serious exegetical loss.

This concludes my plea to interpret Isaiah xxxvi and xxxvii as a single literary unity in which repetition is a literary device in order to clarify the author's intention and to enhance the reader's suspense.

Historical implications

My approach to Isaiah xxxvi-xxxvii has some interesting implications. As there is no opportunity to discuss them fully, I shall confine myself to some observations.

In the first place: the date of the narrative has to be established again. Up till now there was no agreement on this point; distinction was made between earlier and later strands[93]). But if the text is a literary unity, we have to opt for the Persian period because some passages are rather similar to the Second Isaiah[94]). Also Isaiah xxxix cannot have been written earlier than the Persian period, because in its present form it predicts that the Davidic dynasty will not be restored to the Judaean throne[95]). These chapters were probably written after the completion of the Second Isaiah in order to create a bridge between the two parts of the book. This implies that 2 Kings xviii 17-xx 19 have been added to an almost complete book of Kings, as the last part of Kings was written about the middle of the sixth century[96]).

In the second place: the narrative has almost no bearing on the historical reconstruction of the events in 701 B.C.E. This reconstruction must be based on 2 Kings xviii 13-16 and the Assyrian sources[97]). Although there are some differences, in all essentials the Assyrian report can be reconciled with that given in 2 Kings xviii 13-16[98]).

After Hezekiah's rebellion Sennacherib invaded Judah. He laid siege to Lachish but not to Jerusalem which he only surrounded[96]). Hezekiah offered Sennacherib a fair indemnity and the Assyrian king agreed. I concur with CLEMENTS that this was not a case of extraordinary leniency on the side of the Assyrian king, but a convenient solution for both[100]). The tribute was high enough. There is no reason to suppose that Sennacherib had been forced to accept Hezekiah's offer because of an Egyptian counter-attack or a sudden plague-epidemic[101]).

It is reasonable to assume that during the Assyrian attack Sennacherib entered into negotiations with Hezekiah. That this was customary has been proven by the Nimrud letters[102]). Just because the sending of messengers to the enemy was a common feature[103]), we cannot be sure as to whether or not Rabshakeh's speeches have any historical background. But as CLEMENTS noted: "The two speeches of the Rabshakeh reveal themselves to be free compositions of the author"[104]) We have described

Rabshakeh as a pupil of the Israelite prophets. This was, of course, not
meant literally. Rabshakeh is a literary figure who plays the opposite to
Isaiah and has to speak in a similar way. His intimate knowledge is not
the result of the activities of the Assyrian secret service[105]). The author
showed by introducing Rabshakeh in his narrative how easily the
theopolitical view of the prophets can be distorted. His point of departure
must have been Isaiah x; the two speeches of Rabshakeh are actually a
dramatization of the prophecy in this chapter.

   Also Isaiah's reactions in the narrative cannot be regarded as
historical, since in the rest of the book of Isaiah he has a totally different
opinion on Hezekiah's rebellion[106]). I doubt also of the pious attitude
ascribed to Hezekiah in the narrative[107]). What we know for certain is
that he plundered the Temple in order to pay the penalty Sennacherib
imposed upon him[108]).

   But did the author not use any historical tradition when writing this
narrative? Stephan DE JONG made an interesting proposal[109]). He pointed
to the similarity between Isaiah xxxvi-xxxvii and Jeremiah xxxvii. This
similarity had been noted before, but it was assumed that the author
Jeremiah adopted the pattern of his narrative from the first Isaiah account. DE JONG argued that it is the other way around: the Isaiah account
has been based on Jeremiah. If this is the case, Hezekiah is not only a
counterpart of his father Ahaz, but also of Judah's last king Zedekiah.
Where Zedekiah failed to listen to Jeremiah and relied on Egypt,
Hezekiah puts his trust in the Lord alone and takes heed to Isaiah's
words. This results in a miraculous delivery of Jerusalem in contrast to
the terrible fate Jerusalem met in Zedekiah's days. In this way it is
clarified to the readers as to why they had to experience exile whereas
their ancestors have been spared after Hezekiah's rebellion. Seen from
this perspective the Hezekiah narratives do have a historical background
but a rather different one than it appears at first sight.

NOTES

[1]) The argumentation has been given by W. GESENIUS, *Der Prophet Jesaja* II, 2, Leipzig
1821, 932-936, and has been accepted since. "Zweifellos haben die vier Kapitel ihren
ursprünglichen Ort im zweiten Königsbuch", as is stated by H. WILDBERGER, "Die Rede
des Rabsake vor Jerusalem", *ThZ* 35 (1979), 35-47, especially p. 35 n. 3. Sometimes it is
supposed that the Hezekiah- (or Isaiah-) narratives have existed separately before their inclusion into the book of Kings; cf. idem, *Jesaja* III, Neukirchen-Vluyn 1982, 1374 (the
former article of WILDBERGER will be indicated as: WILDBERGER, "Rede"; the latter as:
WILDBERGER, *Jesaja*). But see also A. JEPSEN, *Die Quellen des Königsbuches*, Halle 1956², 77,
who considers it to be possible that the second redactor of Kings (R^II) has used Isaiah
i-xxxix. It is interesting to note that in Chron. xxxii 32 and Sir. xlviii 17-25 these narratives are considered to be a part of the book of Isaiah rather than of Kings.

²) Cf. P. R. Ackroyd, "Isaiah 36-39: Structure and Function", *Von Kanaan bis Kerala*, Festschrift für Prof. Mag. Dr. Dr. J. P. M. van der Ploeg O.P. (*AOAT*, 211), Neukirchen-Vluyn 1982, 3-21, especially p. 15. An exception is made for Hezekiah's psalm in Is. xxxviii, because this is not included in 2 Kings xx.

³) Cf. Ackroyd, *op. cit.* (to be quoted from now on as: Ackroyd, "Structure"); idem, "An Interpretation of the Babylonian Exile: A Study of 2 Kings 20, Isaiah 38-39", *SJT* 27 (1974), 329-352 (to be quoted as: Ackroyd, "Interpretation"); idem, "Isaiah I-XII: Presentation of a Prophet", *SVT* 29 (1978), 16-48 (to be quoted as: Ackroyd, "Presentation"); R. F. Melugin, *The Formation of Isaiah 40-55* (BZAW, 141), Berlin etc. 1976, especially pp. 177f.; R. Rendtorff, "Zur Komposition des Buches Jesaja", *VT* 34 (1984), 295-320; R. E. Clements, "Beyond Tradition-History; Deutero-Isaianic Development of First Isaiah's Themes", *JSOT* 31 (1985), 95-113 (to be quoted as: Clements, "Beyond Tradition-History").

⁴) B. Stade, "Miscellen; 16. Anmerkungen zu 2 Kö. 15-21", *ZAW* 6 (1686), 156-189, especially pp. 172-179.

⁵) Cf. Wildberger, *Jesaja*, p. 1374 ("nach beinahe einhelliger Meinung der Forscher"). Exceptions: A. Šanda, *Die Bücher der Könige* II, Münster 1912, 289-291; J. Le Moyne, "Les deux ambassades de Sennachérib à Jérusalem; Recherches sur l'évolution d'une tradition", in *Mélanges bibliques rédigés en l'honneur de André Robert*, Paris [1957], 149-153 (Le Moyne separates Rabshakeh's first speech from the second which he joins to Stade's second account); M. Hutter, *Hiskija, König von Juda*; Ein Beitrag zur judäischen Geschichte in assyrischer Zeit, Graz 1982, 11-16 ["18,17-19,14 (wahrscheinlich sogar bis 19,19) können als einheitlicher Text gelten"].

⁶) B. S. Childs, *Isaiah and the Assyrian Crisis*, London 1967.

⁷) E. Würthwein, *Die Bücher der Könige 1. Kön. 17 - 2. Kön. 25*, Göttingen 1984.

⁸) Childs, *op. cit.*, pp. 73-76. His division: the first account (B¹) = xviii 17 - xix 9a, 36f.; the second account (B²) = xix 9b-35. According to him (*op. cit.*, p. 87) the first account contains older and younger elements which cannot, however, be separated by literary operation.

⁹) Cf. Childs, *op. cit.*, pp. 96f.: 2 Kings xix 22-32 are an interpolation. Already Stade (*op. cit.*, pp. 178f.) separated 2 Kings xix 21-31 as a later addition; most scholars agree; cf., e.g., R. E. Clements, *Isaiah and the Deliverance of Jerusalem. A Study of the Interpretation of Prophecy in the Old Testament*, Sheffield 1980, p. 57 (to be quoted from now on as: Clements, *Isaiah*).

¹⁰) In Childs' words (p. 93): "On the one hand, the study has shown a large layer of material which reflects ancient tradition with a genuinely historical setting. On the other hand, we have seen also that newer elements have entered into the account." Cf. also Wildberger, "Rede", *passim*.

¹¹) Because he separates two traditions in the first account. Cf. also O. Kaiser, *Der Prophet Jesaja; Kapitel 13-39* (ATD), Göttingen 1973, 302f. (to be quoted as: Kaiser, *Jesaja*). Kaiser separates all the verses in which the motif-words בטח and נצל occur. There is, however, no conclusive argument to do so as unimportant inconsistencies in the narrative can easily be attributed to one author.

¹²) In Würthwein's translation (pp. 415-418 and 425-427) all these layers and traditions are indicated; an extremely difficult patch-work is the result.

¹³) Cf., e.g., C. van Leeuwen, "Sanchérib devant Jérusalem", *OTS* 14 (1965), 245-272. A comprehensive survey of the studies on this question is given by M. Wäfler, *Nicht-Assyrer neuassyrischer Darstellungen* (*AOAT*, 26), Kevelaer etc. 1975, pp. 43f. (+ nn. 179-181).

¹⁴) Cf. Kaiser, *Jesaja*, p. 298; Wildberger, *Jesaja*, p. 1390; Clements, *Isaiah*, pp. 22,92; Würthwein, *op. cit.*, p. 405. Also the solution proposed by A. K. Jenkins, "Hezekiah's Fourteenth Year; A New Interpretation of 2 Kings XVIII 13 - XIX 37", *VT* 26 (1976), 284-298, is not convincing. The dating of Sennacherib's attack in Hezekiah's fourteenth year was necessitated by the granting to Hezekiah of fifteen more years to live in Is. xxxviii, as this event is supposed to have taken place in the same year and Hezekiah reigned twenty-nine years in all; cf. also Wildberger, *Jesaja*, p. 1394.

[15]) See above n. 1.

[16]) See also WILDBERGER, *Jesaja*, p. 1373.

[17]) Cf. CHILDS, *op. cit.*, pp. 137-140. I do not agree with his conclusion (p. 140): "Perhaps in terms of percentage, the Kings text does retain a slight advantage." Cf. also JEPSEN, *op. cit.*, p. 77; WILDBERGER, *Jesaja*, p. 1372; S. NORIN, "An Important Kennicott Reading in 2 Kings XVIII 13", *VT* 32 (1982), 337f. ("It is more probable that the redactor of 2 Kings made use of the Isaiah text", *op. cit.*, p. 338). *Contra* O. KAISER, "Die Verkündigung des Propheten Jesaja im Jahre 701; I. Von der Menschen Vertrauen und Gottes Hilfe; Eine Studie über II Reg 18,17ff. par Jes 36 1ff.; 1. Das literar- und textkritische Problem", *ZAW* 81 (1969), 304-315 (to be quoted as KAISER, "Verkündigung").

[18]) Cf. ACKROYD, "Presentation", p. 24 and CLEMENTS, *Isaiah*, p. 52. Of course, one could point to Jonah, but the book of Jonah is later than Kings and pseudepigraphical.

[19]) We will return to this parallel later.

[20]) I separate Is. xxxviii 21-22 as a later addition based on 2 Kings xx 7,8. In Kings Hezekiah asks for a sign only after his recovery, which is illogical. Therefore, I assume that vv. 8-11 are added afterwards in 2 Kings xx from the example of the Isaiah-version. The motif of a sign in Is. xxxviii is very important as it links this narrative with Is. vii; cf. ACKROYD, "Structure", pp. 17f. It is also important to note that the absence of a passage concerning Hezekiah's submission to Sennacherib in Is. (comparable to 2 Kings xviii 14-16) enhances the internal probability of the Isaiah-version. Possibly the interest in the treasures of the Temple induced the author of Kings to include this passage taken from an earlier chronicle.

[21]) Cf. KAISER, *Jesaja*, p. 291; A. VAN DER KOOIJ, *Die alten Textzeugen des Jesajabuches* (OBO, 35), Fribourg-Göttingen 1981, 17f.; ACKROYD, "Structure", p. 7 and CLEMENTS, "Beyond Tradition-History", p. 98.

[22]) See the studies of ACKROYD mentioned in n. 3.

[23]) See also n. 3.

[24]) Except from the additions by Dtr WÜRTHWEIN separates in 2 Kings xix as later additions: 4b (post-exilic); 14-19 (not before the Second Isaiah); 21-28 (late exilic); 29-31 (exilic/post-exilic) and 34 (late).

[25]) WÜRTHWEIN, *op. cit.*, p. 436.

[26]) The same applies to the *Grunderzählung* as reconstructed by KAISER (see above n. 11). The purpose of Is. xxxix is clarified by ACKROYD, "Interpretation", pp. 332-343.

[27]) These points of relationship are discussed by ACKROYD, "Structure", pp. 17-20.

[28]) *Ibidem.* Concerning the location of the story see also J. A. MONTGOMERY & H. S. GEHMAN, *The Books of Kings* (ICC), Edinburgh 1951, 487 and G. FOHRER, *Das Buch Jesaja II* (Zürcher Bibelkommentare), Zürich 1967², 167.

[29]) Both stories have the same location: "The conduit of the Upper Pool on the causeway which leads to the Fuller's field" (Is. vii 3; xxxvi 2); in Is. xxxviii 8 the stairway of *Ahaz* is mentioned; the theme of a sign.

[30]) For a discussion see J. VAN SETERS, *In Search of History*. Historiography in the Ancient World and the Origins of Biblical History, New Haven etc. 1983, 292ff.

[31]) The parallel between Is. xxxvi 1 and 2 Kings xviii 13 cannot serve as an argument against the primacy of the Isaiah-version as Is. vii 1 refers also to the book of Kings without being originally part of it. *Contra* KAISER, "Verkündigung", pp. 305f. When we accept the primacy of Is. xxxvi-xxxix, another problem can be solved, as it has amazed scholars that other parts of 2 Kings xviii were not included in Is. xxxvi. The inclusion of 2 Kings xviii 4-7 would have enhanced the favourable portrayal of Hezekiah. See also P. R. ACKROYD, "The Death of Hezekiah—A Pointer to the Future?", *De la Tôrah au Messie* (*Festschrift* Cazelles), Paris 1981, pp. 219-226, especially p. 220.

[32]) In my opinion, these verses were borrowed from the Chronicles of the Kings of Judah by the author of Kings and they do belong to the original version of Kings. Note, however, the remarks by A. VAN DER KOOIJ, "Das assyrische Heer vor den Mauern Jerusalems im Jahre 701 v.Chr.", to be published in *ZDPV* (especially nn. 98f.; I am indebted to Dr. Van der Kooij for kindly lending me a copy of the manuscript).

[33]) To wit: 2 Kings xix 7, xix 28b and xix 33 (STADE, *op. cit.*, p. 174).

[34]) *Ibidem.*

[35]) *Ibidem*, p. 175.

[36]) CHILDS, *op. cit.*, pp. 74-76.

[37]) WILDBERGER, *Jesaja*, pp. 1376f. See also KAISER, *Jesaja*, p. 299.

[38]) The exact division of verse 9 between the two accounts is remarkably difficult. In the words of J. GRAY, *I & II Kings. A Commentary*, London 1977[3], 663: "The problem of the end and beginning respectively of the first and second versions will probably never be solved to the satisfaction of all critics." But the problem disappears as soon as one considers Is. xxxvi and xxxvii as a literary unity.

[39]) See also CHILDS, *op. cit.*, p. 74.

[40]) *Ibidem*, p. 75.

[41]) *Ibidem*, p. 96.

[42]) *Ibidem*, pp. 98 and 103.

[43]) Cf. also KAISER, *Jesaja*, p. 304, who suggests the possibility that "die Aufzeichnung der zweiten Geschichte mit der Bearbeitung der ersten zusammenfiel." This interpretation would be rather similar to my view except from the fact that I am not convinced that a *Grunderzählung* ever existed which the author of the second part of the narrative would have reworked into the first part of the story. I cannot preclude the existence of such an earlier source, but in my opinion there are no clues in order to reconstruct it. See also above n. 11.

[44]) CHILDS, *op. cit.*, p. 73.

[45]) It is, of course, possible to argue that Sennacherib sent his letter after concluding an agreement with Hezekiah. It is hard to believe, however, that the biblical author would not have remarked on such a perfidy of the Assyrian king. Cf. also STADE, *op. cit.*, p. 181 and CLEMENTS, *Isaiah*, p. 22.

[46]) Cf. Chicago Prisma II, 78 - III, 5; most recent translation in TUAT I, 4, p. 389. See also ŠANDA, *op. cit.*, p. 265 and WILDBERGER, *Jesaja*, p. 1376.

[47]) We do not know the exact age of Tirhakah in 701 B.C.E. According to M. F. L. MACADAM, *The Temples of Kawa* I. The Inscriptions. Text and Plates, London 1949, Tirhakah was nine years old. This opinion is attacked by K. A. KITCHEN, *The Third Intermediate Period in Egypt (1100-650 B.C.)*, Warminster 1973, 158-172, and A. F. RAINEY, "Taharqa and Syntax", *Tel Aviv* 3 (1976), 38-41. According to KITCHEN, Tirhakah was twenty or twenty-one in 701 B.C.E. Following KITCHEN's calculations, however, one can lower this to eighteen. Anyway, Tirhakah became only king of Egypt in 690/89. Apparently, the biblical author was not aware of this. In my opinion, there was only one Egyptian counterattack which resulted in an Assyrian victory at Eltekeh. It is not very probable that the Egyptian army was commanded by Tirhakah at that time. It is more reasonable to suppose that the biblical author did not know the name of the Egyptian commander and therefore opted for Tirhakah, who is also prominent in Greek writings on Egyptian history; see for the latter: J. M. A. JANSEN, "Que sait-on actuellement du Pharaon Tirhakah?", *Biblica* 34 (1953), 23-42 (especially p. 23 and p. 34).

[48]) Repetition as a literary device in Old Testament narrative is discussed by R. ALTER, *The Art of Biblical Narrative*, New York 1981.

[49]) Q[a] and the LXX combine *wayyišma'* with *wayyāšobh*; see S. TALMON, "Aspects of the Textual Transmission of the Bible in the Light of Qumran Manuscripts", *Textus* 4 (1964), 95-132, especially pp. 107f.

[50]) STADE, *op. cit.*, p. 174.

[51]) See also STADE, *ibidem* (although his approach and conclusions are different). Different interpretations are given by ŠANDA, *op. cit.*, pp. 265f. and KAISER, *Jesaja*, pp. 299-301. According to KAISER (p. 300) it is possible "dass die erste Erzählung eine Taharqa-Szene als retardierendes, die Spannung erhöhendes Moment einschaltet, um den Grosskönig vielleicht gar erst nach einem Sieg über den Pharao plötzlich aufgrund eines Gerüchtes über Schwierigkeiten an anderen Stellen seines Reiches, sei es in Assur selbst, sei es in Babylonien, abziehen zu lassen und so gleichsam den Satz zu illustrieren, dass Gotts Hilfe am nächsten ist, wenn die Not am grössten." In my opinion, retardation

was not the only purpose of the author when introducing Tirhakah, although it is one of the ways by which he tries to enhance the suspense. I cannot agree with KAISER's interpretation of the first oracle. As H. LEENE, "רוח end שמוע in Jesaja 37,7: Een kwestie van vertaalhorizon", *ACEBT* 4 (1983), 49-62, especially p. 52, remarked, nowhere in the text it is said that Sennacherib returned to Assyria because of internal troubles in Mesopotamia. A survey of the various interpretations of this oracle to be found in commentaries on Kings and Isaiah is given by LEENE, *op. cit.*, nn. 8 and 12.

⁵²) See R. A. CARLSON, "Élie à l'Horeb", *VT* 19 (1969), 416-439, especially pp. 424f.

⁵³) In the version of Kings Rabshakeh is accompagnied by Tartan and Rabsaris. Concerning these titles see VAN DER KOOIJ's article (mentioned above, n. 32). Already STADE (*op. cit.*, p. 182) remarked that these two other Assyrian dignitaries must have been added by a later redactor.

⁵⁴) Cf. my article in *ACEBT* 2 (1981), 50-67, especially pp. 58ff. See also ACKROYD, "Structure", p. 11. Cf., however, KAISER, *Jesaja*, pp. 301f. He acknowledges "einen geplanten doppelten Durchgang der in 4b gestellten Frage", but he is still convinced that the speech does not constitute a literary unity. In his argumentation it appears that KAISER does not take into account sufficiently the literary nature of the text, as he is looking for historical probability.

⁵⁵) In the next sentence (Is. xxxvi 5) Rabshakeh underlines the idleness of Hezekiah's expectations and he repeats the question more explicitly: "Now, on whom dost thou trust that thou rebellest against me?"

⁵⁶) Cf. also CHILDS, *op. cit.*, p. 85; KAISER, *Jesaja*, p. 301 and HUTTER, *op. cit.*, p. 15.

⁵⁷) It is remarkable that in this verse Hezekiah is suddenly referred to in the third person (cf. CHILDS, *op. cit.*, p. 79); it indicates that the author was not a contemporary, but a later author who used a sentence from one of his sources.

⁵⁸) Rabshakeh's argument appears to be inspired by Deut. xii 2ff. and 2 Kings xxiii 8ff. rather than by 2 Kings xviii 4.

⁵⁹) See also KAISER, *Jesaja*, p. 307. *Contra* WILDBERGER, *Jesaja*, p. 1387 and p. 1401, who considers this passage as a later addition written by someone opposing the Josianic cult-reforms.

⁶⁰) KAISER, *Jesaja*, p. 307, underlines the fact that this view cannot originate from a period earlier than the sixth century, and is certainly not Assyrian. *Contra* WILDBERGER, "Rede", p. 46.

⁶¹) Cf. Is. xx 1-6, xxx 1-17, xxxi 1-9; Jer. ii 16-18, 36, xlvi 25f.; see also Ez. xvi 26; Hos. vii 11, 16.

⁶²) Cf. also CHILDS, *op. cit.*, p. 84.

⁶³) According to WÜRTHWEIN, *op. cit.*, p. 420, Rabshakeh did not address the people of Jerusalem in general, but only the (mercenary) soldiers. This is, however, not in accordance with Rabshakeh's proposal to surrender and to follow the Assyrian king to a new land. WÜRTHWEIN is forced to consider the passage containing this proposal as a later addition.

⁶⁴) The image of Assyria in the book of Isaiah is discussed by P. MACHINIST, "Assyria and its Image in the First Isaiah", *JAOS* 103 (1983), 719-737 (I am indebted to drs R. J. van der Spek who drew my attention to this article).

⁶⁵) Cf. also CHILDS, *op. cit.*, p. 85; KAISER, *Jesaja*, p. 301 and HUTTER, *op. cit.*, p. 15.

⁶⁶) Cf. 1 Kings v 5; Mic. iv 4; Zech. iii 10. The mentioning of vines and fig-trees must be an allusion to these texts as the offering of bread would have been more sensible to people in starvation. See, however, also Jer. v 17: "(The enemy) shall eat up thy vines and thy fig-trees." Rabshakeh's words are the opposite of historical reality.

⁶⁷) See also Deut. xxxiii 28, ACKROYD, "Interpretation" p. 348 and idem, "Structure", p. 11. GRAY (*op. cit.*, pp. 683f.) who wonders why olives are included in this enumeration, as olives are only grown in the Mediterranean region, misses therefore the point. H. W. F. SAGGS, "The Nimrud Letters, 1952—Part III", *Iraq* 18 (1956), 40-56, especially p. 55, states that Rabshakeh's offer can be historical as he concludes from Nimrud-letters xxiv-xxvi that the Assyrian government was most anxious that the groups of people concerned should be efficiently and contentedly resettled. The content of these letters, however, do not justify such a generalization.

[68]) In the version of Kings the similarity with Deuteronomy is enhanced by adding:
ארץ זית יצהר ודבש וחיו ולא תמתו.

[69]) For more details on the identification of the geographical names I refer to the commentaries of GRAY and WILDBERGER.

[70]) Cf. Is. x 9. The similarity between Is. x and xxxvi is already noted by CLEMENTS, *Isaiah*, p. 55.

[71]) Cf. Is. xxxvii 4 and 17. The expression "to taunt the Living God" occurs also in 1 Sam. xvii 26, 36. The story of David and Goliath offers a close parallel to our narrative; cf. also O. PROCKSCH, *Jesaja* I (*KAT*), Leipzig 1930, p. 446.

[72]) ACKROYD, "Structure", p. 11.

[73]) Cf. Is. xxxvi 22 and xxxvii 1. Hezekiah also covers himself with sackcloth.

[74]) Cf. STADE, *op. cit.*, pp. 176f.

[75]) Cf. also CHILDS, *op. cit.*, p. 98. The difference between Rabshakeh's first and second speech has also been noted by LE MOYNE, *op. cit.* (n. 5), p. 151, but it induced him to divide the speech into two strands. See also FOHRER, *op. cit.*, p. 172.

[76]) I hope to publish in *ACEBT* 8 (1987) an article on the antithesis between Ahaz and Hezekiah, respectively Manasseh and Josiah in the book of Kings.

[77]) The prayer has the following structure:
A. Thou art the God, Thou alone (v. 15)
B. All the kingdoms of the earth (v. 15)
C. Appeal to the Lord (v. 16)
D. The Living God (v. 16)
D'. The work of men's hands (v. 17)
C'. Appeal to the Lord (v. 19)
B'. All the kingdoms of the earth (v. 19)
A'. Thou art the Lord God, Thou alone (v. 19).
By this structure the emphasis is laid on the distinction between the Living God who will rescue Jerusalem and the idols who are not able to withstand the Assyrian agression.

[78]) See above n. 70.

[79]) Cf. also CHILDS, *op. cit.*, p. 100; VAN LEEUWEN, *op. cit.*, p. 259; ACKROYD, "Structure", p. 12 and WÜRTHWEIN, *op. cit.*, p. 428.

[80]) Cf. CHILDS, *op. cit.*, p. 100, but he (*op. cit.*, p. 98) does not choose for this possibility. According to him the author of the second account did not use the first account directly. Note also the opinion of KAISER, *Jesaja*, p. 304 (see above n. 43) and WILDBERGER, *Jesaja*, pp. 1421f.

[81]) Cf. STADE, *op. cit.*, pp. 173-175. See also KAISER, *Jesaja*, p. 299.

[82]) LEENE, *op. cit.* (see above n. 51). In n. 15 he gives a survey of other interpretations of רוח. From Is. xxxvii 28 it becomes clear that רוח indicates a spirit inducing Sennacherib to taunt the Living God and in this way bringing about his destruction.

[83]) Cf. e.g. CHILDS, *op. cit.*, p. 96 and KAISER, *Jesaja*, p. 314.

[84]) To wit: Is. xxxviii 9-20.

[85]) ACKROYD, "Interpretation", p. 345.

[86]) Cf. STADE, *op. cit.*, p. 179. WILDBERGER, *Jesaja*, p. 1430 dates the song in the last days of the Judaean kingdom, but WÜRTHWEIN, *op. cit.*, p. 431, even in the exilic period. The song itself is a parody echoing what the Neo-Assyrian kings say in their own inscriptions, cf. ACKROYD, "Structure", p. 12 and MACHINIST, *op. cit.* (n. 63), p. 723. According to H. TAWIL, "The Historicity of 2 Kings 19:24 (= Isaiah 37:25): The Problem of *Yeʾōrê Māṣôr*", *JNES* 41 (1982), 195-206, *māṣôr* does not mean "Egypt" but "Mount Muṣri". His argumentation is not very convincing.

[87]) He added vv. 21, 22aα, 23 and 24aα. Also v. 26 (which resembles the conceptions of the Second Isaiah; cf. KAISER, *Jesaja*, p. 314 n. 105) could be his work.

[88]) See ACKROYD, "Structure", pp. 12,17f. and MELUGIN, *op. cit.*, p. 178.

[89]) The expression "for Mine own sake and for My servant David's sake" is a combination of an expression typical of Deutero-Isaiah and a Dtr expression; cf. KAISER, *Jesaja*, p. 313.

⁹⁰) This figure almost matches the boast of Sennacherib that during his military campaign against Judah he drove out 200.150 people, young and old, male and female, and considered them booty; cf. Chicago Prisma III 24-27.

⁹¹) Cf. KAISER, *Jesaja*, p. 313; CLEMENTS, *Isaiah*, p. 21 and WÜRTHWEIN, *op. cit.*, p. 429.

⁹²) Concerning Sennacherib's death see S. PARPOLA, "The murderer of Sennacherib", in B. ALSTER (ed.), *Death in Mesopotamia*; Papers read at the XXVIe Rencontre assyriologique internationale, Copenhagen 1980, 171-182. Cf. also TUAT I, 4, pp. 391f. The prophecy is not in complete agreement with the Assyrian sources, cf. VAN LEEUWEN, *op. cit.*, pp. 260ff.

⁹³) Cf. e.g. KAISER, *Jesaja*, p. 305; WILDBERGER, *Jesaja*, p. 1393 and p. 1422; CLEMENTS, *Isaiah*, p. 55 and WÜRTHWEIN, *op. cit.*, p. 424.

⁹⁴) An earlier date (e.g., in the Josianic period) is therefore precluded. Neither can the narrative be dated in the exilic period, as the confidence in Jerusalem's inviolability cannot have been restored before the Persian period. It is interesting to note that in Jer. xxvi 18f. Hezekiah is mentioned in connection with the prophet Micah instead of Isaiah. In this passage Micah iii 12 is quoted. From Micah iii 11 it becomes clear that Micah is opposing people who trust in the inviolability of Jerusalem because of YHWH's presence in the Temple. When they do not keep the commandments, their confidence is without reason: in that case Jerusalem will nevertheless be destroyed. But Hezekiah heeds to Micah's words and beseeks the Lord. Because of the king's repentance the evil did not come in his days. In my opinion, Jer. xxvi offers an earlier stage of the idealization of king Hezekiah compared to the Hezekiah narratives. In this earlier stage Isaiah does not figure, but Micah. The delivery of Jerusalem is in Jer. xxvi the result of the king's repentance, in Is. xxxvii of the king's humility and of Sennacherib's arrogance. Seen from this perspective we must conclude that the Hezekiah narratives are later than Jer. xxvi, which constitutes another proof that they originate from the Persian period. See also ACKROYD, "Presentation", pp. 23f.

⁹⁵) Cf. Is. xxxix 7. It is important to note that Isaiah first speaks about Hezekiah's *fathers*, then of his *sons* which he will beget, and concludes that these will be *eunuchs*. The author wants to indicate that the Davidic dynasty will come to an end in Babylonia (see also Jer. xxii 30).

⁹⁶) If not, one would expect the same conclusion as that in the book of Chronicles (2 Chron. xxxvi 22-23) which is more appropriate than 2 Kings xxv 27-30.

⁹⁷) A survey of the Assyrian sources is given by VAN LEEUWEN, *op. cit.*, p. 245, and by HUTTER, *op. cit.*, pp. 39-51. In my article in *ACEBT* 2 (1981), 50-67 I have discussed the historical value of the Hezekiah narratives more fully.

⁹⁸) See also CLEMENTS, *Isaiah*, p. 13. Pace J. B. GEYER, "2 Kings XVIII 14-16 and the Annals of Sennacherib", *VT* 21 (1971), 604-606.

⁹⁹) Cf. CLEMENTS, *ibidem*.

¹⁰⁰) *Ibidem*, pp. 19 and 62. A complete siege of Jerusalem would have taken the Assyrian king too much time and money; the Babylonian siege of Jerusalem in 588-586 shows this clearly.

¹⁰¹) Cf. also KAISER, *Jesaja*, p. 300 and 304; WÜRTHWEIN, *op. cit.*, p. 429.

¹⁰²) Cf. H. W. F. SAGGS, "The Nimrud Letters 1952—Part I", *Iraq* 17 (1955), 21-50. It concerns text no. 1. According to SAGGS (p. 47) the discussion between Assyrian officials and Babylonian citizens described in this letter resembles Is. xxxvi very much. This is also the opinion of other scholars (cf. e.g., WILDBERGER, "Rede", p. 45). I do not agree. The argumentation the Assyrians given in the Nimrud letter is of a political and strategical nature; Rabshakeh's words are echoing biblical theology.

¹⁰³) Cf. ACKROYD, "Interpretation", pp. 347f. and my earlier article in *ACEBT* 2, n. 32.

¹⁰⁴) CLEMENTS, *Isaiah*, p. 55. Cf. also, e.g., MONTGOMERY and GEHMAN, *op. cit.*, p. 487; GRAY, *op. cit.*, p. 665.

¹⁰⁵) *Contra* MONTGOMERY and GEHMAN, *op. cit.*, p. 487; cf. also WÜRTHWEIN, *op. cit.*, p. 422.

106) Cf. FOHRER, *op. cit.*, p. 162; KAISER, *Jesaja*, pp. 292, 305 (+ n. 62); W. ZIMMERLI, "Jesaja und Hiskia", reprinted in *Studien zum alttestamentlichen Theologie und Prophetie*, Munich 1974, 88-103; CLEMENTS, *Isaiah*, pp. 28-51.

107) Cf. FOHRER, *op. cit.*, p. 163 and also P. R. ACKROYD, "The Biblical Interpretation of the Reigns of Ahaz and Hezekiah", *In the Shelter of Elyon*. Essays on Ancient Palestinian Life and Literature in Honor of G. W. Ahlström, Sheffield 1984, 247-259.

108) Cf. 2 Kings xviii 15-16.

109) S. DE JONG, "Hizkia en Zedekia; Over de verhouding van 2 Kon. 18:17-19:37/Jes. 36-37 tot Jer. 37:1-10", *ACEBT* 5 (1984), 135-146.

1 CHRONICLES XXIV AND THE ROYAL PRIESTHOOD OF THE HASMONEANS

BY

L. DEQUEKER
Leuven

Introduction

In 1910 Solomon SCHECHTER published the "Fragments of a Zadokite Work", from the Cairo-Genizah manuscripts in Cambridge University Library[1]). Since then the fragments have become known as "The Damascus Document"[2]). The term "Zadokite", however, has persisted in English terminology[3]). André DUPONT-SOMMER rejected the term as ambiguous. "Zadokite Fragments" would be the same as "Sadducean Fragments", which of course is not correct for Qumran. The sect had nothing in common with the Sadducean party in Jerusalem[4]).

In spite of the growing consensus for the term "Damascus Document", even in English[5]), the term Zadokites seems to me an appropriate qualification for the members of the sect. They present themselves as fervent adherents of the priests, "Sons of Zadok", governing the community[6]).

"Sons of Zadok" has been understood, recently again, as a purely moral qualification of those who keep the Covenant and follow the Law[7]). In my opinion, "Sons of Zadok" is a genealogical title which determined not only the doctrine, but also the historical development of the sect. In this paper I should like to examine the nature of the conflict between the sectarians in Qumran and the Hasmonean dynasty in Jerusalem. Both the Hasmoneans and the Zadokites in Qumran laid claim to the high priesthood in the temple. Both of them were of Zadokite lineage. Basically, the struggle between Qumran and Jerusalem was a struggle for power and priestly legitimacy.

1. The priests "Sons of Zadok" in Qumran versus the Hasmonean priesthood in Jerusalem

Qumran was at enmity with Jerusalem and the temple. The spiritual leader of the sect, the Teacher of Righteousness, was a priest. His opponent was the high priest in Jerusalem. Sect members refer to him as the

Wicked Priest. Scholars admit that he was a member of the Hasmonean priestly dynasty. He has mainly been identified as Jonathan, the first Hasmonean high priest, or as Alexander Jannaeus[8]). For many years, indeed, the opinion has prevailed that the contest between Qumran and the temple was a dispute about priestly legitimacy. The Teacher of Righteousness and the other priests "Sons of Zadok" in Qumran were of high Zadokite lineage. They contested the Hasmoneans and regarded them as usurpers who appropriated to themselves the high priesthood which traditionally belonged to the family of Onias. The exact grounds on which the sectarians in Qumran rejected the legitimacy of the Hasmonean priests have been understood in different ways. The traditional picture of the Hasmoneans as countrymen belonging to the lower ranks of the priesthood[9]), may lie at the basis of the idea that the priests in Qumran opposed the Hasmoneans as non-Zadokites, or even as non-Aaronites[10]). A. S. VAN DER WOUDE understood the enmity as a rivalry between Zadokites and Ithamarites, as in 1 Chr xxiv[11]). Other scholars hold that the contest between Qumran and the temple was not so much a problem of Zadokite lineage, but a problem of temple discipline and personal morality. G. VERMES holds that it was the sect members' opposition on principle to the offering of sacrifices which caused the rupture[12]). S. TALMON pointed to the peculiar calendar reckoning of the sect as the main reason[13]). J. Le MOYNE follows the same argument[14]). Basically, he says, Qumran and Jerusalem disagreed on ritual prescriptions. The reason for the split could not have been the legitimacy of the priesthood, since the house of Jehoiarib, the priestly family of the Hasmoneans (1 Mac. ii 1) is mentioned in the sectarian list of Mishmarot, Qumran Cave 4[15]). Jacob LIVER strongly opposes the traditional view on the Hasmoneans as priests of a lower rung[16]). The family presumably belonged to the priestly aristocracy in Jerusalem (1 Mac. ii 1). The subject of contention was not a problem of priestly lineage, but of the personal conduct of the Wicked Priest. The Habakkuk-pesher is explicit in the matter.

Whatever the meaning of the calendar-dispute and the impact of personal misdeeds may have been, I am of the opinion that it was the problem of Zadokite lineage that lay at the basis of the conflict between Qumran and Jerusalem. The personal grievances against the Wicked Priest and the introduction of a new calendar may have been signs and signals of the deep rivalry and enmity between two priestly families, which both pretended to be of Zadokite descendance and consequently laid claim to the office of high priest in the temple. I hope to demonstrate this with the help of the list of priestly courses in 1 Chron. xxiv, which reflects the Zadokite claims of the Hasmonean dynasty.

2. The "Sons of Zadok" in 1 Chron. xxiv

1 Chron. xxiv 7-19 publishes a list of priestly courses which remained unchanged until the fall of the second temple[17]). My purpose is to investigate the Zadokite claims which arise from this list. Which of the priestly families mentioned claimed to have a right to the office of high priest in the temple because of their Zadokite lineage?

The list is given as part of the many arrangements made by David towards the end of his life, after the nomination of Solomon as his successor: 1 Chron. xxiii 3-xxvii 34. WILLIAMSON pointed out that the passage on the sons of Aaron, i.e. xxiv 1-19, including the list of priestly courses vv. 7-18, is a secondary level in this larger context. The original strand of 1 Chron. xxiii-xxvii, consisting of little more than a genealogical list, deals with the organization of the Levites by David himself. In the intrusive section on the divisions of the sons of Aaron, David is acting no longer alone, but with the help of Zadok and Ahimelech. WILLIAMSON dates the revision one generation after the Chronicler, i.e. at the close of the Persian period, if Chronicles is to be dated around 350 B.C. He dissociates himself from the Maccabean dating, proposed by many in view of the significant position of Jehoiarib, the Hasmonean family at the head of the list[18]).

The classification of the priestly courses was made, the text says, by David with the help of both Zadok, of the house of Eleazar, and Ahimelech, who is introduced as a son of Ithamar (1 Chron. xxiv 3). Zadok was the priest and brave fighter (1 Chron. xii 28) who sided with David in the struggle for succession against Adonijah (1 Kings i-ii). His counterpart, Abiathar, former priest of Nob, took sides with Adonijah, but was dismissed by Solomon (1 Kings ii 26-27). Abiathar was dismissed from his office, it is said, "in fulfilment of the sentence that the Lord had pronounced against the house of Eli" (1 Kings ii 26-27). The vaticinium ex eventu 1 Sam. ii 27-36 explains to Eli that the eternal priesthood given to Phinehas at the time, after the incident of Baal Peor (Numb. xxv 12-13), would be transferred to Zadok. Zadok is the "faithful priest, who would serve the Lord in perpetual succession before (David) the anointed king" (1 Sam. ii 35). Ahimelech and Abiathar served in the sanctuary of Nob under Saul (1 Sam. xxi-xxii). Kinship with Ahitub (1 Sam. xxii 9) connects them with Eli in Shiloh. The whole house of Eli stands for the old Israelite sanctuaries before a new temple originated in Jerusalem. Zadok, on the other hand, stands for Jerusalem, David's new creation. He represents the symbiosis of El-Eljon and Jahwe[19]).

Abiathar is nowhere mentioned in Chronicles. In the section on the classification of the priestly courses it is his father Ahimelech (1 Sam. xxii 20), who acts next to Zadok. Zadok, however, is one of the most prominent figures in Chronicles. In Samuel and Kings he turns up in the history of David without any genealogical connection. In 1 Chron. v 30-41, he occupies the centre of a long genealogical list of high priests, from Aaron up to the last high priests at the time of the exile (see Table 1). He is number 12 in a series of 24 high priests, from Aaron to Jehozadak[20]).

In 2 Sam. viii 17 Zadok is mentioned as ben Ahitub, next to Abjathar ben Ahimelech. GUNNEWEG understands it as an attempt to legitimize Zadok as a descendant of Eli[21]). Eli is the grandfather of Ahitub in the genealogy of the priests in Shiloh (1 Sam. xiv 3). To me the qualification of Zadok as ben Ahitub seems more like a gloss, referring to the Zadokite genealogy of 1 Chron. v. Any reference to the house of Eli would have been a dishonour, as in the case of Abiathar at the time of his defeat by Solomon[22]).

Before continuing the analysis of the list of priestly courses in 1 Chron. xxiv, let me turn to another Zadokite document in the Bible: the so-called ''Zadokidenschicht'' in Ezekiel xl-xlviii, the prophet's restoration-programme of the Temple. Only the priests ''Sons of Zadok'', the prophet says, would be allowed to serve at the altar of the Lord in the rebuilt temple. The others, those who turned away from the Lord, as did the Israelites in the North, would have to serve in the House as Levites. H. GESE[23]), followed by A. H. J. GUNNEWEG, made clear that the original text of Ezekiel dealt with the traditional distinction between priests sons of Aaron, and Levites, as in Numbers xviii 1-7. The distinction must go back to the centralisation of the cult in Jerusalem. The Levites were the priests of the former Israelite sanctuaries in the North, adopted in Jerusalem as a minor clergy[24]). A Zadokite writer reinforced the thesis by defining the priests serving at the altar as the ''Sons of Zadok'' (Ezek. xliv 10-16; xl 46b; xliii 19a; xlviii 11a''). Only the priests descendants of Zadok are worthy to enter the sanctuary proper and to approach the Holy of Holies (Ezek. xliv 14). The original programme of Ezekiel reflects the situation before the exile. The Zadokite version depicts the situation at the moment of the return from Babylon. The claim of the returnees appears to have been that only the ''Sons of Zadok'', i.e. only the descendants of the high priests before the exile, would be admitted to serve as priests in the temple. Other priestly families, especially those who stayed in the country during the exile, are stigmatized as deserters, the offspring of Israel, the idolatrous people in the North (Ezek. xliv 10.12).

Ezra, the priest and scribe, principal author of the post-exilic reform, claimed to be of Zadokite descendance. His genealogy, Ezra vii 1-5, is remarkably similar to the detailed Zadokite genealogy of Jehozadak, son of the last high priest before the exile, 1 Chron v 30-41[25]). Would it be

98   L. DEQUEKER

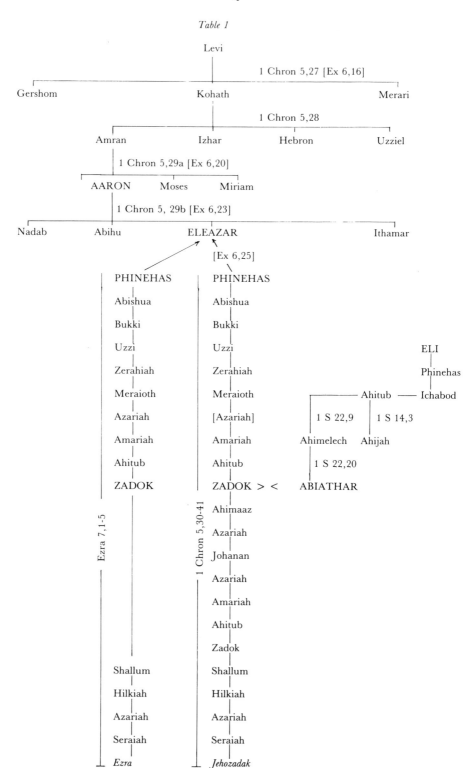

Table 1

hazardous to link the Zadokite program of Ezekiel with the priestly reformation of Ezra[26])?

The Zadokite genealogy of 1 Chron. v points to the fact that
Jehozadak, the last in the line, went into exile (v. 41). It was he who
perpetuated the high priestly dignity when the cult in Jerusalem was in-
terrupted. His son Jeshua was the first to redress the altar after the return
(Ezra iii 2). The descendants of Jeshua are known as the house of
Jedaiah, the first priestly family mentioned after the exile (Ezra ii 36-38;
x 18ff.). The house of Jedaiah appears in the list of priestly courses, 1
Chron. xxiv, immediately after the Hasmonean ascendant Jehoiarib. In
the genealogy of Ezra the name of Jehozadak is missing. Does it reflect
tension and rivalry between the adherents of Ezra and those of Jeshua,
the house of Jedaiah[27])? I do not think so. As said before, Jeshua son of
Jehozadak is mentioned with praise, as the one who reconstructed the
altar, Ezra iii 2.

Let me go on with 1 Chron. xxiv. In the list of priestly courses the
distinction between Zadokites and non-Zadokites, which in Ezekiel was a
distinction between priests and non-priests, is related to the distinction
between sons of Eleazar and sons of Ithamar, which is the distinction
between the high priestly families and the other priests in Jerusalem.
Zadok is presented as a son of Eleazar, according to the genealogy of 1
Chron. v. His counterpart Ahimelech is characterized as a son of
Ithamar, according to a late tradition, the further developments of which
are found in Josephus (Antiq. v 361) and in the Midrash (Yalk. Shof.
68), where Eli himself is classified as an Ithamarite. In 4 Ezra i 2-3, Eli
belongs to the family of Eleazar.

Ithamar, the priest son of Aaron, does not represent an old Israelite
tradition. He turns up for the first time in the Priestly tradition[28]), and is
always inferior to Eleazar. The distinction between Eleazarites—or
Zadokites—and Ithamarites is equivalent to the distinction between high
priestly families and the other priests in the temple[29]). The Ithamarites
were not a minor clergy, like the Levites, nor descendants of a defeated
priesthood, like Eli or Abiathar. The Ithamarites were among the
returnees after the exile (Ezra viii 2), but may not have been accepted to
the priesthood in the temple by Ezra and the sons of Zadok, since they
were not descendants of Jehozadak. 1 Chron. xxiv reflects a new situation. The predominant position of the Zadokites or Eleazarites is
underlined by their larger number vis-à-vis the Ithamarites (v. 4). On the
other hand the Ithamarites are said to have had ministers in the sanctuary and ministers of the Lord, just as the Eleazarites (v. 5). Obviously,
after a few generations the Ithamarites sons of Aaron could no longer be
excluded from the priestly duty in the temple. It was decided to accept

them. But the high priestly office should remain in the hands of the Zadokites.

Do we know from the list of priestly courses which families were considered as Zadokites, and who were the Ithamarites? In contrast to Jacob Liver, who puts that "the entire matter of subdivision into Eleazarite and Ithamarite descent became devoid of any actual content in the Chronicler's time"[30]), I think that the list shows plainly how important was the subdivision. The list groups on one side the Zadokites, sixteen heads of families belonging to the line of Eleazar, on the other side eight heads for Ithamar. The main purpose of the list was to fix the order in which the priestly families should serve in the temple. Since both groups consisted of priests, the order in which the families would serve was decided by lot. But because of the predominance of Eleazar, the lots were drawn in a sequence of two against one, two lots being successively given to the line of Eleazar, against one lot for Ithamar. Two families of the Eleazar-group, the group of the Zadokite high priest, should always serve one after the other.

The proposed explanation supposes an emendation of the verse 6. The reading of the Massoretic text   בית־אב אחד אחז לאלעזר ואחז אחז לאיתמר usually translated as "one priestly family is taken from the line of Eleazar and one from that of Ithamar", contradicts the predominance of Eleazar as stated in v. 4. The LXX reads οἴκου πατριᾶς εἷς εἷς τῷ Ελεαζαρ καὶ εἷς εἷς τῷ Ιθαμαρ. The double repetition of εἷς is obviously due to the conflation of different readings. אחז (taken) and אחד (one) are indeed very similar in writing. The Greek translator may have read twice אחד. The original text can easily be restored as follows: בית אב אחד אחז לאלעזר ואחד ואחז אחד לאיתמר —"they chose one family for Eleazar, and one more, and one family for Ithamar"[31]).

The result of the proposed analysis is shown in Table 2. In the left column are the names of the families considered to be of Zadokite lineage, i.e. high priestly families, in the right one the Ithamarites, who never could lay claim upon the high priesthood.

Let me apply this to the history of the Hasmoneans.

3. Zadokites and Hasmoneans

Onias, the high priest deposed by Antiochus IV Epiphanes in 174 was of Zadokite lineage. Ben Sirach 1 applies the solemn covenant with Phinehas (Numb. xxv) to Simon, the father of Onias. "May the mercy of the Lord dwell on Simon; may he uphold for him the covenant with Phinehas, neither he nor his descendants shall be deprived of this covenant as long as the heavens exist" (Sir. 1 23-24, Hebrew)[32].

Table 2

1 Chronicles 24,6-18

The line of ELEAZAR (16 heads of families)	The line of ITHAMAR (8 heads of families)
1. Jehoiarib	
2. Jedaiah	
	3. Harim
4. Seorim	
5. Malchiah	
	6. Mijamin
7. Hakkoz	
8. Abiah	
	9. Jeshua
10. Shecaniah	
11. Eliashib	
	12. Jakim
13. Huppah	
14. Jeshebeab	
	15. Bilgah
16. Immer	
17. Hezir	
	18. Aphses
19. Pethahiah	
20. Jehezekel	
	21. Jachin
22. Gamul	
23. Delaiah	
	24. Maaziah

The Oniads belonged to the house of Jedaiah, i.e. they were descendants of the high priestly family of Seraiah and Jchozadak before the exile. According to Flavius Josephus the father of Onias I, founder of the Oniad dynasty, was called Jaddua (Antiq. xi 347).

Onias was deposed in favour of his brother Jason, a Zadokite, as a matter of course. Jason did not hold office for long. After two years he was superseded by his brother-in-law Menelaos[33]), from the house of Bilgah, and supported by the wealthy but non-priestly Tobiad-family. According to the Greek text of 2 Mac. iv 23 and iii 4, Menelaos and his brother Simon, the main instigator against the Oniads, were from the house of Benjamin. This would mean that Menelaos was not even a priest. Scholars agree to read with the Vetus Latina: "from the house of Bilgah"[34]). In the list of 1 Chron. xxiv Bilgah is on the side of the non-Zadokites. 2 Mac. iv 25 states that Menelaos had a royal mandate by the Syrians, "but nothing else to make him worthy of the high priesthood."

The rededication of the temple in 164 and a peace-treaty obtained by the Maccabeans at the end of 163, led to the fall of Menelaos. The Syrians made him responsible for the difficulties in Jerusalem. Alkimos, a moderate Hellenist, as he is called by scholars, took his place. Was Alkimos a Zadokite, as commonly held, or even an Oniade? Scholars think he was, on account of 2 Mac. xiv 3-7 dealing with the claims of Alkimos upon the high priesthood and the opposition of Judas. Scholars understand that Alkimos had formerly been high priest, but had been deprived by Judas the Maccabee of his hereditary rights[35]).

The alleged statement that Alkimos had been high priest before Demetrius came to power, is contradicted by xiv 13 which says that Demetrius appointed him. Moreover, in the parallel text 1 Mac. vii 5 it is not said that Alkimos had been high priest before, but that he aspired to the office, and that he fought hard for it (vii 21). 2 Mac. xiv 3 is to be understood in the same way. Ἄλκιμος δέ τις προγεγονὼς ἀρχιερεύς means: Alkimos was advancing himself to the high priestly office[36]), and complained before the king that the Maccabeans rejected his legitimate rights. The text continues with an explanation of the reasons why there was not the slightest possibility for him to be admitted as a high priest and to have access to the holy altar. He defiled himself voluntarily at times when segregation was prescribed: ἐν τοῖς τῆς ἀμειξίας χρόνοις. Scholars understand the expression in the context of Hellenistic reform and the profanation of the temple. I propose to relate it with the personal ambitions of Alkimos and to understand it in the light of what is said about him at the end of his life, 1 Mac. ix. Alkimos died at the very moment he gave orders to demolish the wall of the inner court of the temple. In doing this, he destroyed the work of the prophets (1 Mac. ix 54). The wall under discussion was not intended to separate the Jews and the Gentiles, according to the instructions of Ezek. xliv 9 and Ezra iv 3[37]). I think the segregation is meant of Zadokites and non-Zadokites, i.e. of the high priest and the other priests, in the inner court of the temple, according to the restoration programme of Ezek. xl 44-47[38]). The measures taken by Nehemiah against Tobiad and Sanballat (Neh. xiii 7-9.30) may reflect the same concern.

There are thus no reasons for regarding Alkimos as a Zadokite, even less an Oniad. The Hasidim and scribes supporting him in the beginning trusted him as a priest of the family of Aaron (1 Mac. vii 14). Flavius Josephus refers to him as "from the line of Aaron" (γένους μὲν τοῦ Ἀαρῶνος), but not of the same family as Onias (οὐχ ὄντα δὲ τῆς οἰκίας ταύτης—Antiq. xx 235). Dealing with the nomination of Alkimos in Antiq. xii Josephus is more explicit. When Onias son of Onias heard about the death of his uncle Menelaos and learned that the king had given the office of high priest to Alkimos, although Alkimos was not of the family of high priests (οὐκ ἐκ τῆς τῶν ἀρχιερέων ὄντι γενεᾶς) the young man fled to Egypt. The king, Josephus goes on, had been persuaded to transfer the office from this house to another (μεταθεῖναι τὴν τιμὴν ἀπὸ ταύτης τῆς οἰκίας εἰς ἕτερον οἶκον) (xii 387). Which other priestly house is meant? At the beginning of the passage Josephus refers to Alkimos as: Ἄλχιμος ὁ καὶ Ἰάχειμος—or: Ἰάχιμος—κληθείς. "The high priest chosen after the death of Menelaos was Alkimos, also Iakeimos" (Antiq. xii 385). In the Lucianic text-tradition of Maccabees Ἰάχιμος occurs repeatedly as an addition to the name of Alkimos, may be under the influence of Josephus[39]). It refers, so we understand, to the priestly family of Jakim, which, according to the list in 1 Chron. xxiv, was of the Ithamar-group, thus not of Zadokite lineage.

Although a descendant of Aaron, and trusted, at least in the beginning, by the Hasidim, Alkimos is severely judged in the books of Maccabees, which openly support the Zadokite claims of the Hasmonean family.

Alkimos was a godless man (1 Mac. vii 9), who did not respect the rules of segregation, and despised the proper domain and the liturgical rights of the Zadokite high priest in the temple (2 Mac. xiv 3).

After the death of Alkimos it took seven years (Antiq. xx 237) before the Hasmoneans could impose themselves as high priests, with the agreement of the Syrians. Jonathan assumed the high-priestly vestments at the Feast of Tabernacles in 153 (or 152) (1 Mac. x 18-21). Josephus fills up the "intersacerdotium" of seven years by making Judas already a high priest (Antiq. xii 414.419.434). H STEGEMANN, followed by J. G. BUNGE, fills in the gap by introducing the Teacher of Righteousness as a high priest in Jerusalem before Jonathan[40]).

Did Jonathan the Hasmonean have any legitimate right to the office? His father Mattathias was a priest from the house of Jehoiarib. Mattathias lived in Jerusalem, but left the capital at the time of the persecution by Antiochus Epiphanes and settled at the family estate of Modein in the Shefela (1 Mac. ii 1). In the list of priestly courses 1 Chron. xxiv Jehoiarib occupies the first place. In the older lists of priestly families after the exile he is either absent (Neh. x 3-9) or has a subordinated position (Neh. xii 19). The Hasmonean origin of the list in 1 Chron. seems certain. The list proves that the Hasmonean high priests were, or at least claimed to be of Zadokite origin[41]).

Simon succeeded his brother Jonathan in 142. In 140 a popular assembly in Jerusalem confirmed him as "leader and high priest in perpetuity, until a true prophet should appear" (1 Mac. xiv 40-41). "Until a true prophet should appear" is not to be understood as a restriction, which would leave open the possibility that a prophet arises and contests the legitimacy of the Hasmoneans[42]). On the contrary: the decision of the popular assembly to confirm Simon as ἡγούμενον, i.e. as *nāgīd*—which was the title of David! 2 Sam. vii 8—, is made in anticipation of the anointment of Simon by a true prophet of the Lord. The text alludes to the anointment of David by Samuel (1 Sam. xvi 13).

Conclusion — Qumran and the Zadokite list of 1 Chr xxiv

Who was the Wicked Priest, the main antagonist of the Teacher of Righteousness in Qumran? Why did the "Covenanters of Damascus" segregate from Jerusalem?

The non-Zadokite Alkimos, the ambitious rival for the high priesthood, who made misleading promises to the Hasidim, may have been the Wicked Priest[43]. In the beginning he enjoyed a reputation for truth (1QpHab viii 8-9), i.e. the Hasidim, the ancestors of the Essenes in Qumran, trusted him as a priest of the family of Aaron. But as soon as he had realised his ambitious plans, he grew arrogant and abandoned the Lord (1QpHab ib.). He practised abomination, involving every kind of impurity and filth (ibid.). The picture fits in with the accusations of ritual impurity in 2 Mac. xiv 3.

Apart from the Wicked Priest, the pesher Habakkuk fulminates against "the last Priests of Jerusalem, who amass for themselves wealth and gain by plundering the people. But their wealth and plunder was delivered into the hands of the army of the Kittim" (1QpHab ix 4-7). The "last priests of Jerusalem" are, so I understand, the Hasmoneans. The text refers to their defeat by Pompey.

The Zadokite community in Qumran opposed thus not only the non-Zadokite Alkimos, but also the Zadokite family of Jehoiarib in the struggle for the high priesthood in the temple.

To which priestly family the Teacher of Righteousness and his adherents, the priests Sons of Zadok, belonged, we do not know. Do we have to look in the line of Eleazar in 1 Chron. xxiv? Is there any possibility that the Teacher of Righteousness was a descendant of the Oniads?

CD iii 20-iv 6 applies the Zadokite reform programme of Ezekiel xliv 15 to the priests and members of the sect. The priests are called hereby the "returnees of Israel" (שבי ישראל —CD iv 2)[44]), using a terminology which is familiar to Chronicles-Ezra and Nehemiah in the description of the exiled community, and which might have explicit Zadokite connotations[45]). Moreover, the passage deals with "a list of their names, in their generations" (CD iv 4-5), which might be an allusion to a genealogical list of priestly families as discovered in 4Q and 6Q[46]). Further study of those lists might help to solve the problem.

NOTES

[1]) S. Schechter, *Fragments of a Zadokite Work*, "*Documents of Jewish Sectaries*", Vol. I, Cambridge, 1910.

[2]) L. Rost, *Die Damaskusschrift*, neubearbeitet (Kleine Texte 167), Berlin 1933.

[3]) H. H. Rowley, *The Zadokite Fragments and the Dead Sea Scrolls*, Oxford 1952; S. Zeitlin, *The Zadokite Fragments*. Facsimile of the Manuscripts in the Cairo Geniza Collection in the Possession of the University Library, Cambridge, England (JQR, Monogr. Series I), Philadelphia, 1952; Ch. Rabin, *The Zadokite Documents*, Oxford 1954.

[4]) A. Dupont-Sommer, *Les écrits esséniens découverts près de la Mer Morte*, Paris 1959, 129-130.

[5]) J. Murphy-O'Connor, "A Literary Analysis of Damascusdocument xix 33-xx 34", in *RB* 79 (1972), 544-564; Ph. R. Davies, *The Damascus Covenant. An Interpretation of the "Damascus Document"* (JSOT-Suppl. Ser. 25), Sheffield 1983.

[6]) 1Q S v 1-3.7-10; 1Q Sa i 1-3.24-25; ii 1-3; 1QH iii 22-25; CD iii 20-iv 4.

[7]) P. Wernberg-Møller, "Sdq, Sdyq, and Sdwq in the Zadokite Fragments (CDC), the Manual of Discipline (DSD) and the Habakkuk-Commentary (DSH)", *VT* 3 (1953), 310-315; R. Eisenman, *Maccabees, Zadokites, Christians and Qumran. A New Hypothesis of Qumran Origins* (Studia Post-Biblica 34), Leiden 1983.

[8]) See the survey of opinions in E. Schuerer, *The History of the Jewish People in the Age of Jesus Christ (175 B.C.-A.D. 135)*, New English Version by G. Vermes and F. Millar. Vol. I, Edinburg 1973, 188, n. 42 and 224, n. 21. Further in favour of Jonathan: H. Stegemann, *Die Entstehung der Qumrangemeinde* (Diss. Bonn 1965), Bonn 1971; J. Murphy-O'Connor, "The Essenes and their History", in *RB* 81 (1974), 215-243; J. G. Bunge, "Zur Geschichte und Chronologie des Untergangs der Oniaden und des Aufstiegs der Hasmonäer", *JSJ* 6 (1975), 1-46. According to A. S. van der Woude, "Wicked Priest or Wicked Priests? Reflections on the Identification of the Wicked Priest in the Habakkuk Commentary", in *JJS* 33 (1982) (= Essays in Honour of Yigael Yadin), 349-359, the expression "Wicked Priest" is not restricted to one person, but is used for a series of Priests, from Judas the Maccabee to Alexander Jannaeus.

[9]) E.g. R. de Vaux, *Ancient Israel. Its Life and Institutions*, transl. by J. McHugh, London 1961, p. 402: "The line of Yehoyarib (1 M 2: 1) was an obscure family which was placed at the head of the Priestly classes in 1 Ch 24: 7 only after the triumph of the Hasmoneans; it was a late date for such a correction, and since the family was not Sadoqite, those who were partisans of traditionalism could consider the Hasmonean high priests as illegitimate usurpers."

[10]) J. T. Milik, *Ten Years of Discovery in the Wilderness of Judaea*, London 1959, 92; H. J. Schoeps, "Der gegenwärtige Stand der Erforschung der in Palästina neu gefundenen hebräischen Handschriften. 35. Die Opposition gegen die Hasmonäer, *ThLZ* 1956, 664-670.

[11]) A. S. van der Woude, *Die Messianischen Vorstellungen der Gemeinde von Qumran* (Studia Semitica Neerlandica 3), Assen 1957, 229.

[12]) G. Vermes, *Discovery in the Judean Desert*, New-York-Paris, 1956, 39.212.

[13]) Sh. Talmon, "The Calendar Reckoning of the Sect from the Judaean Desert, in Ch. Rabin-Y. Yadin, *Aspects of the Dead Sea Scrolls* (Scripta Hierosolymitana IV), Jerusalem 1965, 162-199.

[14]) J. le Moyne, Les Sadducéens (Etudes Bibliques), Paris 1972, 63.295.

[15]) J. T. Milik, "Le travail d'édition des manuscrits du Désert de Juda", in *Volume du Congrès Strasbourg 1956* (Suppl. VT IV), Leiden 1957, 17-26.

[16]) J. Liver, "The 'Sons of Zadok the Priests' in the Dead Sea Sect", *RQ* 6 (1967), 3-29.

[17]) J. R. Bartlett, "Zadok and His Successors at Jerusalem", *JThS* xix (1968), 1-18; H. G. M. Williamson, "The Origins of the Twenty-Four Priestly Courses. A Study of 1 Chronicles xxiii-xxvii", in J. A. Emerton (ed.), *Studies in the Historical Books of the Old Testament* (Suppl. VT 30), Leiden 1979, 251-268.

[18]) H. G. M. Williamson, a.c., 266-267; comp. P. Ackroyd, "Criteria for the Maccabean Dating of Old Testament Literature", *VT* 3 (1953), 113-132, esp. 126-127.

[19]) A. H. J. GUNNEWEG, *Leviten und Priester. Hauptlinien der Traditionsbildung und Geschichte des israelitisch-jüdischen Kultpersonals*, Göttingen 1965, 98-104.

[20]) For the restoration of Azariah after Meraioth see A. VAN DEN BORN, *Kronieken* (De Boeken van het Oude Testament), Roermond 1960, 43-44.

[21]) A. H. J. GUNNEWEG, *o.c.*, 104f.

[22]) Comp. A. H. J. GUNNEWEG, *o.c.*, 105: "Wie Zadok ist Abjatar mit fremden genealogischen Federn geschmuckt worden".

[23]) H. GESE, *Der Verfassungsentwurf des Ezechiel (Kap. 40-48), traditionsgeschichtlich untersucht* (Beitr. Hist. Theol. 25), Tübingen 1957.

[24]) A. H. J. GUNNEWEG, *o.c.*, 154-155.

[25]) See Table 1.

[26]) Comp. A. H. J. GUNNEWEG, *o.c.*, 198ff. on the relationship between the "Zadokidenschicht" and P.

[27]) Thus V. APTOWITZER, *Parteipolitik der Hasmonäerzeit im rabbinischen und pseudoepigraphischen Schrifttum*, Wien 1927, and J. LE MOYNE, *o.c.*, § 46.

[28]) A. H. J. GUNNEWEG, *o.c.*, 159.

[29]) A. H. J. GUNNEWEG, *o.c.*, 190.

[30]) J. LIVER, a.c., 21-22.

[31]) Comp. J. M. MYERS, *I Chronicles* (The Anchor Bible), Garden City NY, 1965, 164: "...so that two families were selected for Eleazar for (each) one selected for Ithamar".

[32]) On the Greek, see J. LE MOYNE, *o.c.*, 51; Comp. J. TRINQUET, "Les liens 'sadocites' de l'Ecrit de Damas, des Manuscrits de la Mer Morte et de l'Ecclésiastique", *VT* 1 (1951), 287-292.

[33]) That Menelaos was the brother in law of Onias appears from Antiq. xii 387, where Menelaos is dealt with as an uncle of Onias son of Onias.

[34]) See J. A. GOLDSTEIN, *II Maccabees. A New Translation with Introduction and Commentary* (The Anchor Bible), Garden City-NY, 1983, 203.

[35]) See a.o.: M. HENGEL, *Judentum und Hellenismus* (Wiss. Unters. NT 10), 2. Aufl., Tübingen 1969, 409, n. 679; P. SCHAEFER, *Geschichte der Juden in der Antike. Die Juden Palästinas von Alexander dem Groszen bis zur arabischen Eroberung*, Stuttgart-Neukirchen, 1983. 67; J. G. BUNGE, a.c., 11-13. But see R. de VAUX, *o.c.*, 401: "His successor was called Alkimus, one of the sons of Aaron (1 M 7: 9; 2 M 14: 3, 13), but not of the Sadoqite branch."

[36]) Progignomai: "to come forward" (LIDDELL-SCOTT), "s'avancer" (A. BAILLY).

[37]) Thus R. de VAUX, *o.c.*, 325: "Alkimus wanted to demolish the wall, to please the Greeks".

[38]) Contrast E. SCHUERER (G. VERMES-F. MILLAR), *o.c.*, 175, n. 6. The suggestion might solve the problems of Antiq. xiii 373 and some details of the Temple Scroll.

[39]) R. HANHART, *Septuaginta. Vetus Testamentum Graece ix/2-Maccabaeorum Liber ii*, Göttingen 1959, 23; J. A. GOLDSTEIN, *I Maccabees. A New Translation with Introduction and Commentary* (The Anchor Bible), Garden City-NY, 1976, 333.

[40]) H. STEGEMANN, *o.c.*, 95ff.; J. G. BUNGE, a.c., 27.

[41]) Sh. TALMON, a.c., 171, n. 20 explains the position of Jehoiarib by the assumption that the order of the courses in the Temple was founded on progressing rotation.

[42]) Thus J. T. NELIS, *I Makkabeeën* (De Boeken van het Oude Testament vi/1a), Roermond 1972, 240: "...tenzij een geloofwaardige profeet mocht komen, die anders zou beslissen."

[43]) A. S. VAN DER WOUDE, a.c., 355 includes Alkimos in his series of Wicked Priests: 1QpHab viii 16-ix 2. In his opinion 1QpHab viii 8-13 applies to Judas the Maccabee before the rift between the Hasmonean dynasty and Qumran (353).

[44]) J. MURPHY-O'CONNOR, "The Essenes and their History": *RB* 81 (1974), 215-243.

[45]) Comp. Ph. R. DAVIES, *o.c.*, 93.

[46]) See Sh. TALMON, a.c., 168-169; Ph. R. DAVIES, o.c., 95.

BEN SIRA'S HYMN TO THE FATHERS
A MESSIANIC PERSPECTIVE

BY

JAMES D. MARTIN

St. Andrews, Fife

In an earlier article[1]) I have argued for a consideration of Ben Sira against a background of other intellectual movements of his day and have suggested that we should perhaps approach his "Hymn to the Fathers" (chapters xliv-xlix/1) with such apocalyptic and eschatological and possibly even Messianic possibilities in mind. There were two points which I touched on there but did not have the space to develop. The first is the question whether in his Hymn to the Fathers Ben Sira refers to or develops any Messianic ideas of either a royal or a priestly nature. Connected with this is a second point, namely the particular figures whom Ben Sira chooses to eulogise (or, indeed, chooses not to eulogise) in the course of his Hymn. It is the first of these two areas which I should like to explore briefly here, though I realise that the two are to some extent interconnected.

The idea that Messianic expectations find expression in the Hymn to the Fathers is not unrepresented among older commentators such as SMEND and PETERS. On a verse such as xlvii 11 SMEND can say, "Gemeint ist das ewige Königtum des Hauses David"[2]), while PETERS, on xlvii 22 this time, has, "Der ganze Vers blickt auf die messianische Zukunft"[3]). The pro-Messianic view continues to find expression in works such as those of KLAUSNER[4]) and MAERTENS[5]) and in an article by SIEBENECK which is fairly heavily dependent on the monograph of MAERTENS[6]). The opposite view, that there are no Messianic concepts in Ben Sira, finds expression primarily in an article by André CAQUOT[7]) and subsequently, for example, in the monographs of MIDDENDORP[8]) and STADELMANN[9]). There is still disagreement, then, even in recent literature on him, as to whether or not Ben Sira, particularly in the Hymn to the Fathers, contains references to a Davidic Messiah. Let us look at those passages, brief and isolated though they are, which are usually cited in support of the Messianic theory and try to see whether they are capable of bearing the Messianic interpretations sometimes put upon them or whether such interpretations make these texts say more than they do.

The initially most obvious place to look for indications of Davidic Messianism is in that portion of the Hymn which deals with David (xlvii 1-11), and there we discover that it is the final verse which is usually considered to be the most relevant.

וירם לעולם קרנו: ג[ם] ייי העביר פשעו

וכסאו הכין על ירושלם: וֹיֹתֶן לֹו חק מַמלכת

Two expressions here have been thought to have Messianic overtones: "He exalted his horn for ever" and "He gave him the decree of the kingdom (or a royal decree)". Two questions are raised: Does קרן ("horn") have a Messianic connotation? And what is meant by חק ממלכת ("royal decree")? Primarily, in the Old Testament context, קרן is used as a symbol of strength and power, and it is indeed used twice in that sense in this section on David, in verse 5, where David's defeat of Goliath has the result of "lifting up the horn of his people", that is of exalting the power of the Israelites, and in verse 7, where his defeat of the Philistines and his subsequent settlement of former Philistine territory is described as his having "broken in pieces their power (literally, "their horn") to this day", that is definitively.

A more specifically royal significance for קרן may be found in two places in the Old Testament. The first of these is in Ps. cxxxii 17, a context which is concerned with the establishment of the Davidic dynasty, and, since it is a specifically liturgical context, its concern may well be with an annually recurring reaffirmation of the continuance of that dynasty. The second use of קרן in a royal sense is in Daniel chapters vii and viii, where the word is used as a symbol for various Macedonian and Seleucid rulers. In the Daniel context there is no Messianic idea in the use of קרן as a royal symbol, and even in the case of Ps. cxxxii there is uncertainty as to whether the reference is simply to the "strength" (קרן in that sense) of the Davidic dynasty or whether, as in Daniel, it symbolises the Davidic king or the succession of Davidic kings. It is by no means certain that it refers to a Messianic king[10]). The verb used in Ps. cxxxii 17, however, is אצמיח "I shall cause to sprout", and the same verb is used with קרן as its object also in Ezek. xxix 21. Some commentators follow the Babylonian Talmud in seeing in the Ezekiel passage a reference to the future son of David, but it seems from the context to refer rather to an approaching deliverance for Israel[11]). The verb in Ben Sira, however, is not the potentially Messianic hiphil of צמח but the more frequently occurring hiphil of רום. As we have already noted, קרן occurs twice earlier in the David pericope in the more normal sense of "strength, might", and it seems likely, therefore, that its third occurrence, in verse 11, is in this same sense. The only factor which might give us slight pause in that judgement is the statement that David's "horn" is exalted by Yahweh "for ever" (לעולם). While the expression "to exalt the horn" is not Messianic, the addition of לעולם may add to it Messianic overtones, especially in view of the immediately following idea that Yahweh gives to him a חק ממלכת.

This latter expression recalls the חק יהוה of Ps. ii 7, where the reference is usually thought to be to the royal protocol granted to the king on his accession, but most commentators on Ben Sira refer the expression to 2 Sam. vii 12-16 which is part of Nathan's "decree" establishing the Davidic dynasty. Both CAQUOT and, following him, STADELMANN make much of the fact that Ben Sira omits (and the implication is, "deliberate-ly") any reference to the fact that the dynasty is to be an "everlasting" one[12]). While 2 Sam. vii 16 indeed affirms that David's throne will be established "for ever" (עד עולם), for Ben Sira it is established "over Jerusalem" (or "Israel", if one prefers the reading of the Greek and Syriac texts to that of the Hebrew). Neither CAQUOT nor STADELMANN observes that the expression לעולם has occurred earlier in the verse, so that while the everlasting nature of the dynasty is not made explicit by Ben Sira, the possibility is not to be dismissed out of hand that the im-plicit assumption behind the expressions he uses is Messianic.

The final verse of the pericope on Solomon, xlvii 22, is usually regard-ed as a more secure reference to Davidic Messianism than the verse which we have just looked at.

... ‏[א]ל לא יטוש חסד	ולא יפיל מדבריו ארצה:
לא ... ‏ו. נין ונכד	‏[ואוה]בֿיו לא ישמיד:
ויתן ל. ...	‏ולבֿ[ניֿת] ... ‏.שֿ:

Unfortunately here the for us potentially most significant parts of the verse are fragmentary in the Hebrew text. There are, however, a number of possibly significant vocabulary elements here. The word חסד in verse 22a occurs in 2 Sam. vii 15 and in Ps. lxxxix 34 in contexts where Yahweh vows not to remove it from the Davidic ruler. Here the promise is that "God will not abandon חסד'", will not break faith with the Davidic line. The words missing at the beginning of the second line of the verse (22cd) have been reconstructed, on the basis of the Greek, as

לא יכרית בחירו נין ונכד

and it has been pointed out that בחירו in the singular, "His chosen one", is used of David in Ps. lxxxix 4 and that the verb בחר is used in other similar contexts of the choice by Yahweh of David as king[13]). It might even be argued that in Ps. lxxxix 4 the reference is not so much to the historical David but to the Davidic ruler generally. The significance of this point, however, is somewhat lessened by the fact that the parallel word in the second half of the line, ואוהביו, although again a partial reconstruction, is clearly a plural form and that instead of בחירו ''His chosen one'' we should read בחיריו ''His chosen ones'', a less certain reference to Davidic rulers. The reference is probably to collective ''Israel'', a meaning which the expression appears to have in xlvi 1.

It is the third line of the verse, however (22ef), which is potentially the most significant and which is, unfortunately, the most fragmentary. It can be reconstructed on the basis of, for example, the Greek and taking into account what can be read of the Hebrew:

ויתן ליעקב שארית   ולבית דוד ממנו שרש

Both שארית and שרש are concepts which are found in the Isaianic corpus, the latter more particularly in the context of promises about the Davidic dynasty. In Isa. xi 1 the promise is that from the ''roots'' of the defunct dynasty a new monarch will arise to recover the throne of David, while in verse 10 the ''root'', with a decided shift in imagery from verse 1, has been thought by many to refer to a Messianic Davidic ruler[14]). This final part of the verse in Ben Sira has been thought to refer to the past and to say simply that in spite of Solomon's laxity which brought about the division of the kingdoms (verse 21), nevertheless throughout the remaining history of the kingdom of Judah there was never any lack of a Davidic ruler to occupy the throne in accordance with Yahweh's promise of old[15]). However, SMEND makes the point that the verb at the beginning of this third line should be read not as a Waw Consecutive Imperfect (וַיִּתֵן) but as an Imperfect with simple waw (וְיִתֵן), having a future reference. The earlier verbs in the verse are unmistakable imperfects, almost certainly with a future sense. There seems little justification for a modern translation such as that of SAUER into German, for example, to translate *all* of the verbs as past tenses, as if in a kind of retrogressive assimilation from the opening verb of the third line (ויתן) understood as a Waw Consecutive Imperfect[16]). In fact, in line with SMEND, it might be argued that the future implications of the imperfects of the earlier parts of the verse have their logical outcome in a future sense for the verb of the third line as well: ''He will give...''[17]). If an argument for a future sense of this verse as a whole were to carry conviction, then we would once more need to be cautious about dismissing out of hand, as does, for example, STADELMANN, those assertions of the older commentators that the verse ''looks to the Messianic future''[18]).

Yet another verse which is not so often cited in this connection is xlix 11

:... ל.. אׄ..   מׄה [ננ]דׄל ...

again a fragmentary verse in Hebrew which may perhaps be read as

מה נגדל את זרבבל   והוא על יד ימין כחותם

a restoration which may be made partly on the basis of the Greek translation and partly on the basis of Haggai ii 23 which seems to be being
quoted here. In Jer. xxii 24 it is said by Yahweh of "Coniah the son of
Jehoiakim", that is Jehoiachin, that though he were "the signet ring on
my right hand" yet Yahweh would destroy him, where the "signet ring"
is used figuratively for Yahweh's particular care. The same image is used
by Haggai to refer to Zerubbabel, and it is this image that Ben Sira picks
up here in xlix 11. There are a number of vocabulary elements in the
Haggai verse which give to it a fairly distinctive Messianic character. It
begins with the expression ביום ההוא ("on that day"); Zerubbabel is
described in it (Yahweh is the speaker) as עבדי ("my servant") and the
one whom Yahweh has chosen (בחרתי)[19]. It is in this context that Zerubbabel is also described as a "signet ring" (חותם). As a recent commen-
tator has said, "The final colon of v. 23 corroborates fully this assessment
of Haggai's oracle as a speech in which Haggai addressed the Davidic
Zerubbabel as if he were to have royal status at some future time"[20]).
Ben Sira cannot have been unaware of these Davidic-Messianic overtones when he chose to quote this verse as his cameo portrait of Zerubbabel. In such a light, again, one cannot categorically deny any Davidic-
Messianic concepts and ideas to Ben Sira, as has so readily been done in
the more recent literature on him.

In a verse from his pericope on Elijah, too, it is clear that he was not
unaware of such an area of thought, and here again he goes to the Book of
the Twelve to pick up what Malachi has tentatively said about Elijah.
The verse in question in Ben Sira is xlviii 10:

להשבית אף לפנ[י] .... :   הכתוב נכון לעת
ולהכין ש.. .ל: להשיב לב אבות על בנים

Here the opening word tells us that what follows is a scriptural quotation,
though direct quotation does not in fact occur until the second line of the
verse. Nevertheless, the first line is already sufficiently clearly an allusion
to Mal. iii 23f. where the temporal expression qualifying Yahweh's sending of Elijah, namely "before the great and terrible day of Yahweh
comes" is what is resumed succinctly here in Ben Sira in the single word
לעת. The purpose of Elijah's being in a state of "readiness" (נכון) is expressed by three infinitive phrases. The first of these is incomplete, but
something of the nature of חרון, expressing the all-consuming nature of
Yahweh's wrath, seems likely as the final word of the line[21]). This could
also be regarded as an allusion to Mal. iii 23b since it is "the great and

terrible day'' that would be the occasion of the outpouring of Yahweh's
wrath. The second infinitive phrase is a direct quotation of Mal. iii 24aα
with verse 24aβ included by implication. Elijah's second function, then,
is to restore family harmony and unity in the face of Yahweh's wrath and
judgment, ''to reconcile fathers to sons (and sons to fathers)''. The third,
though again fragmentary in Hebrew, is an allusion to rather than a
quotation of Isa. xlix 6, where one of the functions of the Servant in that
second Servant Song (xlix 1-6) is להקים את שבטי יעקב. The reading of the
infinitive in the Hebrew of Ben Sira (להכין) is not in doubt, but there
seems to be no great difference in sense between the hiphil of קום and that
of כון. The Isaiah phrase speaks of ''the tribes of Jacob'', the immediately following phrase having the parallel expression ''the preserved of
Israel''. What we seem to have in what remains of Ben Sira's Hebrew is
the first letter of שבטי and the final letter of ישראל. It may be worth noting
in passing that in the Isaiah verse the first Isaiah scroll from Qumran
(1QIsaᵃ) has the proper names reversed (''the tribes of Israel''/''the
preserved of Jacob''). This appears to be the reading in Ben Sira as well.
This third function of Elijah in Ben Sira's view is the restoration of national harmony and unity, balancing the restoration of family unity in the
second infinitive phrase. This function is one that the prophetic tradition
attributes to the Servant of Yahweh. Ben Sira associates it with Elijah
here, and he makes a similar allusion to the phrase, though this time in
the MT wording שבטי יעקב, in xxxvi 11: ''Gather all the tribes of Jacob,
that they may receive their inheritance as in days of old.'' The person addressed here by the imperative is Yahweh. Chapter xxxvi is described by
Hengel as a ''prayer for the eschatological liberation from heathen and
Seleucid rule''[22]) and receives qualified acceptance as an expression of
eschatological nationalism even by Caquot[23]). It is in Mal. iii 1, 23f. that
the concept of Elijah as a Messianic forerunner has its roots. It was
Strack-Billerbeck who suggested that this reference in Ben Sira xlviii
10 is the earliest passage to refer to Malachi in this way and that in attributing to a returning Elijah one of the tasks of the Servant of Yahweh
Ben Sira seems to regard Elijah as some kind of Messianic personality, as
an instrument of Yahweh's deliverance of His people[24]). While one
would certainly wish to agree with Stadelmann that for Ben Sira Elijah
was certainly not ''the Messiah''[25]), it can nevertheless scarcely be
doubted that in linking the Malachi passage with the Deutero-Isaiah one
Ben Sira was attributing to the returning Elijah figure some kind of
redemptive function vis-à-vis his people[26]).

   There has been, in those verses which we have looked at so far, no explicit reference to the Davidic covenant, though the expression חק ממלכת
of xlvii 11 *may* be such a one. A specific reference to it does, however, oc-

cur in xlv 25, a verse which is part of the extensive Aaron-Phinehas pericope (xlv 6-26).[27])

ברית שלום לכלכל מקדש: כהונה גדולה עד עולם: בן ישי למטה יהודה: נחלת אהרן לכל זרעו: המעטר אתכם כבוד:	24 לכן גם לו הקים חק אשר תהיה לו ולזרעו 25 ונם בריתו עם דוד נחלת אש לפני כבודו ועתה ברכו נא את ייי הטוב

In verse 24 we are told how Yahweh has established an "ordinance" (חק, the same word as is used in the David context in xlvii 11) with Phinehas, and this חק is then further described as a ברית שלום ("a covenant of well-being"). Then verse 25 goes on to say that Yahweh's ברית is also "with David", and here we have an unequivocal reference to a Davidic covenant. It is when we try to enquire more closely into what the second line of verse 25 might tell us of the nature of this covenant in Ben Sira's view, that we run into difficulties. As BEENTJES rightly says, verse 25, especially 25cd, is a *crux interpretum*.[28])

The majority of the early commentators, basing themselves mainly on the sense of the Greek translation, see in verse 25cd either some kind of contrast or some kind of parallel between the inheritance situation in monarchical circles and that of priestly, and especially high-priestly, circles[29]). In order to achieve this kind of exegesis, however, textual emendation of the first part of the line (verse 25c) has to be resorted to in greater or lesser degree. Everyone regards אש as *scriptio defectiva* for איש ("man"), and LEVI, followed by BOX and OESTERLEY, then emends that to מלך on the basis of the Greek and the Syriac. While SMEND retains לפני כבודו and asserts that "a man before his glory" refers to Solomon, though without explaining why he thinks that is what that phrase means, some of the others emend these two words to לבנו לבדו ("for his son alone"). The outcome of such major reconstruction may be translated as follows:

> The inheritance of a king is for his son alone,
> While the inheritance of Aaron is for all his descendants[30]).

No one, it seems to me, really makes very clear what precisely this means, and in any case one wonders whether one should not be taking the Hebrew text a little more seriously than to subject it to such cavalier emendation.

Only two scholars, STADELMANN and BEENTJES, as far as I can see, take the Hebrew text seriously, and both in very different ways suggest that what this verse expresses is the idea that the Aaronite high-priesthood has taken over the rights and privileges originally accorded to the Davidic monarch[31]). STADELMANN is also one of those who read איש = אֵשׁ, but otherwise he is faithful to the Hebrew as it stands. The double נחלה of 25cd is the predicate of a nominal sentence the subject of which is the בריתו עם דוד of 25a. The sense then is: "(The Davidic covenant) is the heritage of a man in the face of His glory (where the pronominal suffix of כבודו refers to Yahweh), the heritage of Aaron for all his descendants". 25c and 25d, he argues, are in apposition to each other, not parallel or contrasted as earlier commentators had suggested, and what they say is that the Davidic covenant has been "inherited" by the Aaronite high-priests. The "man in the face of His glory" is the high-priest himself, for the sanctuary where he officiates is the dwelling place of the "glory of Yahweh", the כבוד יהוה. It is to Aaron's descendants in the high-priestly office that has fallen the inheritance of the Davidic covenant.

BEENTJES reaches much the same conclusion, but in a different way. He begins in verse 24 and regards the syntax as running on from verse 24 into verse 25, thereby explaining why there is no verb in verse 25ab. The "ordinance" (חק) is established with Phinehas

> ...so that to him and to his descendants should belong
> the high-priesthood for ever,
> but also His covenant with David
> the son of Jesse from the tribe of Judah.

The "covenant with David" is thus to be regarded as in apposition to "the high-priesthood", and both belong "to him (that is, Phinehas) and his descendants for ever". Without even taking verse 25cd into consideration, BEENTJES has made the same point as STADELMANN. BEENTJES does not neglect the difficulty of the next part of verse 25 (cd). He regards it as referring not to David, not even partly so, but to Phinehas and his descendants. To them belong not only the high-priesthood and the Davidic covenant but also

> the heritage of fire before His glory,
> the heritage of Aaron for all his descendants.

Here, too, the pronominal suffix of כבודו refers to Yahweh, but BEENTJES retains איש = אֵשׁ, firmly anchoring the verse within the high-priestly institution of the cult.

BEENTJES' analysis and discussion seem to me to be more refined than those of STADELMANN, perhaps because he discusses the Aaron and Phinehas pericopes together and indeed regards them as a unit[32]), whereas STADELMANN, although he discusses both pericopes (Aaron and Phinehas) in the course of his work, deals with them separately and in

quite different chapters of his book[33]). BEENTJES makes the additional interesting point that, corresponding to what we might call this ''Davidis-
ing'' of the Aaronite (high-)priesthood in the Phinehas pericope, there is
in the David pericope what we might call the ''Aaronising'' of David
with, in xlvii 8-10, an emphasis being laid on his role in the establishing
of the cult and, in xlvii 2, a cultic image being used to depict David's
emergence in Israel[34]).

Both of these views, that of STADELMANN and that of BEENTJES, have the
great merit of taking seriously the Hebrew text of xlv 25. Both of them
reach what seems to me to be a correct view of the verse in question,
namely that it represents an expression of the idea that what was once
promised to the Davidic dynasty has now been ''inherited'' by the
Aaronite high-priesthood. On balance, BEENTJES' approach seems to be
the more comprehensive of the two and is to be preferred. His approach
has the added advantage of reading אש as אֵ֫שׁ[35]), and in this he is surely
correct. I know of no other place where אִישׁ is written defectively. Even if
one were to follow STADELMANN's approach, however, need one
necessarily follow him to his conclusion that Ben Sira had an extremely
negative attitude to any concept of Davidic Messianism?[36]) It is, I hope,
clear from the passages we have looked at earlier that ''Messianic'' ideas,
of however unfocussed a variety, were not entirely foreign to Ben Sira's
thought. Both STADELMANN's view and BEENTJES' view of xlv 24f. assume
the making of promises by Yahweh to the Davidic dynasty, and it is these
promises that are the seed-bed of Davidic Messianism. The growth of
such Messianism had begun long before the time of Ben Sira, and he cannot have been ignorant of such a growth. In his book Ben Sira is not, of
course, propounding Messianic teaching, so Messianic teaching does not
become explicit, but the book is surely not as devoid of an awareness of
such ideas nor of expressions of them as STADELMANN, for example,
would have us believe.

But the main interest of xlv 25 is not that it mentions the Davidic covenant but that it associates it with the Aaronite high-priesthood. Earlier in
the Aaron-Phinehas pericope reference has been made to an ''eternal ordinance'' and an ''eternal covenant''. In the former case (xlv 7) it is
Aaron himself who *is* the חק עולם, while in the latter (xlv 15) it is the in-
stallation to the priesthood and the duties which that involves which has
''become an eternal covenant for him and for his descendants for
ever''[37]). It would perhaps be going too far to speak of priestly Messianism here, but such a feeling is certainly in the air.

I had already pointed out in my earlier article that these motifs were
not far removed from the kinds of expressions Ben Sira was using, even if
he does not make them explicit, and that in xlv 25, where Davidic cove-

nant and priestly aristocracy combine, we are coming close to the two
Messiahs of Qumran, when I discovered an article by PRIEST which suggested just that[38]). BEENTJES dismisses PRIEST in a footnote and says that
no one has followed him in his idea[39]), but he reads rather more into
PRIEST than PRIEST actually says. PRIEST is, in fact, very cautious in what
he suggests, and it is no more than that "Ben Sira holds to the 'two
covenants' as the men of Qumran did to the 'two Messiahs'"[40]). At the
basis of Ben Sira's "two covenants" idea and of the priestly inheriting of
the royal one lies the great esteem which he has for the priesthood as an
institution. This is clear from a number of passages in his book. One
thinks for example of vii 29ff. which begins, "With all your heart fear
God and reverence His priests", but above all of the amount of space he
devotes to "priesthood" in the Hymn to the Fathers, in the combined
eulogies of Aaron and Phinehas in xlv 6-26 and in the final culmination of
the Hymn with its praise of Simon in l 1-21(24). It may even be that Ben
Sira was himself a priest, as has been argued by a number of scholars[41]).
But it is the way in which Ben Sira has the "Davidic covenant", with all
that that implies and has implied through the centuries since the exile,
pass into the hands of those who have inherited the "priestly covenant"
which is significant here and which moves, as PRIEST puts it, "much
more pointedly in the direction utilized by the group which finally shaped
the two Messiah teaching"[42]).

Jeremiah xxxiii 17-26 has often been pointed to as if it were a kind of
forerunner of what Ben Sira is saying here. Chronologically, these verses,
usually thought to be a later addition to the Jeremiah material, may mark
a step along the road which Ben Sira is taking here, but there the two
covenants are simply laid side by side. Ben Sira's contribution to the
development, if development there is, is to suggest the absorption of the
two covenants by a single group. It may well be, too, that the psalm
which occurs only in the Hebrew text of Ben Sira between verses 12 and
13 of chapter li, and thought by many to be not original, is a further step
along this same road, especially with its extolling in adjacent verses of the
horn that is caused to sprout for the house of David and of the choice of
one of the sons of Zadok as priest[43]).

These ideas, then, were in the air in Ben Sira's time and were
doubtless shared by various groups, one of which eventually formed the
Qumran community and developed further an idea which happens to
find expression in a tentative way in Ben Sira but which was almost certainly not his exclusive property. Ben Sira's expression of this idea was
doubtless occasioned by particular political and religious circumstances
of the time[44]), but this raises a host of other questions beyond the scope of
the present article. I shall return briefly to this point in a moment by way

of conclusion, but let us examine briefly a final, potentially Messianic figure in the Hymn, namely Adam[45]).

Adam occurs once in the Hymn to the Fathers, not, as one might suppose, at the beginning, but just before the final panegyric of the high-priest Simon, in xlix 16:

וְעַל כָּל חַי תִּפְאֶרֶת אָדָם: וְשֵׁם וְשֵׁת וֶאֱנוֹשׁ נִפְקָדוּ

"Above all living is the glory of Adam"[46]). In verses 14 and 15 Ben Sira seems to be contrasting Enoch, who was "translated" without experiencing death, and Joseph, who dies in Egypt but whose bones were "translated" to Palestine. Shem, Seth and Enosh were also subject to the same laws of mortality as was Joseph, but in a special category of his own (עַל כָּל חַי) is "the glory of Adam"[47]). It was SMEND who first pointed to the Messianic potential of this view of the first man. This assessment of him, says SMEND, has its roots in the Messianic hope which sought its ideal in the past and carried that back to the beginning of the world[48]). Box and OESTERLEY perhaps sound an early cautious note when, admitting that "this idealization of Adam is a notable feature and occurs here for the first time in Jewish literature", they go on to point out that this idea *later* plays an important part in the development of Messianic doctrine and suggest that it is precarious to impute such an idea to Ben Sira[49]).

JACOB, in a 1957 article, picks up the reference to Adam, and, while it is the term "*eschatologie adamique*" which he uses in his article, there is no real reason why he should not have used the expression "*messianisme adamique*", since he cites SMEND with approval and points out that Ben Sira sees Adam not as the first in a line but as the source and possibility of a new beginning[50]). JACOB believes that this "Adamic eschatology" has its origins in wisdom circles, and STADELMANN, too, regards Enoch and Joseph as well as Adam as figures which are specially important for late Jewish wisdom tradition[51]). The idea of Adam as the first wise man is found already in Job xv 7 and continues, apart from this reference in xlix 16, in Tobit viii 6ff. and in Wisdom x 1f. It appears in Qumran in 1QH xvii 15 ("Thou wilt cause them to inherit all the glory of Adam and abundance of days") and, according to LEBRAM, in the Qumran Psalms Scroll (11QPsᵃ), column 18. CAQUOT is, of course, critical of this "eschatological" view of Adam[52]). He believes that, for Ben Sira, Adam, glorified "above all living" because he was created not by man but by God, is the ancestor not of all mankind but specifically of Israel. Even if one were to suppose that Wisdom was incarnate in Adam, along the lines, for example, of Job xv 7, one could not attribute to such a figure any eschatological role, since for Ben Sira Wisdom was active and present there and then in Israel both in the Law as practised and in the cult as celebrated.

But neither CAQUOT nor those who favour a Messianic/eschatological conception of Adam have observed in this connection the Adam-Messiah relationship which it is perhaps possible to discern in the second Dream-Vision of Enoch (1 Enoch lxxxv-xc). In 1 Enoch lxxxv 3 we read: "I saw in a vision on my bed, and behold a bull came out of the earth, and that bull was white"[53]) and it is clearly Adam who is represented by the white bull. The "white bull" imagery is maintained up to and including Isaac, but with the birth of Jacob/Israel the animal imagery is transformed to that of sheep, a common enough image for Israel as a people. Only towards the end of this second dream vision does the figure of a white bull return:. "And I saw how a white bull was born, and its horns were big, and all the wild animals and all the birds of heaven were afraid of it and entreated it continually. And I looked until all their species were transformed, and they all became white bulls" (xc 37f.). There are two aspects of this about which we must be cautious. The first is the date of the Dream-Visions (1 Enoch lxxxiii-xc). There is fairly general agreement that the author wrote sometime during the early Maccabean period[54]), though NICKELSBURG hints that such a dating might be of a revision of a somewhat earlier original. How much earlier he does not say. The second cautionary aspect is the precise identity of the white bull of xc 37. There are some who would accept that it represents the Messiah[55]), while others, notably MILIK, would argue that it represents, rather, a "second Adam"[56]). It is beyond the scope of this article to enter into a discussion of these views, though it may be noted that BLACK does not feel that MILIK's view necessarily rules out Messianic implications. Suffice it to say that in a period not much later than that of Ben Sira, or possibly, if NICKELSBURG's suggestion that the present form of the text is a revision of a somewhat earlier original is correct, even more nearly contemporary with him, we have, as JACOB had suggested for Ben Sira himself, an "*eschatologie adamique*" or possibly even an "Adamic Messianism". In this case, too, then we should be careful about dismissing, as categorically as does CAQUOT, that this is indeed what we have in Ben Sira's Hymn to the Fathers.

It is here that I come back, by way of conclusion, to CAQUOT. His prime argument against the possibility of any Messianic ideas being found in Ben Sira is that the political, social and religious situation of Ben Sira's day was too stable for Messianic ideas of any kind to have any currency: "He cannot make room for a Messiah who would overthrow an economy believed to be eternal...Situated in a period where the institutions on which the hierocracy of Jerusalem had reposed for more than three centuries, Ben Sira remains satisfied with the internal order in which he lives.''[57]) Whether we can still regard this as the case may be doubted. The usual view is that the stability of the Jewish theocratic state was not really disturbed until the intransigence of Antiochus Epiphanes brought about the Maccabean uprising and that it was not until the subsequent emergence of Hasmonean pretensions to both throne and high-priesthood that we see the real emergence of ''sects'' in Judaism to any great extent. It is, however, worth noting that a recent study by Roger BECKWITH[58]) of the pre-history of the relationships of Pharisees, Sadducees and Essenes suggests that the antecedents of these various groupings are to be found not during the Hellenizing crisis of 175 B.C. and later but before it. Just as the beginnings of apocalyptic writings are to be found back in the mid-third century B.C., so the tensions which give rise to the various later sects are also to be found in that earlier period. BECKWITH dates the emergence of proto-Essene and proto-Sadducean movements, both as reactions to proto-Pharisaic lay conservatism, in the mid-third century B.C. He does not feel that there was open division before about 187 B.C., the date of the accession of Onias III as High Priest, but one of his pieces of evidence, namely that the names of the three parties did not exist before then, is an argument from silence. He admits that the very existence of the two reforming schools of thought (proto-Essenism and proto-Sadduceeism) was a major cause of change in the early second century B.C. That early second century world in which Ben Sira lived and wrote may have been not at all as stable and secure as CAQUOT has suggested. If that is so, CAQUOT's main argument against Messianic elements in Ben Sira is decidedly weakened. Most of those who accept CAQUOT's view on this simply cite him with approval and adduce no fresh arguments in defence of their point of view.

Just as Ben Sira, in various parts of his book, may, as I have tried to show in my earlier article, have been influenced by the apocalyptic thinking of those who were his near contemporaries, simply because all these ideas were in the wind, so too ideas about Messianism, though never formulated by him into any kind of ''doctrine'', are nevertheless present in his work and especially in parts of the Hymn to the Fathers, however much, for various reasons, we might prefer not to find them there.

NOTES

[1]) 'Ben Sira—A Child of his Time'', in *A Word in Season. Essays in Honour of William McKane*, ed. James D. Martin and Phillip R. Davies (JSOT Supplement Series 42), Sheffield 1986, 141-161.

[2]) R. SMEND, *Die Weisheit Jesus Sirach* (Berlin, 1906), 452.

³) N. Peters, *Das Buch Jesus Sirach* (Exegetisches Handbuch zum alten Testament, Vol. 25; Münster, 1913), 408.

⁴) J. Klausner, *The Messianic Idea in Israel* (ET y W. F. Stinespring of the 3rd Hebrew edn., London, 1956), 252-8.

⁵) Dom Th. Maertens, *L'Eloge des Pères* (*Ecclésiastique XLIV-L*) (Collection Lumière et Vie, 5; Bruges, 1956).

⁶) R. T. Siebeneck, "May their bones return to life!—Sirach's Praise of the Fathers", *CBQ* 21 (1959), 411-428. A. A. Di Lella, *The Hebrew Text of Sirach* (The Hague, 1966), in the course of a discussion on the genuineness of the Psalm which occurs in the Hebrew text between li 12 and li 13, also points to "Davidic Messiah" references in a number of verses in the Hymn.

⁷) A. Caquot, "Ben Sira et le Messianisme", *Semitica* XVI (1966), 43-68 (L'eschatologie du Siracide n'a rien de messianique", 67).

⁸) Th. Middendorp, *Die Stellung Jesus ben Siras zwischen Judentum und Hellenismus* (Leiden, 1973, 117) ("Ben Sira selbst hat keinen davidischen Messias erwartet").

⁹) H. Stadelmann, *Ben Sira als Schriftgelehrter* (Tübingen, 1980), 160-167 ("So fehlt bei Ben Sira jede ausdrückliche Messiaserwartung", 166).

¹⁰) See, e.g., A. A. Anderson, *The Psalms* (New Century Bible, 1972), Vol. II, 885.

¹¹) W. Zimmerli, *Ezekiel 2* (ET J. D. Martin, Philadelphia, 1983), 120.

¹²) Caquot 55; Stadelmann, 161.

¹³) E.g. 2 Sam, vi 21; 1 Kings viii· 16; Ps. lxxxix 20.

¹⁴) The idea that it may be collective and be a figurative representation of the post-exilic community of Judah which will act as "an ensign" for the still scattered diaspora is favoured by R. E. Clements, *Isaiah 1-39* (New Century Bible, 1980), 125.

¹⁵) So, e.g. Middendorp, 67 ("Vermutlich...") and Stadelmann, 161f. ("...die historische Notiz...").

¹⁶) Georg Sauer, *Jesus Sirach* (Jüdische Schriften aus hellenistisch-römischer Zeit, III, 5; Gütersloh, 1981), 625. Oesterley has a very ambivalent attitude to the terse sequence. In his Cambridge Bible commentary (1912) he has: "will never forsake...will not destroy...nor blot out...will not take away...*he gave*". In his translation (along with G. H. Box in R. H. Charles, *Apocrypha and Pseudepigrapha*, Vol. I (1913), 498f., he has: "did not forsake...nor did he suffer...will not cut off...nor will he destroy...*he will give*". In the translation published in SPCK's series "Translations of Early Documents" (1916) he has (136): "did not forsake...and suffered not...will not cut off...will not destroy...*he gave*". The 1912 volume is a commentary on the Revised Version which was translating the Greek. In the 1913 version he is translating the Hebrew text where available, and his commentary is substantially indebted to that of Smend (1906). The 1916 volume follows Smend's edition of the Hebrew text where available, and his comment on xlvii 22 is that his translation is a "reconstructed text".

¹⁷) The imperfect with simple waw "is common in all periods of the language" (A. B. Davidson, *Hebrew Syntax*, § 85), and by the time of Mishaic Hebrew "the Consecutive Tenses have practically disappeared" (H. M. Segal, *A Grammar of Mishnaic Hebrew* § 156). See also S. R. Driver, *Hebrew Tenses* §§ 130-134.

¹⁸) So Peters (1913), 408; Smend (1906), 457 speaks of the "Messiashoffnung" of the verse, and he is followed by Box and Oesterley (1913), 499 "a reference to the Messianic hope". Baumgartner, "Die literarischen Gattungen in der Weisheit des Jesus Sirach", *ZAW* 34 (1914), 188 describes the verse as a whole as a "Verheissung von der Endzeit und ihrem König".

¹⁹) See the discussion above on the occurrence and significance of בחיר/בחר in the context of xlvii 22.

²⁰) David L. Petersen, *Haggai and Zechariah 1-8* (SCM Old Testament Library, 1984), 102-6, quotation from 104.

²¹) So, e.g. M. S. Segal, *Sēpher ben Sira ha-shālēm*, ad loc.; P. C. Beentjes, *Jesus Sirach en Tenach* (Nieuwegein, 1981), 40.

²²) M. Hengel, *Jews, Greeks and Barbarians* (ET London, 1980), 47.

²³) Caquot, 49f. Hengel also points to the concluding formula of the prayer (xxxvi

llcd), with its varied echoes of Deutero-Isaiah, as showing "that universal breadth which becomes typical of Jewish apocalyptic in Hellenistic times" (48).

[24]) H. L. STRACK-Paul BILLERBECK, *Kommentar zum Neuen Testament aus Talmud und Midrasch* (Munich, 1926), IV, 779f.

[25]) STADELMANN, 165f.

[26]) C. R. NORTH, *The Suffering Servant in Deutero-Isaiah* (Oxford, 2nd edition 1956), 7 is correct in stating that this passage tells us nothing about Ben Sira's view of the figure of the Servant of Yahweh, whether he is to be seen as an individual or as a Messianic figure. What Ben Sira is doing is borrowing language describing a redemptive function, which in Deutero-Isaiah is attributed to the Servant of Yahweh (whoever or whatever that might be), and using it to amplify the functions of the returning Elijah, who has already been singled out for some kind of "end time" activity by Malachi. It may be worth noting here the definition of Messianism given by J. LUST in a paper read to the 1983 IOSOT Congress in Salamanca and recently published in J. A. EMERTON (ed.), *Congress Volume, Salamanca 1983* (SVT XXXVI, Leiden 1985), 174-191: "Messianism is the expectation of an individual human and yet transcendent saviour. He is to come in a final eschatological period and will establish God's Kingdom on earth. In a more strict sense, messianism is the expectation of a royal Davidic saviour at the end time" (175). The looser sense of this definition seems to fit Ben Sira's Isaiah-coloured view of Elijah.

[27]) Although this section deals with Aaron in verses 6-22 and with Phinehas separately in verses 23-26, there are strong linguistic and structural grounds for regarding these two component parts as forming a single unit. See BEENTJES, 186f., part of his discussion of the combined section, 175-199.

[28]) BEENTJES, 188.

[29]) I. LÉVI, *L'Ecclésiastique. La Sagesse de Jésus, fils de Sira. Texte original hébreu*, Vol. I (Paris, 1898), 107: "Le premier hemistiche doit se rapporter à David, et le second à Aron: il doit donc y avoir un parallèle entre les deux." SMEND (1906), 427f.: "Parallelisiert wird die hochpriesterliche Succession mit der königlichen...und *nach Gr. Syr.* (my italics) will der Verf. nur sagen, dass das Hohepriestertum allein dem Pinehas und seinen Nachkommen gehört wie das Königtum allein dem Salomo und seinen Nachkommen." OESTERLEY (1912), 312: "Ben Sira wishes to draw a parallel between the succession of the high-priesthood and the royal succession...As God made a covenant with David that his descendants should succeed him on the throne, so He made a covenant with Aaron that his descendants should succeed him in the high-priesthood." Box and OESTERLEY (1913), 498f.: "Apparently the second line forms the antithesis to line one. If so the meaning may have been: the power and the privileges of the king, as sovereign, are transmissible only to his son, viz. by direct succession: whereas the power of the priesthood belongs to, in a sense, and is inherent in every member of the priestly tribe, all Aaron's descendants, in fact, together with Aaron himself. Others see no antithesis but, on the contrary, a parallel statement...There is probably some allusion intended to contemporary events..." PETERS (1913), 392: "Der Sinn ist: Wie die königliche Würde an die Familie des David, so ist die hohepriesterliche an die des Phinees gebunden."

[30]) Even those who retain איש = איש still take the first part of the line to refer to royal succession.

[31]) STADELMANN's discussion of the verse is on 149-159, while BEENTJES' is on 186-192.

[32]) See above n. 27.

[33]) Phinehas, 146-176 in a chapter entitled "Ben Siras Stellung zu Priestertum und Kultus"; Aaron, 275-281 in a chapter entitled "Schriftgelehrsamkeit und weisheitliche Volkserziehung bei Ben Sira". He deals with xlv 25e-26 in *both* places, 173-176 *and* 282-284. STADELMANN's way of dealing with the text is determined by the thesis of his book.

[34]) BEENTJES, 187. The emphasis on David's "cultic" role is in line with the Chronicler's presentation of him, as BEENTJES says. I have in my earlier article drawn attention to another association between Ben Sira and Chronistic historiography where the Chronicler's schematised presentation of history may possibly be paralleled in Ben Sira's "historical cameos" in the Hymn to the Fathers, and his "cult-centred historiography" is

certainly paralleled in Ben Sira's emphasis in the Hymn on the cult figures Aaron and Phinehas on the one hand and the High Priest Simon (1 1-21) on the other. The image in xlvii 2 is the strange expression "As the fat is 'lifted' from the offering, so was David from Israel".

[35]) The only other scholar who has this reading as far as I am aware is L. G. PERDUE, *Wisdom and Cult* (SBL Dissertation Series 30; Scholars Press, 1977), 193, but he follows the old line of a simple comparison between Davidic and Aaronic covenants and fails to see the full implications of the text in question.

[36]) STADELMANN, 166: "So fehlt bei Ben Sira jede ausdrückliche Messiaserwartung. Sein Augenmerk gilt nicht dem davidischen Königshaus, nicht einer zukünftigen Messiasgestalt, sondern der herrschenden Priesterklasse."

[37]) The final phrase is literally "as the days of heaven" (כימי שמים). BEENTJES (184f.) refers to this as an "unieke woordencombinatie". I find it difficult to know in what sense he is using the word "uniek". There is a similar but not identical usage in Deut. xi 21; it occurs in Ps. lxxxix 30, an occurrence which BEENTJES himself cites; and it occurs also in Ben Sira in l 24. But whatever he means by the word "uniek", BEENTJES is right to point to its significant occurrence in Ps. lxxxix 30, where it is found in the royal context of the Davidic covenant and of the promise that the Davidic throne will stand "for ever".

[38]) J. PRIEST, "Ben Sira 45, 25 in the Light of the Qumran Literature", *RQ* 5 (1964-66), 111-118.

[39]) BEENTJES, 188 n. 36.

[40]) PRIEST, 118.

[41]) This view is fundamental to STADELMANN's thesis, and it has been argued also by J. F. A. SAWYER, "Was Jeshua Ben Sira a Priest?", *Proceedings of the Eighth World Congress of Jewish Studies. Division a: The Period of the Bible* (Jerusalem, 1982), 65-71, with no reference to STADELMANN's work which was published in 1980.

[42]) PRIEST, 118.

[43]) The reference is to verses h and i (or viii and ix) of the psalm. The second of them is often translated in a plural sense, e.g. OESTERLEY (1916): "...that chooseth the sons of Zadok for *priests*', but the word כהן is singular in the Hebrew.

[44]) This was suggested already by SMEND (436) and others. STADELMANN has a brief discussion of the question, 155f.

[45]) SIEBENECK, in his article (426 n. 28), cites MAERTENS (95), who suggests that the descriptions applied to Moses by Ben Sira have so many eschatological overtones to them that what Ben Sira says of Moses can be regarded only as a prophecy of the new Moses. I find their arguments highly speculative and have therefore omitted Moses from consideration here.

[46]) There are problems with the meaning and originality of the verb נפקדו in the first part of the verse. LÉVI suggests reading נכברו on the basis of the Greek, and he is followed by PETERS and by BOX and OESTERLEY . SMEND prefers to follow the Syriac and read נבראו. נפקדו could perhaps be defended in the sense of "were buried", a sense which the same verb form is sometimes thought to have in reference to Joseph in verse 15. See, e.g., SAUER's translation, 630, where there is no indication that he is emending the text (to נקברו or the like?). For a further discussion of the verb and of the verse in general see now also S. D. FRADE, *Enosh and His Generation* (SBL Monograph Series, 30; Scholars Press, 1984), 12-16.

[47]) LÉVI takes אדם here not as a proper name but in the sense of "humanity". The sense of verses 14-16 in his view is that Enoch, Joseph, Shem, Seth and Enosh were all honoured (נכברו) and "were above all living, the glory of humanity"; so, too, Simon the High Priest as "the greatest among his brothers and the glory (תפארת again) of his people".

[48]) SMEND, 476.

[49]) BOX and OESTERLEY, 507.

[50]) Edmond JACOB, "L'histoire d'Israël vue par Ben Sira", in *Mélanges bibliques rédigées en l'honneur de M. André Robert* (Paris, 1957), 288-294; the point cited is from 294.

[51]) STADELMANN, 213. He refers to J. MARBÖCK, *Weisheit im Wandel. Untersuchungen zur*

Weisheitstheologie bei Ben Sira (BBB 37; Bonn, 1971), 131 n. 4 where there is, in turn, a reference to J. C. LEBRAM, "Die Theologie der späten Chokmah und häretisches Judentum", *ZAW* 77 (1965), 202-211. LEBRAM's article has, in turn, its starting point in an article by J. A. SANDERS on two of the non-canonical psalms from Column 18 of the Qumran Psalms Scroll (11QPsª) in *ZAW* 76 (1964), 57-75.

    [52]) CAQUOT, 64-67.
    [53]) The quotations from 1 Enoch are in the translation of M. A. KNIBB in H. F. D. SPARKS (ed.), *The Apocryphal Old Testament* (Oxford, 1984), 169-319.
    [54]) See e.g., G. W. E. NICKELSBURG, *Jewish Literature between the Bible and the Mishnah* (London, 1981), 93: "The author writes (*or the apocalypse is revised* [my italics]) during the campaigns of Judas Maccabeus..."; and M. BLACK, *The Book of Enoch or I Enoch. A New English Edition* (Leiden, 1985), 20: "History for the authors ends with their account of the struggles of the Maccabees; thereafter apocalyptic or transcendent eschatology takes over."
    [55]) R. H. CHARLES in *APOT*, Vol. II, 260; NICKELSBURG, 93; BLACK, 20f., 279f.
    [56]) J. T. MILIK, *The Books of Enoch* (Oxford, 1976), 45.
    [57]) CAQUOT, 48 (my translation).
    [58]) R. T. BECKWITH, "The Pre-History and Relationships of the Pharisees, Sadducees and Essenes: A Tentative Reconstruction", *RQ* 11 (1982-84), 3-46.

THE SENSE OF HISTORY IN JEWISH
INTERTESTAMENTAL WRITING

BY

TESSA RAJAK

Reading

In post-Biblical and pre-Rabbinic Judaism, forms of historical thought
are ubiquitous but also elusive. They are present in such diverse literary
types and contexts that even a summary survey would be a lengthy affair.
I shall take up two lines of approach, relatively narrow in themselves, but
for that reason perhaps a little less familiar, and through them seek to
make some general observations. The first is a matter of theory, the second of practice.

The historian Josephus is at this most original and interesting (all his
readers will know how laboured and derivative he can be at other times),
in his remarks on Jewish history at the opening of the polemic against
Apion. There he has to confront the claim, which he says has sprung up
in response to his published *Jewish Antiquities*, that the Jewish race is
proved of recent origin by the silence of Greek historians and other
writers[1]). Antiquity, in the Classical world, meant distinction—as the
early Christians were to discover to their cost. So the argument is an important one. And Josephus' demonstration of Jewish antiquity has attracted a good deal of attention, not least because of its direct exploitation
(often, be it said, with due acknowledgement) by Christian writers such
as Tatian, Theophilus of Antioch, and Origen[2]). But what is less familiar
is the first stage of that discussion in *Contra Apionem*. Because the issue is
one of proof through written sources, the age and reliability of such
Greek literature as deals with prehistory has first to be evaluated, in contrast with oriental traditions, and above all with the internal Jewish
evidence, which naturally tells quite a different story about the earliest
peoples. This whole evaluation deserves notice because in fact, going
beyond the immediate case, it adds up to a brief but wide-ranging exploration of what constitutes a historical tradition and especially—once
the Greeks have been got out of the way—of the meaning and uses of
history among the Jews.

There is no reason to suspect that Josephus has borrowed these
arguments from some literary source, and, to the best of my knowledge,
for once no such claim has been made about him. While some of the ex-

position of the Jewish Law in book II (145-219) has uncomfortably close affinities with surviving fragments of a work by Philo referred to as the *Hypothetica*[3]), the historically-orientated book I would have had no place in the *œuvre* of the philosopher. On the other hand, it is directly connected with many of Josephus' own preoccupations. Some of the claims made by the Hellenistic Greco-Oriental chroniclers, like Manetho of Egypt and Berossus of Babylon, may come the closest to some of Josephus' conceptions, but there is nothing to suggest that those writers stopped to expatiate separately upon the meaning of what they were doing—they seem to have been writers of an extremely matter-of-fact kind[4]). The same applies to Josephus' Hellenistic-Jewish predecessors, as we shall see.

The argument shapes itself around the contrast with Greek culture—a contrast which is never far, implicitly or explicitly, from this writer's mind. It is in the course of criticizing the Greeks that he establishes the leading themes, as is natural enough, since this is the immediately point of attachment to the polemic—"my first thought is one of intense astonishment at the current opinion that in the study of the earliest events the Greeks alone deserve serious attention, that the truth should be sought only from them, and that neither we nor any others in the world are to be believed" (I.6). Such cultural arrogance was incidentally quite regular in Greek literature; it has been succinctly summarized in A. Momigliano's *Alien Wisdom*[5]).

Josephus counters with a sharp picture of the poverty of the evidence for early Greek history—a point which, if obvious, is none the less true for that, and one which has indeed been made in recent times in strikingly similar terms; take, for example Sir Moses Finley, who writes (not in any way recalling Josephus): "we, too, cannot write a history of early Greece. The reason is very simple: there are no documents. Before the year 700 B.C. such documents never existed"[6]). Josephus analyses this poverty as springing both from inadequacy in the record, determined in the first place by the late arrival of the alphabet to Greece, and then by the loss of the archives through climate and natural disaster, as well as, more generally, by an absence of the recording habit. In a passage much adduced in quite other contexts, he stops momentarily to consider the status of the Homeric poems as history; a status much diminished, he says, by the work's oral formation. Here Josephus is no doubt dependent upon Alexandrian scholarship, but it is remarkable that it is his perceptive formulation which has survived alone, to serve eventually as (in Theodore Reinach's words) one of the "pierres angulaires" of Wolf's famous *Prolegomena* to the Homeric poems. There Josephus is brought in to underpin the argument that Homer consists of separate traditional "lays" joined together[7]).

However, my interest lies not in what Josephus has to say about Greek history and historiography *per se*, but about the way he perceives the essential difference between the Greek and the Hebrew approach. He puts up the paradoxical and in some ways even absurd argument that the Greek historical tradition exposes its weakness through the contradictions between its various authors. The charge sheet reaches its climax with the statement that ''on many points even Thucydides is accused of error by some critics, notwithstanding his reputation for writing the most accurate history of his time'' (I.18). Today, we would be inclined to think that the spirit of debate and criticism, if serious, is just what stimulates and strengthens a historical enquiry and that it is just as well that no reputation should be immune; specious and ostentatious controversies, like some of the ones to which Josephus refers, are, of course, another matter. In this outlook, our idea of history-writing is closer, I suppose, to that of the Greeks. Josephus, however, expresses the plain view (we cannot help feeling that there is a touch of the Greek rhetoric schools about his neat presentation of it!) that contradiction must mean unreliability, a case which could only hold, in fact, in a situation where true knowledge was demonstrably visible and did not have to be proved. And Josephus asserts that that is exactly how it is for the Jews: their records contain no discrepancies. The tradition is the soundest and the most reliable.

He claims, in effect, that the Jews as a nation are distinguished for being historically-minded, that their historical documents are qualitatively different from others'—though nearer to those of Orientals than those of Greeks—and that their entire attitude to the past, above all the distant past, is unique. The formulation is one which suits his calling, as a Greek historian, and his purpose, to vindicate his *Antiquities* by taking on his critics. Without that challenge, and without the Greek orientation of the debate, he perhaps would not or even could not have formulated the matter thus. Yet, at the same time, he is positioning himself outside the framework of Greek thought and he will satisfy us that he is drawing directly on Jewish practices and conceptions. In other words, there is a genuine fusion here of the two cultures: in the context of Josephus' writing career, this is hardly surprising, and is no different in principle from the blend which, for example, H. A. ATTRIDGE has recently pinpointed in the Biblical parts of the *Antiquities*[8]).

Contra Apionem I then, offers an explicit, perhaps the only explicit statement there is, of a first century Jew's ideas about Scripture as history. Josephus deserves acknowledgement in this sphere, as much as for another (in a sense parallel) contribution made by his *Contra Apionem*, that of offering us a ''theological précis compiled by a contemporary of the New Testament writers which is probably the earliest Jewish theological system'' (to take words from G. VERMES)[9]). In many ways, indeed, this short tract has hit the mark. The work was issued in the 90's A.D., and cannot have been put together before the publication of the *Antiquities*, which came in 93/4 at the earliest. In this Josephus confronts us with another paradox, for his eulogy of history emerges from well into that post-70 era when the central tradition of the Jewish people is commonly said to have become profoundly ahistorical, following upon the loss of nationhood and Temple. That diagnosis may indeed apply to the inner core of the Rabbinic tradition—and Jacob NEUSNER some years ago suggested an explanation, in the disillusion which made it unattractive in those circles to think too much about a Messianic future and therefore pointless any longer to contemplate the sweep of the past. The Rabbis, it is said, felt that interest had to be removed from the ultimate direction of history and the uncertainties of redemption; the question (it is asserted) became not when but how this might come[10]). Now, at this time in his life, if not before, Josephus adheres manifestly to the mainstream, incipiently Rabbinic, erstwhile Pharisaic element in Judaism[11]). None the less, perhaps due to his being now a Diaspora resident; perhaps because of his surface Hellenization as a writer (the two are not the same thing, as HENGEL's work has shown us)[12]), and perhaps because of his essentially personal orientation as a relic of a lost generation and, through circumstance, an essentially backward-looking individual; for whatever reason, Josephus' historical view constitutes a powerful exception to the alleged post-70 dismissal of history (not only in *Contra Apionem*, but, it could be said, in his whole career). All in all, it is probably most correct to analyse the situation by seeing him as the *conclusion* of a period of great activity and variety in Jewish historical thinking.

We have looked at Josephus' claim that the Jews had accurate archives. What is even more interesting is his view of what constitutes the authoritative tradition and of the people's relation to it; the underlying assumptions are in some ways as revealing as what is stated. He claims that among the Jews the records are so good because they are valued and that one reason why they are valued is that they are in active use. The memory of the past is protected by its use in the present and this guarantees, rather than, as we might think, diminishes it[13]). The intimate link between history and practice is in Josephus' view and in Jewish tradition itself provided by the Law, since this is at the heart of the Scriptural record and inseparable from the narrative. Divine injunction is the source, and does not go unmentioned by Josephus; but it has in fact been shifted from its key position, evidently because such an emphasis would have been unpersuasive to pagans and weakened the argument. At the same time, there is *no concealment* of the divine contribution, as we shall see; and it is always implicitly there.

I have defined what I think is the essence of Josephus' understanding, but his own presentation is, of course, concrete and specific. A personal slant guarantees that this is the author's own voice, a point which does not detract from its broader interest. For he says that the keeping of records was assigned by "our ancestors" to high priests and prophets (29). He will have some more to say about prophecy, but first he spells out an aspect of the special role of the priesthood, in an unashamedly anachronistic fashion: it is because of the obligation to keep priestly genealogies pure and thus to supervise priestly marriages (see Lev. xxi 7) that the archives have been cherished, the names of remote ancestors preserved, and two thousand years' worth of high priests' names record-ed (30-36). Josephus' pride in his own priestly and also Hasmonean (therefore high priestly) descent comes out in the curious focus of this statement: he had not so long ago boasted about those origins in the opening sentences of his autobiography, earlier, the prophecy to Vespa-sian which had secured his survival had been explained as a priestly gift; and at various times he had presented Judaea as a theocracy under priest-ly rule; his consciousness of his priesthood is an enduring trait[14]). He perhaps does not mean here literally to bring the whole of Scriptural tradition under the priestly umbrella; and he may in part be influenced by thought of the priests' role in maintaining the Temple archives of Egypt and Babylon, phenomena about which Herodotus had already had much to say, and which Josephus himself does like to bring up as a parallel. But the deeper and more serious point in what he writes is that the Jewish tradition is something alive to each observing generation, and each generation has a vested interest in it correctness.

He continues with a careful explanation of what Scripture is, showing us unequivocally that a canon was taken for granted in his day and infor-ming us of the way it was divided in the circles in which he moved: five books of Moses—of laws and traditional history—(παράδοσις), prophets in thirteen books, and four for hymns and precepts, giving a total of twenty-two, and, in fact, corresponding closely to what has become the accepted Jewish tripartite classification[15]). In this classification the historical books are, it should be noted, not separated off from the rest; and *all* the history is attributed by Josephus to prophetic inspiration, star-ting with that of Moses. The prophets, according to Josephus, received their insight from God; but this succession ceased in the time of Arta-xerxes (to which time Josephus ascribed the book of Esther)[16]). So subse-quent writing has been without the same authority. What is more, the Bi-ble itself really records events over the whole of time (37-8). This implies, as HENGEL has pointed out, that authority has constantly to be sought in the past. Such a view of the prophetic succession again corresponds to

Rabbinic ideas, as expressed, for example in *M. Aboth*'s statement on the chain of tradition travelling from Moses to the prophets and then to the men of the Great Synagogue, or perhaps in the utterance of IV Ezra, where the prophet is told that after his day "truth shall go far away and falsehood shall come near"[17]). Documents were preserved through the agency of priestly care. The formula of Deuteronomy (vi 2 and xiii 1), invoked also in Rabbinic literature and previously by Josephus himself in explaining the procedure of his *Antiquities* (I, 5) is rechoed here in the statement that nothing has been added to the original texts nor taken away from them[18]).

The links between history and Law and between history and life are most forcibly asserted in the statement that Jews adhere to their writings because they take them as God's decrees and would endure martyrdom, as did indeed occur in the theatres, rather than deny the Laws or the other writings (the reference is probably to quite recent events, in 66 or 70, or possibly even later, and not just to the long-gone martyrdoms of the Maccabean era)[19]). The people was always ready to carry the "burden of history", however heavy[20]). Far from there being a separate sphere for history, for Josephus, and for the Jews of his time, the dependence of precept and of faith upon the written report of the past is self-evident. It is all quite different for the Greeks, whose writings are composed, as Josephus would have it, to suit the tastes of the authors—something on which he puts, for the purposes of his argument, the most derogatory implication; still, his concentration on the role of Greek historians as entertainers or rhetoricians is, we may feel, not entirely unjustified.

Though it is mainly the remote past which is in question, the line of tradition is drawn as continuous and as continuing to be in some sense authoritative; thus Josephus does not shrink from extending his theory to cover contemporary history and then, more particularly (this need not surprise us, knowing his personality) to defend his own eye-witness account of the Jewish War by contrast with others "published by persons who never visited the sites nor were anywhere near the action" (46). The descent from the sublime to the ridiculous calls for no further comment. And Josephus' defence leads into a digression about his own first book which replaces the expected conclusion to the whole first section of the *Against Apion*, winding up the discussion about the two kinds of history and leading on to the criticisms of his critics.

Some excesses in Josephus' observations can easily make us lose sight of their value. In general terms, he is right to insist that having the Scriptures caused the Jews to be continually recalling their past, that in many respects they had as a people a peculiar interest in such matters, and that

that interest was part and parcel of the business of their daily lives. Having analysed the theory, we now must examine contemporary practice. In what ways, beyond mere possession of a sacred text, did the Bible create a special relationship with the past among the Jews of Josephus' day? It would be foolish to spend much time seeking appearances of pure "history" in our accepted meaning of the word in intertestamental literature: perhaps even not in those works, and they are not so very numerous, which are formally designated "histories" (both the books of the Maccabees embody major distortions and fictions). Moreover, we must be aware that the boundaries between the categories in Jewish literature correspond neither to those of the Greeks nor to our own[21]). But in what respects was there a developed historical consciousness in this literature? And of what kind was it?

What we should not look for is proof of straight, disinterested, scholarly enquiry. Indeed, it is probably a mistake to seek such manifestations in any consistent form, even in the admired historiography of the Greeks and Romans, as Classical scholars are now beginning to note (some of them, perhaps, with a degree of overreaction)[22]). Our own academic aspirations in this field—even supposing them to be attainable—may be themselves no more than a temporary aberration, some kind of "historical accident", as Hayden WHITE has called it[23]).

On any broader conception of history, intertestamental Judaism is a culture that is historically-minded and notably prolific in historical thought. A sense of history is, after all, no more than an interest in the past, seen as some sort of continuity, within a context (even if a false one) of time. Furthermore, whatever uses this past be put to—understanding the ways of God, describing one's own identity or relating to others, interpreting current events or predicting future ones, defending one's nation or justifying one's party, producing social cohesion, controlling the younger generation or understanding the older one (and there may be many more)—it is a prerequisite for something of an attitude of enquiry and curiosity to be present among creators and consumers. For one thing, without such a shared attitude, the past simply could not be a potent force.

So, even if it is true that, as FINLEY has reported, drawing on the anthropologists, "wherever tradition can be studied among living people, the evidence is that it does not exist apart from the connection with a practice or belief"[24]), it must also be the case that the same practices and beliefs depend upon an independent momentum of remembering and asking, within the tradition. Visions of the past, if they are allowed to, will exert their own spell. Intertestamental Judaism—as Josephus perceived—was a paradigm case of movement in both directions.

The most characteristic modern way of doing history is distinguishing truth from fiction. Josephus, following the Greeks, talks a great deal about historical truth, but since he believes himself to adhere to a tradition which is all true, his prime concern will be different. Certainly, the truth/fiction distinction is not a central one in the Hebrew tradition; and, by all accounts, the application of this distinction to memories of the past has been, everywhere a rare activity[25]). It will be apparent that when this distinction is left out of account, there is still ample scope for historical enquiry: it can ask questions about how or why things happened, or about what things were like in the past; it can try to fill disturbing gaps in the record (even though this may require imaginary incidents) and it can make links between events. These tasks, surprising as it may seem at first sight, become not less but more pressing the more a tradition is respected and the more it is felt that the content, however problematic, has to be saved. Even before the Biblical books had become canonical, their importance to the Jews was such that continuing interpretative and expansionist labour of this nature was called for. Thus, in the intertestamental period just as the legendary is not sharply divided from the historical, so there is no clearly-marked distinction between literature which is described as exegetical and that normally categorized as historical[26]). The fusion of history with Aggadic Midrash is displayed in clear and extended form in the Biblical parts of Josephus' own *Antiquities*, especially the first six books, where the amplifications and interpretations of scripture are at their most abundant. S. RAPPAPORT, G. VERMES and T. FRANXMAN have demonstrated the intimate connection of this material with contemporary and later traditions of exegesis, and the strength of the cumulative case they have built up cannot be resisted[27]).

Now, however, we cannot dwell on the strange amalgam that is the *Jewish Antiquities*. We shall look at earlier texts to see how Biblical writings prompted post-Biblical historical questioning and how history was conceived within a Biblical framework. I think that this viewpoint and the perspective of Josephus' idea of Biblical history, offer a fresh approach to literature that is not unfamiliar. Here I shall concentrate on a limited area, on historical or quasi-historical works which are Biblical in subject matter. This seems appropriate to the present occasion; and the major historians whose subject matter was contemporary, both in Hebrew and in Greek—that is to say, the author of I Maccabees on the one hand, and on the other Jason of Cyrene and his Epitomator (who is the author of II Maccabees), must be left for another time[28]). It would be possible, too, to pursue the theme further in a different direction, and to explore the presentation of the historical process, past, present and, above all, future, embodied in some of the Testaments and in the Apocalypses, which are perhaps the era's most distinctive literary form.

Most of the present subject matter will consist of works surviving (insofar as they do survive) in the Greek language. Yet it would be wrong to assign Judaeo-Greek historiography particularly to the Diaspora: the Epitomator of Jason of Cyrene appears to have written in Palestine, as Jason himself may well have done, in view of his likely first-hand acquaintance with the Maccabean revolution[29]); again, not all of those normally regarded as Alexandrian Jewish writers can, from their fragments, be assigned even as a probability to that milieu. The identification of Eupolemus, whom I shall be discussing shortly, with the Palestinian ambassador of that name is strongly favoured by some scholars. We shall also find that there are points of similarity between this literature and Jubilees or the Genesis Apocryphon. Samaritan writing, too, fits in an interesting way into this group. It is, indeed, particularly important to note that no sharp differentiation can be made from the point of view of either language or provenance between Palestinian and non-Palestinian material[30]).

The now fragmentary Hellenistic-Jewish writers who precede Philo have never been fully restored to the place in Judaism from which they were displaced by the closing in of the religious tradition after the disaster of 70, by the subsequent destruction of the Alexandrian community under Trajan, by the interest shown in them on the part of early Christian writers, and by their own severe limitations as authors and thinkers. The fragments are too few to build very much on (while, by contrast, Philo's works are perhaps too copious for comfort); but they are part of a culture which is in its own way a remarkable phenomenon. Recent editions and commentaries (sometimes, it must be admitted, inflated to disproportionate size) stimulate a fresh look, and FREUDENTHAL's book of 1874-5 provides a solid, if to our taste over-speculative foundation[31]).

The retelling of Biblical history, with expansions, contractions and even modifications was everywhere, as I have said, a major branch of literary activity in the period, notwithstanding the special status held by the canonical books and the obligation not to add or subtract emphasized by Josephus. We may take it that this was regarded as permissable activity, in that it could be viewed as another way of expressing what was already there in the text[32]). Now this is a kind of activity that leaves little room for concerns about distinguishing truth from fiction: rather the opposite: it adds further accretions of fiction to a tradition where invention is already inextricably intertwined with true recording, in a mixture hallowed by respect for the text. With such an ever-expanding tradition, it is never really possible to get anywhere with distinguishing the well-founded from the invented (even were that desired) except, to a very limited extent, using the tools of modern scholarship. Once a version is accepted, there is no longer room for disbelief. Morton SMITH's formulation catches the point, when he talks, in relation to the role of the ancient "editors", of an old-established historical interest in Israel, "extending itself to organize what was apparently a body of non-historical texts"[33]). This is not to say that writings will not contain visibly differing proportions of pure romance; nor to deny that they will be different valued, within specific circles or more generally; and some authors may begin and end their careers in an altogether fringe role. To take one case, it may be that no group of readers set much store as literal truth by the flights of fancy of that dubious Jew Artapanus on the subject of Moses/Mousaios, the teacher of Orpheus, who founded Heliopolis and buried his wife Merris at Meroe[34]). But for us it is usually difficult if not impossible to judge their impact; the ancient criteria for setting a value will have been complicated ones, with factual accuracy playing at most a minor role.

In his authoritative book on literary falsification[35]), W. SPEYER classes the remains of the so-called Hellenistic-Jewish historians as "geschichtliche Verfalschungen". Such a description (which is accommodated, of course, to the theme of the book) rests on positivistic premises which seem inappropriate to this literary context; its logical consequence is to present, as he does, these figures as pure propagandists, *Tendenzschriftsteller*; but this, even on the very limited evidence we have, seems unjustifiably narrow. Such they may have been; but not only that, and perhaps not mainly that.

Without making excessive claims for what these writings could ever have contained, I would suggest that we should not hesitate to treat them as a species of historical narration genuinely stimulated by Scripture, and to regard them as works with an internal role within the Hellenized-Jewish culture. This is not an altogether new view—a fact from which I take some comfort. For one scholarly approach has been precisely to hold that the psychological needs of the Alexandrian community are the primary explanation of its own curious literature. Most important, V. TCHERIKOVER in two justifiedly well-known articles, one of a general nature and one dealing with the letter of Aristeas, set out to establish this position[36]). Martin HENGEL, N. WALTER, Salo BARON (in brief) and B. Z. WACHOLDER in his monograph on Eupolemus[37]) have all by and large supported him. The influential voice on the other side, asserting the extra-mural and competitive character of the writing, was E. BICKERMAN, in a classic paper on Demetrius the chronographer. BICKERMAN makes apologetics seem dominant, and the author's principal objective is defined as countering "Hellenocentric" history; J. J. COLLINS has recently taken up a similar line[38]). Much of TCHERIKOVER's case rested upon the social and political realities of the Alexandrian milieu, but, in relation to Aristeas (itself, incidentally, a legend written up as a historical document, and incorporated by Josephus into the *Antiquities* as history), TCHERIKOVER puts forward a very interesting argument which draws on the text itself. In the account of the Jewish way of life (128-171) offered by the high priest Eleazar, the choice of material is quite unexpected: specialized dietary rules like those about animals with the "parting hoof" and the "cloven foot", and esoteric habits like the use of *tefilin* and *mesusot* are scarcely of a kind to make sense to pagans; they tended to be entirely ignored and indeed there is no hard evidence in pagan literature that these customs ever caught the attention of outsiders (for all that Eleazar has opened his exposition with the earnest declaration that the question of unclean animals is one that arises great interest in "most men", 128-9).

Such detailed observation of content is the right way forward and there is room to exploit it in the case of other authors. I shall look, therefore, more at the texts themselves than at any hypothetical setting for them. While TCHERIKOVER's instance is of a halakhic nature, the concern of this paper is with what falls under the heading of *aggadah*. The earliest so-called historian of the tradition is the writer Demetrius, probably of the third century B.C.[39]). Some have called him the "father of Hellenistic-Jewish history", while others have claimed him as an exegete: but the disagreement is an empty one[40]). What is visible in his work is the exploitation of Midrashic-type questions and answers, which aim mainly at disposing of historical difficulties in the text. Primarily, these difficulties are matters of chronology and it is, after all, any historian's first job to make his chronology work out. Peter FRASER has offered a surprisingly simplistic judgment: "the Jews of Alexandria did not need a chronological study of the book of Genesis"[41]). Such a statement is only possible when an author like Demetrius is taken entirely out of the context of Jewish culture.

The hazards of transmission make it difficult to grasp the overall purpose of Demetrius' original work, for with this author as with the other fragmentary writers in the group, there has been a double process of selection: we now have only the Christian authors by whom the fragments were cited—principally Eusebius in book IX (mainly) of the *Praeparatio Evangelica*, but also, to a lesser extent, Clement of Alexandria, in *Stromata*, book I; but they took them all from a volume on the Jews by a first century B.C. Roman freedman called Alexander Polyhistor, who made excerpts about different peoples[42]). Two sets of specialist but obscure criteria therefore governed the selection. Of Demetrius we have only six fragments altogether (not that the other authors are better represented) and only one of them (fragment two) is even as much as several pages in length. Fragment 1, moreover, is technically unattributed. But the reader does not get the impression that the chronological investigations are there for polemical purposes at all; that is to say, the surviving fragments do not reveal a Demetrius busy impressing pagans by slotting Biblical history into Greek or, still less, into universal history; nor does he seem preoccupied with establishing priority for the Hebrews (in the fashion of the *Contra Apionem*). What he offers is an artless, though not entirely charmless, retelling of the Biblical narratives—in his case, it would appear, exclusively drawn from the Greek version; and the retelling has a distinct numerical focus reminiscent of Jubilees. The flavour of his writing is best conveyed directly. This is part of fragment 2: "Jacob set out for Haran in Mesopotamia, leaving behind his father Isaac who was 137 years old, whereas he himself was 77 years old. Thus, after he had spent seven years there, he married Leah and Rachel, the two daughters of his maternal uncle. At that time he was 84 years old. Now in the next seven years twelve children were born to him: in the eighth year and tenth month Simeon; and in the tenth year and sixth month Levi ... Now because Rachel was not bearing children, she became jealous of her sister and made her own handmaid Zilpah lie with Jacob. (There is an error here). This was at the time that Bilhah also became pregnant with Naphtali, that is, in the eleventh year and fifth month..."[43]). The interest in ages and dates here comes across as almost domestic, suggesting perhaps a sort of affection for the text and its characters. However, in the end, we remain at a loss to know quite why it should be a matter of importance to the author or his clientèle that when Dinah was raped by Shechem, son of Hamor, she was 16 and four months, while Simeon and Levi were 21 and four months and 20 and six months respectively when they avenged her. The Biblical dates are such that, as will be obvious, a figure like Jacob's seventy-seven years requires careful extrapolation: he died at age 147 (Gen. xlvii 28), he was 14 years in Laban's service (Gen. xxxi 41), and at the end of this period Joseph was born; 30 years later Joseph entered Pharaoh's service (Gen. xli 46) and spent 7 years of plenty and two years of famine there before his brothers came (Gen. xlv 6); 17 years later Jacob died (Gen. xlvii 28). So this total ($14 + 30 + 9 + 17 = 70$) has to be subtracted from 147 to give Jacob's age when he left for Haran to enter Laban's service.

The text as we have it contains some simple mistakes vis-à-vis Biblical narrative, such as the just-noticed case of Zilpah, who was in fact Rachel's handmaid. Editors have been ready to emend the text (they always are) but it is not impossible that Demetrius was capable of crude mispressions arising from his own need to make simple personal sense of the characters' interaction and to turn them into flesh and blood individuals.

That the author did not have the outside world in view as audience emerges from his readiness to ascribe social inferiority and also dishonesty to the patriarchs (contrast Josephus who tends to remove all such elements from the *Antiquities* and certainly never multiplies them). This is an indicator that appears not to have been noticed. Demetrius is happy to say, of Joseph in Egypt, that "though Joseph had good fortune for nine years, he did not send for his father because he was a shepherd as were his brothers too, and Egyptians consider it a disgrace to be a shepherd. That this was the reason he did not send for him, Joseph himself declared. For when his kin did come, he told them that if they should be summoned by the king and were asked what they did for a living, they were to say they were cowherds". The text, at Gen. xlvi 31-34, conveys a different impression in several respects: attention is *not* drawn to Joseph's unfilial delay in sending for his father; the embarrassment about being shepherds in juxtaposed but not linked by way of motive with the delay (and it can hardly be said to be a worthy one), and lastly there is no question of real dishonesty in the brothers calling themselves herdsmen, as they are said to have had both flocks *and* herds; still less was there any contrived deception. It is instructive, by way of contrast, to see how Josephus (*AJ* II, 184-6) turns the motif in yet another direction. Like Demetrius, he regards the Jews as in principle *exclusively* shepherds, but says that they were advised by Joseph to show goodwill towards the Egyptians by putting aside this forbidden occupation (presumably he would now provide for them!). Thus in Josephus' version the thrust of the story is acutely apologetic; the Jews are shown to be positively eager to accommodate themselves to the customs of others, thereby evincing the opposite of the misanthropy and peculiarity of behavious commonly ascribed to them[44]).

Here our concern is with Demetrius, and it would be absurd to suggest that his interpretation is designed to *discredit* the patriarchs: rather he seems to be struggling simply to make everyday sense of the events in terms of the data provided in the original version: the text is processed to provide an explanation for what happened, and this is standard Midrashic procedure of a primitive kind[45]). It is also primitive history-writing—especially as the explanation offered is one which catches up and builds upon a specific datum of social history about the gap between shepherd peoples and others supplied by the book of Genesis (whether there is any foundation in that, I leave open here). One might recall the term "historiated Bible" which M. GASTER used to describe such writings.

It is worth noting, however, that fragment 2 as we have it does engage in one telling apologetic device, by way of what looks like deliberate omission; for Genesis says of the dinner given to greet Jacob that "They served him (Joseph) by himself, and the brothers by themselves, and the Egyptians who were at dinner were also served separately; for Egyptians hold it an abomination to eat with Hebrews" (Gen. xliii 32). That last, unhappy statement, so close to the heart of many difficulties between Jews and their neighbours, is not to be found in Demetrius: instead, he fills the story out at this point by his favourite game of numerology, building on the information that Benjamin's portion was five times as large as any of the others' (xliii 34) with the observation that seven sons had been born to his father by Leah and only two by Rachel, so that Benjamin had five portions and Joseph himself two[46]) making a total of seven, as many as all the sons of Leah received.

With the next historian, Eupolemus[47]), we have an author who is likely to be some three generations later in date (from the second half of the second century, it would seem) and has, perhaps for this reason, a little more sophistication in the five surviving fragments (one could hardly have less). Another reason might be that he is closer to the mainstream of the scholarly traditions of his time, since his affinities are Palestinian, his orientation is towards the Temple, his style and syntax are Hebraic, and his Bible may sometimes be the Hebrew one; furthermore, according to a now-favoured identification (which still, it should be said, falls short of proof), he wrote in Jerusalem, was of priestly family and is the same man as Eupolemus, son of John, son of Accos, who served as aide to Judas Maccabeus and is named as one of his envoys to Rome in 161 B.C. at I Macc viii 17-20 and II Macc iv 11[48]). B. Z. Wacholder has sought to position this author within Jewish literature, comparing his re-writings, additions and contractions to those of the Chronicler operating upon Kings, describing as Biblical his way with architectural minutiae and measurements, and tentatively reviving EWALD's comparison between the Solomonic correspondence in Eupolemus and Apocryphal material. In spite of some dubious evidence of the subsidiary use of a pagan historian (or romancer), in the shape of Ctesias[49]), there is no unequivocal sign of the outside world being addressed.

It is true, however, that in presenting Moses as a *Protos Euretes* (like the Moses of Artapanus[50]) and like Abraham in pseudo-Eupolemus), who invents the alphabet and teaches it to the Phoenicians (fragment 1) and in incorporating Solomon's correspondence with Vaphres king of Egypt and Souron king of Tyre, Eupolemus does betray a concern with placing the Hebrews on the map of general history, at least for his and their own self-satisfaction. None the less, if we are to judge from the fragments, a principal objective seems to have been the same as that of Demetrius, simply to illuminate the historical sections of Scripture. The inclusion of correspondence between monarchs—like the Solomonic one here—is an accepted mode in Jewish history-writing, with direct precedents in Solomon's letters from Kings and Chronicles[51]); and in this mode fictional elaboration takes its place beside possibly authentic documentation rather in the way that speeches are treated in the classical writers. (Here the fiction is compounded by the fact that Vaphres, the Egyptian correspondent chosen is extra-Biblical, while the properly attested Hiram king of Tyre is turned into Souron—Josephus was to claim that the Tyrian monarch's correspondence with Solomon was in his own day extant in the Tyre archives: CA I, 111). Eupolemus, however, may have believed all the letters he cited to be authentic, as suggested by WACHOLDER[52]). The hypothesis of an *apocryphon* from which Eupolemus actually derived his material can neither be proved nor refuted; nor can the case for direct dependence upon the *Letter of Aristeas* (which need not even be prior in date). What can be clearly seen is the business of the forger: he seeks, at this point, to stress Solomon's piety, to visualize how the king collected and how he fed his enormous labour force, and to conjure up in graphic form the respect paid to the pious king and his God by foreign powers: "when I read your letter I rejoiced greatly. I and my entire administration set aside a feast day upon the occasion of your succeeding to the kingdom of such a kind man and one approved of by so mighty a God"[53]). It is interesting that the basically Palestinian Eupolemus is, on the showing of the fragments, more interested than Demetrius, the supposedly Diaspora writer, in clarifying the Jewish people's place in a wider world.

When it comes to the (undated) fragments of Artapanus' *On the Jews*[54], we are, as I have indicated, in a different realm, that of historical extravaganza or romance, with links with the text that seem often slighter than its associations with Egyptian animal cult and other unexpected matter. There are, however, touches of the flesh and blood realism that we have seen in the other two authors, and there may be some affinities with Jewish tradition, for example, in the description of Moses' appearance—"tall, ruddy complexioned, with long flowing gray hair and dignified" (frag. 3).

Artapanus' subject matter (as it survives) is Moses; Demetrius had retold the book of Genesis; Eupolemus harmonized Kings and Chronicles. An author who is scarcely more than a name to us, another Aristeas[55]), gives early testimony to traditions about Job, whom he makes the son of Esau (perhaps in the sense of "descendant"). Cleodemus Malchus[56]), cited by Josephus, attaches Abraham's descendants to Libyan legend. The scholarly theory that the latter was a Samaritan sprang principally from his name; but yet another identifiable author, generally and unattractively termed pseudo-Eupolemus[57]) (though described by Eusebius in one case as "Eupolemus" in another as "some anonymous writings") may well more properly (though still not certainly) be designated Samaritan, because he recounts that Abraham was received by the city at the temple Argarizin, which is interpreted Mountain of the Most High, where the patriarch met Melchizedek the priest. This author also embodies themes found in the Samaritan book *Asatir*[58]). The fragments again are quite slight and only two in number, but the procedure is in principle similar to what we have already seen in Jewish authors, as is evident from Eusebius' erroneous conflation of this figure with Eupolemus.

HENGEL has given us a brilliant portrait of this anonymous writer[59]), whom he dates to before the Maccabean revolt; he emphasizes the way that pagan deities are demythologized, for example Bel and Kronos through the identification of both with Noah/Nimrod; this reduces them to being not only mortals, albeit of giant frame, but markedly evil ones, whose descendants had to be punished. The universalizing traits and the cultural interests of the author emerge in the extraordinary idealization of a Biblical figure, Abraham, who is here the discoverer of astrology and divination (as also, later in Josephus). But I should like to draw attention to the significance of other aspects, not overlooked by HENGEL but easily overshadowed: the probability that the author knew Hebrew[60]); and the connections with what might be called Jewish apocryphal traditions (Genesis Apocryphon, Jubilees and I Enoch), above all in the notion that Enoch learnt astrology from the angels[61]). Another such case are the details of what happened to the Pharaoh who tried to have intercourse with Sarah: her chastity was providentially protected, and his household began to perish until diviners came and revealed to him the lady's identity; similar aggadic elaborations, again, are in Genesis Apocryphon and Jubilees, as well as in Josephus, Philo and even, on the other side, Genesis Rabbah[62]). But the closest parallel here is the Samaritan *Asatir*.

We must accept that the Samaritans of this period (before the great rift) shared in the Jewish world of Bible interpretation and allowed it to feed their historical consciousness in the same way. Here we have a phenomenon of the first importance, and it reveals a community whose culture and self-awareness may have had different overtones from that of the Jews, yet which ran parallel to theirs. We need not take too seriously, however, the information derived from Eusebius (*PE* IX, 17-1-9) that Alexander Polyhistor reported the title of this work by "Eupolemus" as "Concerning the Jews of Assyria". In general the titles ascribed to the

various works cited by Polyhistor in his Jewish collection seem either ar-
bitrary or obvious, and in this case, where even the author's name has
had to be rejected, there is even more room for doubt⁶³). If this historian
is Samaritan, he constitutes a literary correlative of newer archaeological
evidence: I refer here to the discovery made on the island of Delos of two
steles, found near the προσευχή erected by οἱ ἐν Δήλῳ Ἰσραελεῖται οἱ
ἀπαρχόμενοι εἰς ἱερὸν Ἀργαριζείν. The steles are dated palaeographically to
250-175 to 150-50 B.C., respectively. This Diaspora community of
Samaritans was located, it seems, near the Jewish place of assembly,
and, it has been suggested, the two Bible-based groups may have drawn
together in conditions of exile and remained close even after the schism of
129⁶⁴).

Most of the Hellenistic Biblical historians, whether Jewish or
Samaritan, were not named by Josephus in his *Antiquities* (hence our
dependence on the pagan-Christian line of transmission for our limited
knowledge of them)⁶⁵). We might be tempted on this basis to form the
view that they had little importance or at any rate no influence. But that
view would be ill-founded. The reasons why Josephus referred little to
them are discernible and specific. He had direct access to the Hebrew Bible and also to richer veins of tradition and interpretation (oral and
perhaps even written) in Hebrew and Aramaic Midrash; where he drew
from Greek originals, it was always where the style and Hellenized form
as well as the substance had something to contribute to his history, and
could ease the labour of composition in Greek (the letter of Aristeas and
the additions to Esther, both utilized by Josephus, are obvious
examples). None of the historians considered here could be so described,
even if Eupolemus may have been too harshly judged by some of his
critics⁶⁶). In any event, Josephus, in keeping with other Classical
historians, is not given to naming his sources except for special purposes,
and we should remember that even Philo lacks proper mention, though
was demonstrably used by the historian.

Though the Hellenistic Jewish and Samaritan writers rose beyond Septuagint Greek, they seem to have written like the antiquarians which,
much of the time, they were. For it remains an open question, on the
evidence of the fragments, how far their authors were concerned with the
larger processes of history: the indications of a broader vision are, it
might be said, just sufficient for us to call their thinking historical, if we
take into account a phenomenon like Eupolemus' overarching,
chronological and outward-looking geographical frameworks. It is certainly hard to imagine that any of them could have achieved a grand
opening like that of *Jubilees* (a book which, of course, is deeply concerned
with the future as well as the past and especially with the working-out of

covenantal history): "this is the history of the division of the days of the Law and of the testimony, of the events of the years, of their (years') weeks, of their Jubilees throughout all the years of the world, as the Lord spake to Moses on Mount Sinai when he went to receive the tables of the Law and of the commandment, according to the voice of God as he said unto him, 'Go to the top of the Mount'", or that any of them could have aspired to the supreme theme tackled by *Jubilees'* author: "and Moses was on the Mount forty days and forty nights, and God taught him the earlier and the later history of the vision of all the days of the Law and of the testimony" (i 5). This education is followed in *Jubilees* by a directive from the angel of God to Moses to "write a complete history of the creation".

In the face of that blinding prospect, it is difficult to know how to proceed. *Jubilees* is, in its overall conception, more historical than our author, in its minor features perhaps less. In date it is quite likely to be contemporary with the Maccabean revolt since there is a fairly explicit hostile reference to the Hellenizers at one point, and thus it may be contemporary with Eupolemus on one side, with the non-extant Jason of Cyrene on the other[67]). The Epitome and I Maccabees come a generation or more later. It was undoubtedly the great events of the persecution, the revolt and the ensuing wars of liberation that enabled Jewish history-writing to grow, in what was already fertile soil (just as the great revolt produced Josephus).

These events were to call forth, in I and II Maccabees both a Biblical and a contemporary historiography, written in the shadow of the Bible. In the first book we find not only an imitation of Biblical form but even a modelling of narrated incidents upon Biblical prototypes; the model of David for example in the narrative of the wars of Judas, where echoes extend even to the battle numbers, to the nature of the fighting for the sanctuary and to the description of the victory (I Macc iii-iv); and also the model of Joshua (chap. ix ff.)[68]). In II Maccabees, we are struck first and forcibly by the Hellenistic format of the original (whether we call it pathetic historiography or temple propaganda or epiphanic history or whatever) and with the avowedly secular, pleasure-giving aims of the Epitomator, extending even to the comparisons he draws from dinner parties, architecture, and the mixing of wine. But we soon discover that the Old Testament theory of punishment and forgiveness is at least as prominent[69]): punishment, it is said, always comes to the people of Israel even before their sins have reached their height (vi 14), and falls upon the *whole* people, even innocent children; yet anger turns to mercy when Maccabaeus organizes his band (viii 5). All understand that God's rebuke is to be shortlived (vii 33). The pattern is a familar one, with occasionally a special twist. Here, then, in yet another way, new life has been breathed into the old mould and an Old Testament schema has engendered something new.

That single crisis should produce two major histories, each with its own strengths and weaknesses, its own accuracies and inaccuracies and, above all, its own very distinctive character, as well as historical reflections of itself in other works (Jubilees, Daniel), is testimony to the power of the Bible-based tradition from which those works spring. It is not, I think, fanciful to include the Graeco-Jewish historical fragments in that tradition, and thus to challenge Martin GOODMAN's sceptical assertion that there exists no such thing as a school of Judaeo-Hellenistic historiography[70]. I hope that I have managed to cast a little new light on that tradition and on the forms of its historical awareness. Although it is not possible to disentangle the historical ideas of the Jews, whether Biblical or post-Biblical, from either theology or Law, I believe it to be worth the effort occasionally to adopt a change of perspective and to give history, even if not true history, pride of place.

NOTES

[1]) We may presume the claim to be not a new one: in both books of *Contra Apionem*, Josephus' named opponents are all of earlier generations than himself.

[2]) Tatian, *Address to the Greeks*, 37-8; Theophilus, *ad Autol* III, 21-2; Origen, *Contra Celsum* I, 16; IV, 11.

[3]) See F. H. COLSON in the Loeb Classical Library *Philo* IX (1941), p. 409 n. *a* and nn. passim, pp. 422 ff.; and now G. VERMES, "A Summary of the Law by Flavius Josephus", *NT* 24.4 (1982), pp. 301-2, n. 50, citing other discussions.

[4]) On this type of writer, see T. RAJAK, "Josephus and the 'Archaeology' of the Jews", *JJS* 33, 1-2 (1982): *Essays in Honour of Y. Yadin*, pp. 472-3. The importance of Josephus' discussion of historiography is noted by A. MOMIGLIANO, "Time in Ancient Historiography", in *Essays in Ancient and Modern Historiography* (1977), p. 195; also in *History and Theory*, Beiheft 6 (1966).

[5]) Arnaldo MOMIGLIANO, *Alien Wisdom: The Limits of Hellenization* (1975).

[6]) M. I. FINLEY, "Myth, Memory and History", in *The Use and Abuse of History* (1975), p. 20.

[7]) *Flavius Josèphe, Contre Apion*, ed. Th. REINACH (Paris, 1930), n. *ad* I, 12.

[8]) Harold W. ATTRIDGE, *The Interpretation of Biblical History in the Antiquitates Judaicae of Flavius Josephus* [Harvard Dissertations in Religion 7] (1976); ATTRIDGE emphasizes the "apologetic" character of this fusion.

[9]) *Op. cit.* (n. 3), pp. 301-2 with n. 50. In conclusion, VERMES proposes that Josephus' "internalization" of the Torah, with its bias towards the religious and ethical, may even be Palestinian Jewish, rather than Hellenized or for the benefit of a foreign readership.

[10]) J. NEUSNER, "The Religious Uses of History", *History and Theory* 5 (1966), pp. 153-71.

[11]) I have argued that this was always his basic affiliation: see *Josephus: the Historian and his Society* (1983), pp. 32-4. In any event, there is little room for doubt, when it comes to the 90's A.D.; see SHAYE, J. D. COHEN, *Josephus in Galilee and Rome: his Vita and Development as a Historian* (1979), pp. 236-9, where self-interest is described as the main explanation for this choice; H. A. ATTRIDGE, *op. cit.* (n. 8), concludes that "many of the interpretative

elements in the *Antiquities* are not inconsistent with Rabbinic Judaism, and thus perhaps with Pharisaism. These agreements, however, are not so specific that we are compelled to call Josephus a Pharisee because of them'' (p. 178). Josephus' lack of interest in the food laws and such aspects of ritual purity, not only in *Contra Apionem*, but even in the *Antiquities* (III, 258 ff.) would have been remedied by his projected work *On Customs and Causes*: see VERMES, *op. cit.* (n. 3), p. 292.

¹²) Martin HENGEL, *Judaism and Hellenism: Studies in their Encounter in Palestine during the Early Hellenistic Period* (English edition, 1974).

¹³) Cf. Josephus, *Vita* 6, on Josephus' own priestly genealogy as recorded in the public archive.

¹⁴) T. RAJAK, *op. cit.* (n. 11), pp. 14-22; VERMES, *op. cit.* (n. 3), p. 295.

¹⁵) Even if Josephus' total of twenty-two, instead of twenty-four, raises problems, as does his division by which only four books are assigned to the third section. The Septuagint's general grouping is markedly different. See G. W. ANDERSON in *The Cambridge History of the Bible*, vol. I (1970), pp. 114-7, 124-5, 136-9.

¹⁶) *AJ* XI, 184 ff.; Ezra and Nehemiah are transferred by Josephus to Xerxes' reign, in a correction of Scripture—see *AJ* XI, 120 ff.

¹⁷) *M. Aboth* I, i; IV Ezra xiv, 18. Talmudic texts generally put the beginnings of the Great Synagogue in the generation of Ezra; but the chronological implications are sometimes confused; on this see *Enc. Jud.* XV, s.v. "Synagogue the Great".

¹⁸) *CA* I, 42; RAJAK, *op. cit.* (n. 4), pp. 471-2; VERMES, *op. cit.* (n. 3), p. 290, n. 4, who prefers, however, the interpretation of W. C. VAN UNNIK (*Flavius Josephus als historischer Schriftsteller*, 1978), pp. 26-40, that Josephus seeks to make no substantive point with this formula, beyond reassuring his readers of his trustworthiness. My reading is closer to that of L. H. FELDMAN, "Hellenizations in Josephus' Portrayal of Man's Decline", *Religions in Antiquity: Studies in Honour of E. R. Goodenough*, ed. J. NEUSNER (= *Numen* suppl. 14, 1968), p. 338.

¹⁹) In addition to *CA* I, 42-3, see also II, 232-4; 272. There were massacres in A.D. 66 at Gaza, Ascalon, Ptolemais, Tyre, Philadelphia, Gerasa, Pella, Gadara, Hippos, Scythopolis, Damascus and Alexandria, as well as Caesarea; in 67 at Antioch; "*sicarii*" were suppressed in 72/3 in Alexandria and Cyrenaica; under Domitian, the harsh exactions of the Jewish tax and the emphasis laid upon the imperial cult appear to have led to local persecutions, though the evidence is weak. On all these events, see E. M. SMALLWOOD, *The Jews under Roman Rule* (1976), chap. XIV. HENGEL, *Die Zeloten* (1961), p. 267, cites this passage of Josephus in connection with Essene martyrdoms.

²⁰) On this conception of history as expressed in the twentieth century, see Hayden V. WHITE, "The Burden of History", *History and Theory* 5 (1960), pp. 111-32. The Jewish people might be conceived of as in a special way subject to this burden.

²¹) It is worth noticing in this connection the implications of the chapter division in the recent volume *Writings of the Second Temple Period, Compendia Rerum Iudaicarum ad Novum Testamentum* II, 2 ed. M. STONE (1984): "The Stories", "the Bible Rewritten", "Historiography", "Testments" etc.

²²) I refer to the approach in e.g. T. P. WISEMAN's *Clio's Cosmetics* (1979) (on the early Roman tradition) or in A. J. WOODMAN's inaugural lecture, "From Hannibal to Hitler: the literature of War" (Repr. from the University of Leeds Review, 1983). What must be avoided, in this new realism, is reducing all historiography to the same level; judged as mere rhetoric or romance; for a reaction, see the words of Arnaldo MOMIGLIANO in "Biblical Studies and Classical Studies: Simple Reflections about Historical Method", *Biblical Archaeologist* 45, 4 (1982), p. 225: "There is a widespread tendency both inside and outside the historical profession to treat historiography as another genre of fiction".

²³) *Op. cit.* (n. 20). On the roots of the modern approach in Greek evaluations of reliability, see MOMIGLIANO, *op. cit.* (n. 4), pp. 190-2.

²⁴) *Op. cit.* (n. 6), p. 27.

²⁵) FINLEY, *op. cit.* (n. 6).

²⁶) See the introductory remarks to the chapters by G. W. E. NICKLESBURG, *op. cit.* (n. 21).

²⁷) Salo Rappaport, *Agada und Exegese bei Flavius Josephus* (1930), G. Vermes, *Scripture and Tradition in Judaism* [Studia Post Biblica 4] (1961), Thomas W. Franxman, *Genesis and the "Jewish Antiquities" of Flavius Josephus* [Biblica et Orientalia 35] (1979). The depth and seriousness of Josephus' concurrent Hellenization of the narrative still awaits a definitive description: for Attridge, *op. cit.* (n. 8) this is one essential component of the author's apologetic theology, while for L. H. Feldman in various studies, they lie at its very heart: see especially his review of Franxman, "Josephus' Commentary on Genesis", *JQR* 72 (1981), pp. 121-3, with nn. 23 and 31 referring to his other papers on the subject.

²⁸) But see some preliminary comments below, pp. 23-4.

²⁹) On the long-standing debate about Jason's date and sources, see Hengel, *op. cit.* (n. 12), pp. 95-8 and nn., with the cautious conclusion that "the suggestion of Niese, that Jason spent at least some time in Palestine in those decisive years after 175 B.C. ... still has a certain degree of probability".

³⁰) The remarks of G. Vermes with M. Goodman in R. Arnaldez etc. (eds.) *Études sur le judaïsme hellénistique* [Association catholique française pour l'étude de la Bible, Congrès de Strasbourg 1983] (1984); and Hengel, *op. cit.* (n. 12), I, pp. 104-5.

³¹) J. Freudenthal, *Hellenistische Studien. Alexander Polyhistor und die von ihm erhaltenen Reste jüdischer und samaritanischer Geschichtswerke* (2 vols, 1874-5); Nikolaus Walter, *Fragmente jüdisch-hellenistischer Historiker: Historische und legendarische Erzählungen* [Jüdische Schriften aus hellenistisch-römischer Zeit I, 2, 1976); ibid., in: *Fragmente jüdisch-hellenistischer Exegeten: Unterweisung in lehrhafter Form* (*JSHRZ* III, 2, 1975); Carl R. Holladay, *Fragments from Hellenistic Jewish Authors*, vol. I: *Historians* (1983); of the latter two series, only Holladay's gives the Greek texts; the fragments are also in A. M. Denis, *Fragmenta Pseudepigraphorum quae supersunt Graeca* (1970), pp. 175-228.

³²) Cf. above, n. 18. On Midrash as part of the text, see Vermes, *op. cit.* (n. 27), pp. 176-7.

³³) "Pseudepigraphy in the Israelite Literary Tradition", [*Fondation Hardt*], *Entretiens sur l'Antiquité Classique* 18 (1972), pp. 191-227.

³⁴) Holladay, *Fragments*, pp. 209-13 (Artapanus, frag. 3).

³⁵) *Die literarische Fälschung im heidnischen und christlichen Altertum: ein Versuch ihrer Deutung* [Handbuch der Altertumswissenschaft I, 2,] (1971), pp. 150-60.

³⁶) "Jewish Apologetic Literature Reconsidered", *Eos* 48, 3 (1956) [= *Symbolae R. Taubenschlag Dedicatae* (1957)], pp. 169-93; "The Ideology of the Letter of Aristeas", *HThR* 51 (1958), pp. 59-85.

³⁷) *Eupolemus: A Study of Judaeo-Greek Literature* [Monographs of the Hebrew Union College No. 3] (1974).

³⁸) E. J. Bickerman, "The Jewish Historian Demetrius", in *Christianity, Judaism and other Greco-Roman Cults. Studies for Morton Smith at Sixty*, III (1975), pp. 72-84; reprinted in Bickerman, *Studies in Jewish and Christian History* II (1980), pp. 347-58; J. J. Collins, *Between Athens and Jerusalem: Jewish Identity in the Hellenistic Diaspora* (1983), chap. I.

³⁹) Holladay, *Fragments*, pp. 51-92, with bibliography on pp. 57-61; Jacoby, *FGrH* no. 722.

⁴⁰) Collins, (*op. cit.*, n. 38), p. 28.

⁴¹) Quoted by Collins, p. 29, from P. M. Fraser, *Ptolemaic Alexandria* I (1973), p. 693.

⁴²) See M. Stern, *Greek and Roman Authors on Jews and Judaism* I (1974), no. 30, pp. 157-64.

⁴³) Holladay, *Fragments*, frag. 2, 2-3 (pp. 64-5).

⁴⁴) See M. Stern, "The Jews in Greek and Latin Literature", *Compendia Rerum Judaicarum ad Novum Testamentum* I, 2 (1976), pp. 1101-1159; J. N. Sevenster, *The Roots of Ancient Anti-Semitism in the Ancient World* [Novum Testamentum Suppl. 41] (1975).

⁴⁵) Cf. Wacholder, *op. cit.* (n. 37), p. 280 ff. On Midrash in Graeco-Jewish literature, cf. Howard Jacobson, *The Exagoge of Ezekiel* (1983), pp. 20-3. The question-answer procedure implicit here has been likened by Freudenthal and by Y. Gutman, *The Beginnings of Jewish Hellenistic Literature* I (1969; Hebrew) pp. 138-44 to that of early Greek literature and of the Homeric scholia. But there is little or no real similarity in form or content between these very different types of literature; Gutman, in any case, accepts that any influence would be superficial.

[46]) The MS texts read "one", but a correction is necessary: see HOLLADAY, n. *ad loc.*

[47]) HOLLADAY, *Fragments*, pp. 93-156, with bibliography on pp. 105-111; JACOBY, *FGrH* No. 723; note also WACHOLDER, *op. cit.* (n. 37).

[48]) WACHOLDER, pp. 1-21.

[49]) The dependence is supposedly shown by Eupolemus' introduction of Astibares, a king in Ctesias, as a Median collaborator with Babylon in the attack on Jerusalem: HOLLADAY, p. 153, n. 110. But WACHOLDER, p. 255, was wrong to take this as proof of a direct literary debt.

[50]) This is undeniably a Greek motif: see, for the classical precedents, A. KLEINGUN-THER, *Philologus* Suppl. 26, 1 (1933); K. THRAEDE in *RAC* V (1962), 1191-1278, s.v. "Er-finder II", especially 1242-6 on the Jewish adaptations.

[51]) I Kings v 2-6; II Chron ii 3-10: The letters in Chronicles are generally longer and more elaborate than those in Kings: HOLLADAY, *Fragments*, 114, n. 47.

[52]) On Eupolemus' own stance, WACHOLDER pp. 157-8. The letter of Vaphres (HOLLA-DAY, frag. 2, p. 118) is headed ἀντίγραφος (copy). The name Vaphres appears to be con-nected with the name of the Pharaoh Hophra in Jeremiah (xliv 30), Οὐαφρης in the Egyp-tian king lists and Ἀπρίης in Herodotus (II, 161; IV, 159); see HOLLADAY, *Fragments*, p. 141, n. 23.

[53]) HOLLADAY, frag. 2, p. 119.

[54]) HOLLADAY, *Fragments*, pp. 189-243, with bibliography on pp. 199-203; JACOBY, *FGrH* 726. In this, as in most cases, reliance cannot be placed upon the ascribed title.

[55]) HOLLADAY, *Fragments*, pp. 261-76; JACOBY, *FGrH* 725.

[56]) HOLLADAY, *Fragments*, pp. 245-60; JACOBY, *FGrH* 727.

[57]) HOLLADAY, *Fragments*, pp. 157-88, with bibliography on pp. 166-8; JACOBY, *FGrH* 724. See especially B. Z. WACHOLDER, "Pseudo-Eupolemus' Two Greek Fragments on the life of Abraham", *HUCA* 34 (1963), pp. 83-113 and WACHOLDER, *op. cit.* (n. 37), pp. 287-93.

[58]) Though none of these traditions appear to be unique to Samaritan sources; however, the Samaritan parallels are the closest when it comes to matters of detail: e.g. Armenians as the antagonists of Israel; Enoch's astrological revelations (see M. GASTER, *The Asatir* (1927), pp. 9-41). The reading of the association Salem/Shechem as a Samaritan version may be thought to require reexamination in the light of the LXX version of Gen xxxiii 18, "Jacob went to Salem, city of the Shechemites", where Salem is not present in the MT; this suggests the Salem-Shechem link to be an interpretation with wide currency. See HOLLADAY, *Fragments*, p. 183 (n. 21); HENGEL, II, p. 59, n. 239.

[59]) *Judaism and Hellenism* I, pp. 88-92.

[60]) *Judaism and Hellenism* II, 60, n. 242.

[61]) See HENGEL, p. 89 and n. 243.

[62]) HOLLADAY, *Fragments*, p. 184, n. 24.

[63]) See HOLLADAY, p. 159, for disputes on the subject; there is no use in pursuing them.

[64]) See P. BRUNEAU, "Les Israélites de Délos et la Juiverie délienne", *BCH* 106 (1982), pp. 465-504.

[65]) Josephus refers to Alexander Polyhistor only once; he cites Cleodemus Malchus once; and he regards Eupolemus as pagan (*AJ* I, 239-41, *CA* I, 218), See ATTRIDGE, pp. 34-5.

[66]) See FREUDENTHAL, *op. cit.* (n. 31), p. 109; WACHOLDER, pp. 256-7.

[67]) For the dating of Jubilees, see G. W. NICKELSBURG, *Jewish Literature between the Bible and the Mishnah* (1981), pp. 78-9 (a date between 175 and 100 B.C.).

[68]) See Jonathan A. GOLDSTEIN's *I Maccabees* (Anchor Bible, 1976), in which the "typology" is fully annotated.

[69]) See Christian HABICHT, *II Makkabäerbuch* [Jüdische Schriften aus hellenistisch-römischer Zeit I, 3] (1976), intr., pp. 185-191; Robert DORAN, *Temple Propaganda: the Pur-pose and Character of II Maccabees* [CBQ Monograph 12] (1981).

[70]) M. GOODMAN, *loc. cit.* (n. 30).

REGISTER VAN BIJBELPLAATSEN

(In het register zijn uitsluitend de belangrijkste Bijbelplaatsen opgenomen, waarnaar in de voorafgaande opstellen wordt verwezen. Aan het register is een supplement betreffende de geciteerde teksten uit de pseudepigrafische literatuur, de Qumrângeschriften en Josefus toegevoegd).

Genesis		*Jozua*	
i-xi	28	xvii 11	47
i 1-ii 4a	24, 26	xix 17-23	47
i 26, 28	25	xxiv 22	66
i 27	26		
ii 4b-iii 24	26	*Richteren*	
ii 7f.	22, 25	i 27	47, 49
ii 8b	31	iii 31	48
ii 17	26	v 6	48
ii 19	22	v 19	40
iii 5	26		
iii 17	23	*1 Samuël*	
iii 19	22	ii 27-36	96
iii 22a	26	xiv 3	97
iv 12	23	xvi 13	104
iv 17f.	23	xxi-xxii	96
iv 23f.	23	xxviii 7	20
iv 25f.	23	xxxi 7	48
v 29	21ff.		
ix 8-17	23	*2 Samuël*	
ix 20	22f.	ii 8-9	47
ix 20-27	27	ii 13	45
xi 10-32	23f.	v 17-25	47
xliii 32,34	137	vii 8	104
xlvi 31-34	136	viii 1	47
xlix 14-15	47	viii 17	97
Exodus		*1 Koningen*	
xxiv 3-8	56	i-ii	96
xxiv 9-11	56	iv 12	47
xxxii 4	51	iv 17	47
		ix 15	47
Numeri			
xviii 1-7	97	*2 Koningen*	
xxv	100	v 23	51
xxv 12-13	96	xvi 5	73
		xvi 7	82
Deuteronomium		xviii 13	73
vi 2	129	xviii 13-16	74, 85
viii 8	80	xviii 13, 17-xx 19	70ff.
xiii 1	129	xix 9	75
xxvi 17-19	66	xix 35ff.	75
xxvii 9-10	66	xx 12-19	73
xxviii	62	xxv 22-26	72

SUPPLEMENT